D1251246

Pocahontas, Powhatan, Opechancanough

University of Virginia Press · *Charlottesville and London*

Helen C. Rountree

POCAHONTAS
POWHATAN
OPECHANCANOUGH

Three Indian Lives Changed by Jamestown

ALEXANDRIA LIBRARY
ALEXANDRIA VA 22304

UNIVERSITY OF VIRGINIA PRESS
© 2005 by the Rector and Visitors of the University of Virginia
"HCR" maps © 2005 by Helen C. Rountree
All rights reserved
Printed in the United States of America on acid-free paper

First published 2005
1 3 5 7 9 8 6 4 2

Library of Congress Cataloging-in-Publication Data
Rountree, Helen C., 1944–
Pocahontas, Powhatan, Opechancanough : three Indian lives changed by
Jamestown / Helen C. Rountree.
p.   cm.
Includes bibliographical references and index.
ISBN 0-8139-2323-9 (cloth : alk. paper)
1. Powhatan Indians—Virginia—Jamestown—Biography. 2. Powhatan
Indians—Virginia—Jamestown—History. 3. Jamestown (Va.)—History.
4. Pocahontas, d. 1617. 5. Powhatan, ca. 1550–1618. 6. Opechancanough,
d. 1646. I. Title.
E99.P85R665 2005
975.5'4251—dc22   2004017384

Dedicated to

The Modern Indian Tribes of Virginia

Survivors Descended from Survivors

CONTENTS

ILLUSTRATIONS

PREFACE

THIS BOOK ABOUT Indian people has been written by a non-Indian. "Rountree" may sound "Indian" to some people, but it is English: a corruption of "rowantree," the mountain ash tree. It is also a name that is common only in one small part of eastern Virginia, near where I grew up and then spent my teaching career. I grew up as a white Virginian, hearing all the mythology—good, bad, and indifferent—about Pocahontas, Powhatan, Opechancanough, "Chanco" the (supposedly only) warning giver, and so on. I had already gone through a master's degree in anthropology, with fieldwork on an Indian reservation in Nevada, before I began looking at the eyewitness records about the native people in my home state and realized that mythology was what I had been hearing.

I have now been studying—and restudying—those early Virginia records for thirty-five years. With learning about other aspects of eastern Virginia such as ethnobotany interspersed between sessions, I manage to get something new out of each restudy of the material. The records were, however, indisputably written by nonnatives. No matter how much sifting out of Eurocentric biases I attempt, I suspect that I will never be able to "get it right" until someone invents a time machine.

Meanwhile, the 400th anniversary of the founding of Jamestown is approaching, and as far as I know at this writing, no one—including anyone from the modern Indian people—is trying to write about Jamestown from the native perspective. Nor has anyone assayed to write a biography of either Powhatan or Opechancanough, even though there are more early seventeenth-century records about those two men than about little Pocahontas.

That seemed to me to be another gap that ought to be filled before 2007. So I set out to do the latter and have ended up doing the former as well. Sad but true, most of what we can know about any Virginia native people, especially their leaders, consists of their responses to the invasion of their country by foreigners. It would be fascinating—to an anthropologist, at least—to know what went on behind the scenes in the Indian towns on the days when no European visitors came to call. But only so much of that behavior can be reconstructed without resorting to fiction. And this book is emphatically not a work of fiction, as the endnotes prove.

I have received assistance along the way from a number of people. Both Chief Anne Richardson, of the Rappahannock Indian Tribe, and Keith Smith, from the Nansemond Indian Tribe, read and commented on the chapters. Nancy Egloff and Thomas Davidson of the Jamestown-Yorktown Foundation facilitated my restudy of the Virginia Company records and my first-ever reading of the Ferrar Papers. Wayne Clark and Mary Louise de Sarran of the Maryland Historical Trust helped me locate the reference giving the Nanticoke Indian terms for rulers. Mr. Paul Relf of St. George's Church in Gravesend, Kent, U.K., pointed me to that church's website, where Pocahontas's burial record can be viewed. Mary Theobald, Morris Bander, and Thomas Finderson kindly researched the phases the moon was in at the time of the Great Assaults of 1622 and 1644. Daniel Richter steered me to where Don Luis's Algonquian name was published, and Jeffrey Ruggles and Greg Stoner of the Virginia Historical Society assisted me with information on some of the illustrations. Bob and Lynne Ripley, the current owners of the Werowocomoco site, allowed me to wander on their farm and assisted me in photographing some of the surface finds from it. And two anonymous readers for the University of Virginia Press made extensive, constructive comments for the improvement of the manuscript. Any remaining faults in the book, of course, are mine.

Introduction

THE POWHATANS' SIDE of the Jamestown story comes only indirectly from the people themselves. They did not have a written language, nor did they need one in their somewhat less complex culture. So we must rely entirely on what the Jamestown English wrote about them and, in some cases, on what those writers remembered them as saying. Such sources of information obviously cannot be taken at face value.

The Sources Available

Aside from testing the native people's reported behavior against the culture that John Smith and others recorded in the early days—because the people would have behaved logically, based upon that culture—it helps to find out as much as possible about the English writers, to discover their personal and cultural biases. Some historians have made a specialty of doing that research, with the result that information about most of the writers is readily available.[1] A book-length biography has been written about William Strachey, besides the multiple books about John Smith's life.[2]

Historians have a standard against which to measure accounts of past events: an account is more likely to be reliable if it is written by a neutral party very soon after the events described in it. Thus letters home, if they are not self-justifying ones, are more trustworthy than later accounts written for the public, especially self-aggrandizing accounts written many years later. That comparison encapsulates the writings of Captain John Smith, who stayed in Virginia between only April 1607 and September 1609. Smith's 1608 *True*

Relation was a report sent home to an unknown person and quickly published without the writer's knowledge. Virginia's native people appear in the narrative as unknown quantities, which they were to Europeans at the time: people who were potentially either friendly or hostile. Smith's "Map of Virginia," written in 1612, was a factual account of the Powhatans' way of life, but it was followed by a history, the "Proceedings of the English Colony," that was produced with his approval by several friends and composed for public consumption during a period in which the Jamestown colony was expanding successfully. The Powhatans appear as formidable adversaries but not monstrous ones. Yet the time lapse and the story's tendency to upgrade Smith and downgrade the colony's other leaders should make a skeptic's radar go off occasionally. Smith wrote his *Generall Historie* in 1624, adding to the "Proceedings" and taking the story onward during a period of vicious war with the Powhatans that often led Smith, who was unwillingly on the shelf, to say, "I told you so!" The Powhatans appear repeatedly in that work as unpredictable and murderous, when they are not cowering with fear at Smith's bravado. The one shining exception—in 1607–9—is Pocahontas, who is given a much-inflated role for a prepubescent female child in her culture. When we read some passages, the radar is screaming now.

All of the writers from Jamestown had the general biases of men of their time: they thought English culture was superior; they considered women, English or Powhatan, to be weak and inferior; and they were uninterested in personalities and motivations (those are twentieth-century concepts). But their accounts can be used, with the same caveats about timing and audience, to corroborate or disprove Smith's versions of things. For that reason, the writings of George Percy, Gabriel Archer, and Edward Maria Wingfield are useful, even though they detested Smith personally: very often they back up his early writings about the native people's actions.

William Strachey's *Historie of Travell into Virginia Britania* corroborates Smith by plagiarizing him. Copying passages from the works of others was not a faux pas in those days: it was more of a compliment, with citing of the original writer being optional. Fortunately for anthropologists, Strachey added many paragraphs of his own, based upon information he had gathered to satisfy his curiosity (unusual for the time) about other cultures. He also, unlike Smith, had competent interpreters to help him during his stay in Virginia in 1610–11.

The time at which a writer made his observations understandably affected his views of the land and the people. Smith, Archer, Percy, and Wingfield all represent the early days, when the Virginia colony, always an economic enterprise, was in its exploratory, treasure-seeking phase and was badly undersupplied from home. The native people, not surprisingly, figure often as potential helpers or obstructors of the enterprise, while the colony's leaders quarreled enthusiastically with one another. After a new regime began in 1610 (governors instead of presidents), and the stockholders in the Virginia Company of London caught on that they would have to send more food and livestock with the additional personnel, the colony became established, and the local Powhatans nearly faded out of sight, even when Pocahontas was captured, converted, and married (1613–14). William Strachey's, Samuel Argall's, and Ralph Hamor's writings date from this period, with Strachey being the standout for his interest in the native people. Then the migrants' enterprise really took off when mild Orinoco tobacco was brought in and found to grow well enough to become a cash crop (1616–21). Assuming that the age-old holders of the land—who put on a friendly face during this time—would soon convert to English religion and culture, the newcomers spread out like a fungus, while making only the most perfunctory mentions of the Powhatans in their writings. The Great Assault of 1622 brought the immigrants up short: the native people weren't acquiescent after all! Well, down with them! It was during the ten-year war that followed that Smith produced his *Generall Historie*. That book, written for a thoroughly anti-Powhatan audience, was the only early account of Jamestown available to the public for two and a quarter centuries, Strachey having failed to get published. Other writers of the 1620s were not concerned with the native people except to curse them in passing.

The Great Assault showed that the Virginia Company's enterprise was far from perfect. After an investigation the Crown took over the colony in 1624, after which the preservation—and, at times, the making—of records became more chancy. A sort of Dark Age set in from the mid-1620s until the late 1640s. Some of the records that were copied and sent to England survived, in spite of the English Civil War (1642–49). Some colony-level ones, like the General Court records and those made by the counties that began to form in the 1630s, remained in Virginia and were subject to the destruction of the American Civil War and other calamities. The surviving records show that

Virginia's counties, like the governors, dealt with the Powhatans living in or near them. But the rush for riches from tobacco was still on, so most of what little appears about the native people after the peace of 1632 concerns problems about land. The last Great Assault (1644) and Opechancanough's defeat (1646) both occurred during the English Civil War, when the colony was unstable and literate men worried more about their own property than about details of what the native people, even hostile "royal" ones, were doing.

Fleshing out the lives of our protagonists, Powhatan, Pocahontas, and Opechancanough, can therefore be done only up to a point, even with in-depth knowledge of the culture they came from. My reconstructive efforts on that culture have been published in a number of places,³ and the early writings themselves have now all been gathered together in Edward Haile's collection, *Jamestown Narratives.* But it would take a time machine to view all the details of the culture or of the protagonists' lives. Thus, because the amount of information about them and their people at various times is uneven, the amount of detail in the chapters that follow is also uneven and occasionally frustrating. However, in my view, anything is better than the cardboard cutouts that have been the rule heretofore.

Manipulating the Sources

I am acutely aware that most of the people reading this book will be non-Indians. Even the Indians today—who like the rest of us are the products of mass education—have been taught to see colonists as brave people who had a right to set up shop in the New World and to see the native people as treacherous "savages" who were simply in the way. After working with the modern Virginia tribes for thirty-five years, I know that being an Indian in Virginia means having a less-than-total acceptance of that scenario, but varying degrees of acceptance have been ingrained in the people nonetheless. That means that in this book I have to bring the Powhatan side of the story alive even for my Indian readers to some extent. And I have to do it in detail: just saying "those #$%!! English" is not enough.

One of the ways I have tried to present the Indian side, in telling the old colonial story from a different point of view, has been to try to reconstruct the native people's motives for behaving the way they did. Those motives stemmed in a logical way from the culture in which the people grew up, so to some extent I bring that culture in, too. The hardest part of the reconstructive endeavor, though, turned out to be eliminating what the English knew about their own activities—which they wrote about in tremendous detail—and sticking to what the Powhatans would have been able to observe or deduce about the newcomers for themselves. That reduced the body of usable records considerably! And then sticking to what the three subjects of this biography would have been aware of reduced the records further. Because, as usual, I was writing with a word-processed, chronologically arranged, footnoted verbatim compilation of the primary sources in front of me, it meant that I had continually to remind myself to ask: How much of this did Powhatan know? How would he have known it? What would he have made of it? And why?

Another way I have tried to put readers into a native-centered frame of mind has been by deliberately playing tricks with language in this book. People are infected with a European point of view if they grow up hearing the English and the colonists spoken of favorably (or, in my case, spoken of literally as ancestors), and the Indians as scarcely human, completely alien-behaving creatures. Such people have a hard time seeing the native side of things as logical or right—which, of course, is how the real-life Powhatans saw their world. So, in attempting a cure for both the readers and myself, I adopted the following practices.

The words *people, men,* and *women* are used for Indians only. The Powhatans were an ethnocentric lot (just like the English!), and evidence shows that much of the time they felt the invaders were subhuman: much too cowardly and incompetent to be "real" men and too lazy and incompetent to be "real" women. Sometimes I call the Powhatans the "Real People," which is how a great many Native American groups have felt historically about themselves compared to outsiders, including other Indian tribes.

I do not use the word *English* in the book unless I absolutely have to, either in a direct quote (or in an aside, in parentheses). Too many of us Americans have been brought up to think anything English is good—not to mention higher-status. The Powhatans did not see the English people as either one. I eschew the word *colonist* altogether because of its semantic nuance of having the right to settle somewhere. In the Powhatan view the English did not have any right whatever to be colonists in Tsenacomoco (eastern Virginia). Therefore I have had to use other words for the denizens of Jamestown, and those words are meant to be distancing: taking *tassantassa*, the Powhatan word for *stranger*, and using it as an ethnic name: the Strangers or the Tassantassas, plus the words *aliens, foreigners, outlanders, invaders, interlopers*, and—because with very few exceptions they did not ask anybody's permission before taking up land—*squatters*. I also try to tell the story in terms of the Powhatan seasons (with occasional English dates inserted parenthetically). Seasons were tied to different kinds of food getting, which seems to have mattered more to the Powhatans than where the moon was at any given time, much less what month or year of the Christian calendar it was.

John Smith has become such a legendary character that I have manipulated his name, too. In native eyes he was not the indomitable captain of the *Generall Historie*. The Powhatans first saw him up close, and remembered him vividly, as a foreign prisoner who agreed to become a subject of their paramount chief in order to be let loose; everyone, even Pocahontas,[4] judged his later actions by how he kept that promise. They must have learned his name early in his captivity, but from what we know of their language, they probably pronounced it "Chawnzmit."[5] So in this book I use that spelling of his name when viewing him through the eyes of a Native American person.

The unpleasantnesses of 1622 and 1644 are not referred to as "massacres" in this book, although of course technically they were: a lot of people got killed at once. From the native people's point of view, though, those events were great (i.e., large-scale) assaults on enemies, so that is what I call them. On another occasion, in 1623, many people died at once, only this time it was native people dying at the hands of the English. I call that occasion a "massacre"—with the full connotation of the innocent being victimized—because that is exactly what it was from the native people's point of view.

My personal opinion has always been that all three events were massacres. But I am not writing about my personal opinions in this book, nor am I trying to keep a scholarly distance and explain both sides, as I did in *Pocahontas's People* (1990). This volume is about one side only, the side that happened to lose, and thus the side that it has been unpopular to try to study or talk about in much depth. This book is an attempt to tell "the other" side of the story, with native leaders who are not mere cardboard cutouts. Otherwise the 2007 commemoration literature might be overwhelmingly about "heroes" who were also squatters, people with pale complexions who also didn't bathe nearly as often as the natives did.

Lastly, a word on pronunciations. The surviving records do not indicate where emphasis was put in people's multisyllable names, and the English sound system's undergoing a change during those decades does not help us either. So here are the ways in which modern Virginians pronounce the names of the main protagonists in the book: POW-ah-tan, poh-cah-HAHN-tuss, oh-pee-CHAN-can-oh.

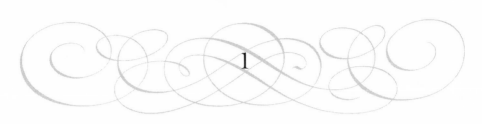

Setting the Scene

THE ANCESTORS of the people of this book had lived in Tsenacomoco (their word for eastern Virginia, possibly meaning "our place") since time immemorial, or so they thought.[1] Archaeology shows that they may have arrived around A.D. 200, after which they peacefully joined an even older people already living there. Their way of life, which was the culture that eventually supported the paramount chief Powhatan, was that of other coastal Algonquian-speaking people from North Carolina to Maine. Since the coming of agriculture around A.D. 1000, the people's way of life was a foraging and farming one adapted to hardwood forested necklands that are interlaced with shallow fingers of the sea.

The European invaders, when they came, would call the region a wilderness or a "desert," but it was not so to the native women, children, and men who knew it intimately. Women and girls who spent part of every year gathering wild food and utility plants had to know where, in their tribe's territory, the plants grew. Men and boys who spent all year hunting animals that were herbivores, like deer and wild turkeys, had to know the locations of the plants the animals ate. Once a person had absorbed a detailed mental map of the territory, based on watercourses and highlands, then navigating through vast spaces of woodland became relatively simple.[2] And it was possible back then to see a long way through much of the woods, unlike today when most of the woodland in Virginia is second-growth, crowded with young trees and underbrush. Mature forest can be a different place. The huge old trees—many of them oaks that bear the acorns so useful to deer, wild turkeys, and people—blot out enough sun that young trees and underbrush do not thrive. An early visitor to Maryland, Father Andrew White, wrote (overenthusiastically) of the "great variety of wood . . . commonly so far distant from each other as a coach and four horses may travel without molestation." Even on the old river floodplains, where the women built the houses and practiced shifting culti-vation, the second-growth woodland was constantly being cleaned of burn-able wood for cooking fires, so that, as John Smith noted, "a man may gallop a horse amongst these woods any way but where the creeks or rivers shall hinder."[3]

People who got much of their meat from hunting fast-moving animals like deer found it simpler not to erect fences or set firm boundaries around tracts of land.[4] A deer belonged to the hunter who killed it, but the land belonged to everyone who foraged there—as long as they were "Real People," that is, Algonquian speakers whose language could be understood when they were encountered in the woods. It also made no sense to the people to claim per-manent ownership of fields that would only be used two or three years before they began to wear out because nobody used fertilizer. So the law of the land was a usufruct system: fields left fallow reverted to general ownership.

Though paths through the woods connected the towns, the major way of moving people and goods was by canoe along the waterways. The rivers and creeks were the very heart of the native people's territories, instead of being the boundaries they are with us today. From the waterways the people drew fish and shellfish and washing water (and, if fresh, drinking water); in them they bathed daily; and along them they traveled to visit relatives, go poli-ticking or warring, or gather reeds to make mats to cover houses. Children of both sexes grew up knowing how to manage the log canoes that their par-ents used almost daily. Because those *quintans* (boats) were heavy and cum-bersome,[5] children learned early to work together to make them go. Very im-portant people might be exempt from paddling on ceremonial or diplomatic occasions, but the comfort level in a canoe, even for a paramount chief, was minimal. If a storm came up, or darkness fell, before a journey was complete, the canoe was beached and the party camped out onshore under a hastily built framework and the mats the sojourners always carried with them.[6]

It is safe to say that religion had always played a major part in the people's lives. Anthropologists working worldwide have found that people appeal to higher powers than themselves, especially when faced with hazards. And Tse-nacomoco had many hazards, some of which are still with us today. People

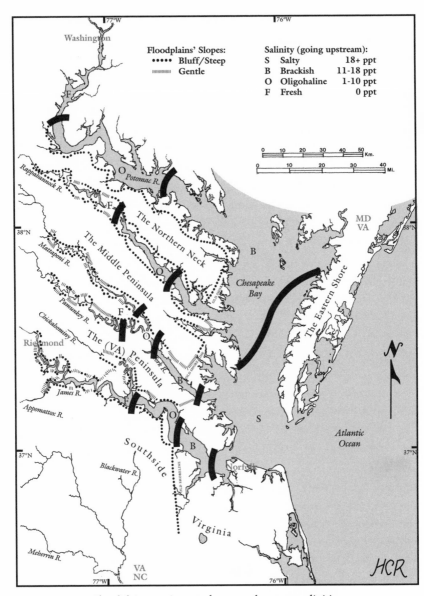

Floodplains, ancient seashores, and average salinities

venturing into the forest might meet with a poisonous snake or an accident that broke a leg far from home. Large predators also were present back then: bears (a few of which still survive in the tidewater), wolves, and bobcats. Many of the waterways of the region are wide enough to develop serious wave action during the thunder squalls that are common in late spring; even modern shipping is occasionally endangered. Log canoes are hard enough to manage on a choppy day that only the hardy—or the very religious— would venture out in them very far. The invaders would record regrettably little about the rituals that people performed in order to stay safe or to give thanks for coming home unscathed.

People like the Powhatans—and the English, who in A.D. 1600 lived in a prescientific age—needed religion not only to face hazards but also to deal with injuries and diseases that shortened people's lifespans. In both cultures thirty-year-olds were middle-aged, and some of those women were grand-mothers. Many women died in childbirth, so that women's life expectancy was lower than men's (that was true worldwide until recently). So many people lost a wife, mother, or daughter in childbed that a young woman's death— like Pocahontas's, at age twenty-one—was not so great a tragedy as it is today, except for those closest to her.

Pre-Columbian Virginia was not a disease-free environment, but the people's living conditions were far healthier than those in English cities, so that epidemics of alien diseases could not wreak nearly the same havoc that they did in urban Mexico and Peru, which endured an estimated 90 percent mortality.[7] Corroboration comes from archaeology in Virginia, where no mass burials of articulated skeletons (i.e., people who had just died) have been found. If anything, the foreign invaders, coming from unhealthy living con-ditions and meeting new "bugs" in Virginia, would suffer a higher mortality rate than the Powhatans ever did from European diseases. The better health of the native people had several reasons. The pre-Contact Powhatans had no dealings with domestic animals other than dogs (hence their hunting for meat).[8] Europeans, on the other hand, often lived cheek by jowl with their an-imals, whose ailments could and did mutate into maladies that killed humans (e.g., smallpox, which mutated from cowpox).[9] Powhatan people preferred to live in smallish hamlets, most of them with houses—and therefore latrines— scattered among gardens and groves of trees.[10] Contrast that with the densely crowded, filthy European towns and cities of the time. The native people in

Virginia also bathed every day,[11] while their contemporaries across the ocean considered bathing unhealthy (and reeked accordingly). Finally, the Powhatans dispersed out of their towns for two seasons each year, instead of inhabiting them year-round. Across the ocean only the wealthiest families, owners of multiple great houses, did such a thing, and they did it for reasons of health. The Powhatans seem to have done it primarily from economic necessity.

People Who Farmed and Foraged

People who all but lacked domesticated animals—for deer and raccoons can be tamed but not domesticated—had to rely on fish and shellfish, wild land animals, or protein-rich plant foods instead. Seafood and wild animals were plentiful year-round in eastern Virginia, while the plant foods were only seasonally available. Nuts are protein-rich, but the deer and wild turkeys also live on them, so it was not wise to overgather nuts in the fall. Corn and beans have been the staple source of proteins for Mesoamerican populations for millennia, but these plants are not native to Virginia. Their watering requirements—rainfall scattered throughout their 120-day growing cycle—are often not met in the tidewater. Even wetter-than-average years are not good crop years if most of the rain falls in the wrong months; 1617 would be such a year. The Powhatans' ancestors therefore had learned long ago not to rely too heavily on farming to get themselves through the winter. Instead, they kept up their ancient foraging skills, which John Smith gave the derogatory label of "living from hand to mouth."[12]

Whenever last year's stored corn and nuts ran out and before the summer corn and beans ripened enough to eat, in the seasons called *cattapeuk* (during spring fish runs) and *cohattayough* (the planting and weeding season),[13] Powhatan families would go out foraging, with an emphasis on gathering tuckahoe, the starchy tuber of arrow arum, or *Peltandra virginica*, from the freshwater marshes. Districts lacking freshwater streams, such as Kecoughtan and Accomac,[14] had to raise more corn each year, even if no drought set in, or else make up some of the calories by eating more seafood. In a drought year everybody had to extend the foraging season far into the summer or even the fall. That would happen in 1607. Whenever the corn matured enough to eat—corn that was green, not "ripe" by our standards—was the season of *nepinough*, when people fattened on garden produce, held major ceremonies,[15]

dried some corn for winter, and paid corn and other valued goods to Powhatan as tribute (similar to taxes). In fall, in the season they called *taquitock,*
whole families would go out again, this time to gather nuts and acorns and
to carry out well-organized communal hunts, aimed at getting in large quantities of venison and hides for the winter. It was poetic justice that John Smith,
who implied that the Powhatans were little better than scavengers, was captured during such a hunt. Winter, called *popanow,* was the coldest and least
active time outdoors for the people. In Powhatan thinking that season did not
complete the year; it began a new one, just as it does for us today. For details
of what women and men did during each season, see Appendix A.[16]

The eyewitness European writers—and nearly all of their readers since—
failed to appreciate several matters stemming from this "mixed economy" of
foraging and farming. First and foremost, that economy affected the avail-
ability of people when the English wanted to go trading—or retaliating. What
season it was determined where in their territories the people were working.
Thus the English sometimes would arrive at a town and find hardly anybody
at home. When times were really awful, in a multiyear drought such as the
1606–12 one,[17] the English traders would find an empty town and assume that
their "enemies" were running away from them. They weren't.

Second, foragers came in both sexes, because the work of both sexes was
a necessity for survival. Feeding a family by hunting and gathering is labor
intensive and requires many hands, as well as knowledgeable brains. All Powhatan mothers were working mothers, and when trade goods were being
sought, the tools for women's work, knives and hoes, were as important for
a family to acquire as those for men's work, knives and hatchets. Both sexes
also would have spotted the utility of English swords as machetes. Though
direct evidence is lacking, it is likely that Powhatan women had considerable
say over the corn that was traded for those tools. Women raised the corn, not
men, and the women were not the "drudges" that the English witnesses wrote
about.[18] That fact of life with which Pocahontas was raised may have caused
her some difficulty during her second marriage, to an Englishman, who believed women were "weak" and therefore "inferior."

Third, the Powhatans' mixed economy meant many fewer people on the
land (about 15,000) than the English were accustomed to in 1600 or than we
have in the region today (about 3 million). Tsenacomoco felt "empty" to the
invaders of 1607, and it would feel even more so to us nowadays. The

Powhatans' lower population was not due to epidemics or to being "uncivilized." The reason is more complicated than that.

A piece of land's carrying capacity (number of individuals it can support, of whatever species) is limited by the natural resources on it. That land's carrying capacity for humans can be increased if the humans make food species increase at the expense of nonuseful species. This is what farming does and why so many people hate weeds. It is also what livestock husbandry does and why so many people hate wild predators except in zoos. The English had been practicing both kinds of intensive food production—using plants and animals—for several millennia, which vastly enlarged the carrying capacity of their land and allowed their population to grow big—perhaps too big. In 1600 England (excluding Scotland, then a separate nation) had a population of about 5 million, nearly 350 times as many people as the Powhatans, living in an area not quite 10 times the size of the Powhatan region. Not surprisingly, England was then experiencing widespread unemployment and food shortages.[19] The Powhatans, on the other hand, only practiced one method of husbandry, gardening, and they only did that part-time. That was their choice, albeit one the climate and available animals pressured them into, and they kept on making that choice until the invaders nearly crowded them completely out of Tsenacomoco in the eighteenth century.[20]

That choice meant that a limited amount of food was available in hard times such as early summer, after the spring fish runs had subsided but the year's crops had not yet ripened. Even less food was available in really hard times, such as the dry years that are known to have afflicted the region in 1562–71 and 1606–12.[21] Hard times made people thin. John Smith wrote, "It is strange to see how their bodies alter with their diet, even as the deer and wild beasts they seem fat and lean, strong and weak."[22] Lean people have fewer reserves to live on if they get sick or if the food runs out. If they are malnourished, they are more likely to get sick. Very lean women often have a harder time conceiving; if they are malnourished, they will have more difficulty carrying fetuses to term. Annual hardship would take its toll on the birthrate, along with other cultural practices that kept husbands and wives apart, such as not sleeping together the night before a deer hunt or for several nights before going to war. Therefore Virginia's human population had never grown as dense on the land as the English one was. And the Powhatans' territory would be seen by the invaders as "empty," even though in their own traditional way the native people were using every square foot of it.

Lastly, Powhatan families produced everything that they themselves needed for a relatively simple lifestyle. Their way of life did not include writing or very intrusive government. They only raised enough food and made enough clothing and housing for their families' needs, plus some corn for tribute to support their chiefs' expenses on diplomatic occasions. Tsenacomoco's people were not accustomed to making the land produce as much as possible of any one thing and then trading for life's other necessities, real and imagined. They therefore had limited corn to spare, even in bountiful years. They certainly were not prepared to begin supporting—temporarily, much less for the long term—a horde of intrusive "visitors" who were unable or unwilling to feed themselves. That kind of lavish support would have required a major change in lifestyle for the native people. Because it was their country and their ways had worked for their ancestors for many hundreds of years, they saw no need to change those ways just because some foreigners began coming around. Let the foreigners learn how Real People lived instead.

2

The VIP Lifestyle

VIRGINIA ALGONQUIAN leaders, called *weroances* (literally, "com-manders")[1] in the Powhatan language, were what cultural anthropologists call "chiefs," not kings or emperors. Chiefs by definition are only moderately powerful hereditary leaders. That is true, too, of paramount chiefs like Powhatan, who rule over other chiefs. They lack standing armies but can command large numbers of personally loyal followers. They do not tax their subjects but instead collect tribute that is supposed to be paid voluntarily, as though to a relative. They may have life-and-death power over their people, but only in the most elaborate chiefdoms, like the one in pre-Contact Hawaii, did they have that power on a daily basis. They are more likely to be able to wield such power only on diplomatic and religious occasions, when they act as the official representatives of their people. Finally, they themselves are bound by customary law, and they cannot intrude too deeply into their subjects' lives: they usually cannot forbid them to trade, for instance, even if a war is going on. And people who wrong one another are not considered to be wronging the chief as well, by breaking "the king's peace." A chief is not responsible for keeping the peace all the time, because he has no constabulary force to deploy. Unless the person wronged is a relative of the chief, the chief stays out of the dispute: custom says that victims and their relatives take revenge.[2]

It is too bad that most of the foreign writers about Powhatan culture were people who saw weroances only on special occasions—special because a foreigner was present. The writer who was an exception, the interpreter Henry Spelman, did not include enough detail in his account to give a clear impression of their lives on ordinary days. There are only two hints about there usually being few status differences between weroances and their subjects. One is from John Smith, who said that even the greatest chief in the land, namely Powhatan, was proud of knowing how to do all the things that lower-status men did, such as making moccasins. Knowledge of that sort would have been spurned as degrading by European royalty of the time. The other hint is from William Strachey, who reported that although Powhatan had the title of *mamanatowick*, or "great king," he was always addressed, "himself in presence," by his personal name of Wahunsenacawh.[3]

Powhatan's Chiefly Duties

Wahunsenacawh was a moderately powerful chief, as chiefs go.[4] His duties seem to have been primarily military and diplomatic, although at times— probably when relatives were involved—he was known to preside over the execution of criminals. So was his son-in-law, the priest Uttamatomakkin.[5]

Most warfare in the Native American world was of the guerrilla kind, with local men being able to determine when and how they fought. That was also true in Virginia, for judging by the events of 1607, the paramount chief let his district weroances and even their subject (i.e., hamlet) weroances make up their own minds about whether and how often to engage in hostilities with the newcomers. However, Powhatan (and later Opechancanough) had the additional power and influence to make large numbers of men turn out for a mass assault. He seems not to have used that power often, though, perhaps because it was a fragile commodity, dependent upon success each time. Powhatan's main military usefulness to his district weroances probably was as a planner of overall strategy. For one thing, he himself came from a frontier area (Powhatan town, near the falls of the James River) where hostilities with the non-Algonquian Monacans to the west were an annual event. He may also have lived among the Carolina Iroquoian speakers and learned from them. Thus he probably had wider-than-average experience of dealing face-to-face with enemy forces. For another thing, as paramount chief Powhatan had access to the priests at Uttamussak on the Pamunkey River, which was the holiest temple and had the most highly rated temple staff in all the land.[6] Those priests were especially adept at communicating with and getting advice from their deity and, more than senior warriors, had "the resulting voice" in war councils.[7]

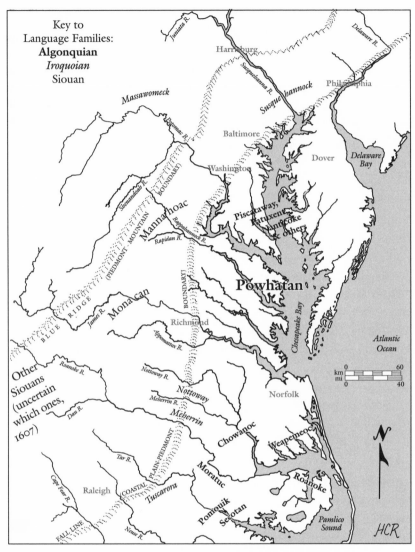

The mid-Atlantic region, showing language families

Chiefs, especially paramount chiefs, usually draw some of their influence over their people because of that access to priests and temples. The Powhatan religion was not well recorded by the evangelistic English, but it is plain that temples were not equivalent to churches by any means. The general public did not go into them; they went to ceremonies held outdoors. That lack of access made the buildings and their contents seem mysteriously powerful to the common folk, and that power rubbed off on the weroances and priests who could enter them. In Virginia and other parts of the prehistoric Southeast, temples doubled as mortuary buildings, for chiefs' bodies were kept there. They also served as treasure houses and sometimes as armories. That meant that they represented ancestral, economic, and military power.[8] A late seventeenth-century writer mentioned that specimens of medicinal plants were kept there as well, which would add the power of curing to the aura of the temple.[9] All those things made a potent combination.

The other major function of a chief, especially a paramount chief, is diplomatic. He or she represents all the people when foreign dignitaries come to town. The requirements of that job therefore are genuine capability as a negotiator and the ability to project great "presence" in a formal meeting. Both Powhatan and Opechancanough had these attributes in abundance, but tradition provided that the setting in which they met emissaries enhanced their qualities considerably. As it happened, Virginia Algonquian culture used some of the same ploys that English culture (and the cultures of other potentates around the world) used.[10]

A weroance did not go out to meet visitors; they were escorted in. A moderately important weroance, like Powhatan's son Pochins at Kecoughtan, met foreigners outside his house, sitting on a mat. In the case of a paramount chief, the visitors had to be led through the town, through the anterooms of the meetinghouse, and into the special reception room, where the mamanatowick sat on a bedstead built across the end of the house. Powhatan sat there, resting comfortably on a bed of fine furs with a lovely young woman on each side of him (his wives, of course). Everyone else sat on mats on the floor: more wives, and also councillors.

The weroance, the wives, and the councillors were all dressed up, showing off their finery. The leading guest was seated facing the chief, and in silence both parties smoked a pipe of tobacco. Then the best orators in the town welcomed the visitors with long, flowery, emphatic speeches, after which a

"Powhatan Held this state & fashion." Detail of John Smith's map, originally engraved by William Hole in 1612 and published that year in London along with Smith's *Map of Virginia*.

feast was laid on. The food was high-status cakes of corn (not tuckahoe from the marshes), nut milk (a great delicacy), and the meat of deer and wild turkeys (the premier game animals)—all of it in embarrassing profusion intended to demonstrate the chief's wealth and put the guests off-balance. Leftovers, and there would be plenty, went to the leading guest's retinue. If the visitors were only making a very short stay, negotiations were conducted thereafter. Otherwise, the rest of the day was spent in watching the townspeople dance to honor the guests and in more feasting and oratory. That night the townspeople put up the visitors, and the leading guest (assumed by the English reporters to be male) was given an added perquisite: "a woman fresh painted red with puccoon and oil, to be his bedfellow."[11]

Powhatan's Chiefly "Luxuries"

Anyone who entertained dignitaries on that scale needed to have luxuries—visible ones and out-of-sight ones—that were in fact necessities in fulfilling the job. In other words, chiefs had expenses.[12]

Weroances, like other potentates and celebrities in the world, got some of their mystique by attracting the opposite sex, preferably in large numbers. Where ordinary men had one wife, weroances would have more than that. (Regrettably, the English writers are silent about whether the *weroansquas*, the female chiefs, had multiple husbands; in some other parts of the world, such women did.) A mamanatowick like Powhatan had a horde of wives. They were not just for show, either: they were working women who happened to share a husband. In the Powhatan world women and girls did the farming, the firewood collecting, and the wild edible plant gathering, so these women (and Powhatan's daughters) partially supported themselves and also added significantly to the store of corn that could be used in feasts. The wives also did the corn pounding and any other food preparation (such as butchering) that had to be done in advance of important guests' arrival, so the feast would be ready for others (such as Powhatan's daughters) to cook while they themselves went to the reception to adorn their husband's presence. And where did those wives get the meat in their diet? No ordinary male mortal, however proficient in food getting, could bring in enough deer and fish to support them all at even the poverty level. No eyewitness writer answers this conundrum, but a mamanatowick did surround himself with forty or fifty bodyguards.[13]

Some of those men could go out hunting and fishing on the boss's behalf each day, with the boss's wives and children being the beneficiaries. It is also likely that the mamanatowick's sons, who left their mothers and joined his household when they were older children, brought in food as well.

Weroances had bigger houses than other people, but then they needed larger accommodations. First, sleeping room was required for all the wives-in-residence and at least some of the children. Second, the house had that extra room with the bedstead across the end, where official callers were received. That room had to be large enough to seat not only the visitors but also the wives-in-residence and the councillors.

Weroances and their wives needed to look good on dress-up occasions. That did not mean having an elaborate wardrobe in the Powhatan world, although important people could have some exquisite garments.[14] Instead it meant having many fine furs to pile onto the weroance's bedstead, many well-tanned deerskins to drape over his and his wives' shoulders and around their torsos, plenty of red paint made from puccoon (which had to be imported), and a large supply of copper, freshwater pearl, and shell jewelry (much of which also had to be imported).[15] These things were the stuff of wealth in the native world, and weroances acquired them through trade and, in the case of the mamanatowick, partly as tribute from distant subjects who made them.

Other luxuries claimed by weroances were perquisites of their elevated status. A chief who wanted to marry a girl did not have to dicker with her parents over the amount of the bridewealth. (Bridewealth is the opposite of a dowry, indicating that a Powhatan man paid for the privilege of acquiring a working woman in his household.) He (and possibly she, a weroansqua) simply stated how much he would pay to acquire a spouse, and the marriage was on. A girl chosen by a male chief did not have any say about the marriage, either, unlike women courted by commoners, who had the right to say no. But because a mamanatowick's marriages, at least, were only temporary, marriage to one was not lifelong bondage; instead it was a bit like being drafted into the army for a couple of years, without having to go through boot camp.

Weroances were permitted to go into temples, unlike ordinary mortals. But, then, they had to make important decisions about handling foreigners, so they needed to consult with their priests and perhaps directly with the local deities themselves. And each time a weroance went into a temple, he came up against his own mortality, for that is where his corpse would lie after he died.[16]

Ordinary people were buried in the ground soon after death. Chiefs' bodies, on the other hand, were allowed to rot until defleshed, after which the bones were collected, wrapped into a bundle along with jewelry, and placed on a bier in the temple. Great ceremony probably was connected with each stage of the process, though the only hint of it comes from a record of 1621 that merely mentions in passing the "taking up of Powhatan's bones." The bones of Powhatan were probably stored in the temple at Uttamussak.

Becoming a Chief in Tsenacomoco

One inherited the right to be a weroance through the mother's line. The common folk seem not to have followed that rule, insofar as their kinship system can be reconstructed, but weroances differed: they were matrilineal. However, that was not the same thing as being matriarchal, meaning rule by women. Powhatan chiefly women passed the position to their children, but they did not rule themselves unless they survived their brothers. Let us look at Powhatan's own family to make sense of it.[17]

Powhatan inherited his right to rule from his mother. His heir was his next-eldest brother, Opitchapam, and after that, his brothers Opechancanough and Kekataugh. All these men except Kekataugh did in fact rule the paramount chiefdom, one after the other. All of them are known to have had multiple wives and children, but none of the children could inherit from them—which is just as well, because a man with multiple wives could easily have two or more children born at the same instant. A woman's children, even if they are quintuplets, come out one at a time, in a definite order. Powhatan had two sisters; the elder would rule after all her brothers had died, and her younger sister would succeed her, if one or both of them lived long enough. That did not happen in real life, because Opechancanough outlived everybody. If Opechancanough had died as young as Kekataugh seems to have done, then at least one of the sisters would have had a turn, after which the elder sister's children would have ruled, first her sons and then her daughters. If that family failed for heirs, then the younger sister's children would have ruled, first her sons and then her daughters. In real life, Opechancanough was succeeded by a male, who would have been his nephew (sister's son), great-nephew (sister's daughter's son), or great-grandnephew (sister's daughter's daughter's son); no one knows which.

This system, so strange to Euro-Americans, had a number of advantages over the European system of royal inheritance. The Powhatan system lacked a Salic law, a males-only law that disinherited even competent adult daughters in favor of a son, even if he was a baby or an idiot. Chiefly women who had children of either gender had heirs. The Powhatan system also made it nearly impossible to come up with an underage monarch and a long regency by quarreling courtiers, something that was the bane of several European countries (especially Scotland) in the fifteenth through the seventeenth centuries. A paramount chiefdom in Virginia could not have afforded such instability. The mamanatowick had no bureaucrats to run the country while he could not, and enough enemies regularly intruded into his territories that he had to be an adult who could make sensible military decisions. So the Powhatan system provided that a whole set of siblings would rule before the position descended into the next generation, giving the sisters' children plenty of time to mature. The sisters themselves would have to live a long time to come to power, but by the time they succeeded, they would have seen and heard enough, even though they had (presumably) never been warriors themselves, that with the priests' advice they could make sound military decisions for their people. Sometimes they got earlier training by being appointed chief of a satellite town, as the Appamattuck chief's sister Opossunoquonuske did.[18]

The way that Powhatan chiefs inherited their position meant that though a weroansqua's daughter was her heir, a weroance's daughter, like Pocahontas, was not an heir. Pocahontas was therefore not a princess in the European sense. Her importance was always limited, and later on she would be a ruler's niece, and still later a ruler's cousin. The seat of power would recede from her as time went on. Everyone in her native world understood that just as weroances' wives were temporary VIPs, so too were weroances' children. In any case, everyone including the chiefs themselves had to work for a living on most days of the year. It was only on special occasions that the rulers and their spouses—but not children like Pocahontas—would paint themselves up and shine in public, to be seen and admired by foreigners who came to call.

3

Introducing the Chiefly Family

P O W H A T A N , Opechancanough, and Pocahontas were surrounded by a great concourse of people for most of their lives. Part of this intensely social life was due to the retinue required by the chiefly position of the two men, which rubbed off for a time on the daughter of one of them. But some of it was due to the size of the chiefly family itself. Thanks to the chiefs' ability to be prodigiously polygynous (multiple wives; polygamy = multiple spouses), the immediate family of a weroance was always big and the family of a mamanatowick was huge. Children could get lost there, unless a child had the personality of a Pocahontas.

Powhatan, Son of . . .

The paramount chief Powhatan was one of at least six children, four boys and two girls. But neither John Smith, the one who asked him about his siblings, nor any other writer ever recorded who the parents were, so that nothing is known about them. Perhaps nobody asked Powhatan or his brothers (whom Smith met) who their parents were. Or somebody asked but did not bother to write down the answer. Of the six siblings, only the boys' names come down to us, most likely because they were the mamanatowick himself and his three next heirs, any one of whom could make difficulties for the invaders of their country. Seventeenth-century Europeans were not nearly so interested in celebrities and personalities as we are today, the "cult of celebrity" being a twentieth-century phenomenon. And the general public's fascination with genealogy was invigorated in 1976, thanks to a novel/film called *Roots.* We cannot "upstream" our present-day interests and expect seventeenth-century authors to write for us in detail.

An equally probable explanation for the information gap, though, is that Smith or someone else asked about Powhatan's parents and got a refusal to talk about them. Many traditional Native American cultures had a custom of not mentioning the names of the dead, either to reduce the survivors' grief or for fear of their ghosts returning to earth and making people sick (for that is what ghosts were believed to do). Refusing to speak of the dead in order to spare their families' feelings was recorded for linguistic relatives—and therefore distant biological kin—of the Powhatans in what is now the New York City area. If the kinfolks did it, the Powhatans may have done it. William Strachey was regrettably vague when he mentioned Powhatan people swearing "by the manes [departed spirits] of their dead father[s]." Those "fathers" may or may not have been named in the oaths.[1]

Whatever the reason, this silence doubly frustrates our curiosity because another fairly famous character has been suggested as Powhatan's father, as well as perhaps the same person as Opechancanough:[2] Don Luis. It would be best deal with Don Luis here.

In 1559 or 1560 a youth (age uncertain, native name: Paquinquineo)[3] was visiting in the Carolina Sounds region when the Spanish came calling. The youth voluntarily departed with the foreigners, who converted him and named him Don Luis after his patron. In 1570 he led a missionary party back to his homeland, which was the Paspahegh territory at the mouth of the Chickahominy River.[4] After the demise of the mission, he remained among his relatives, and he disappears thereafter from the historical record—except for one tantalizing entry. In 1615 Ralph Hamor wrote that the Chickahominies (and perhaps others in the region) detested the Spanish, and he gave a rather vague reason: "For Powhatan's father was driven by them from the West Indies into these parts."[5] Neither Hamor (who had a good interpreter to work with) nor any other English writer gave any further information to explain that statement. If the "father" referred to was a social one rather than a biological one,[6] then anything is possible, including an adoptive relationship of some kind. It is a pity that no one recorded the personal name of Powhatan's father (or "fathers") so that we could compare it with that of Paquinquineo, aka Don Luis. Instead, to consider biological relationships between Don Luis and others, we must try to compare the ages of some of the people involved.

The result shows that Don Luis probably belonged to Powhatan's generation rather than that of the mamanatowick's parents.

Most accounts agree that Don Luis was a youth or even a boy when he joined the Spanish. It was young people that the Spanish and other Europeans wanted as captives, because they could learn a new language fast while retaining their original one.[7] That would put Don Luis's probable birth date between 1540 and 1550. John Smith wrote that Powhatan was about sixty in 1607, with William Strachey saying "eighty"; a later writer (with information from Pocahontas's retinue in England) cautioned that the age given for him (probably the "eighty") was exaggerated because of the native people's preference for counting spring and fall as separate years.[8] Smith's estimate means a birth date of about 1547, Strachey's anywhere from 1527 to 1567. Smith, who saw Wahunsenacawh in the flesh, was probably right, but let us try another tack as well. Powhatan had a grown son (Pochins) in 1596–97, for when he conquered the Kecoughtans in that year, he installed the son there as weroance.[9] Assuming that Powhatan, known as a talented hunter and warrior, acquired his first wife and began reproducing early, and that the son was something of a prodigy as well, a late birth date for Powhatan would have been around 1560, when the youth Don Luis was first meeting the Spanish. This numbers game all but eliminates the possibility of Don Luis as Powhatan's biological father. It seems more likely that Powhatan was born into the same generation as Don Luis.

Opechancanough was one of Powhatan's heirs, usually called his "brother," which probably meant full or half brother (sharing a mother). The word may also have meant a mother's younger sister's son. No one knows how much younger than Powhatan he was—or even whether he was, in fact, biologically younger. If he was a mother's-sister's-son kind of "brother," he could have been older but farther down the line of heirs. The seventeenth-century writers did not think to inquire closely, and it is really an anthropologist's question anyway. At the time of his death in 1646, Opechancanough was said by a contemporary (albeit a foreigner) to be nearly one hundred years old,[10] which if not an exaggeration could make him Powhatan's contemporary or elder. In any case, he had little more chance to be Don Luis's son than Powhatan did, for the same reasons of timing. He also was not Don Luis himself (any more than Powhatan was), because he came from the wrong family.

All the seventeenth-century accounts that mention the matter at all agree that at the beginning of his career, Powhatan had inherited six chiefdoms:

Pamunkey, Youghtanund, and Mattaponi in the York River drainage and Powhatan (town), Arrohateck, and Appamattuck in the James River basin near the fall line. He inherited them through his mother, not his father, for inheritance among weroances was matrilineal. In native terms his father's identity was not very important; it was his mother who bequeathed him the right to rule, once she and all her siblings were dead. We do not know whether Powhatan's mother outlived her brothers and reigned over those six territories herself. But what was true for Powhatan was true for Opechancanough; he was heir to those six territories, because of who his mother had been in her home area. Don Luis, on the other hand, came from a chiefly family—and had a right to rule—downriver in Paspahegh,[11] which in 1570 was not part of Powhatan's paramount chiefdom. The scanty Spanish reports suggest that Don Luis, too, got his rights as a weroance because of who his mother was. At least, the Spanish recorded the same passing along of the position from brother to brother. If the Paspaheghs were indeed matrilineal, then Don Luis's having chiefly rights among them would mean that his mother and Powhatan's and Opechancanough's mother(s) were entirely different people, belonging to different families because their ruling rights were in different places. Therefore, Opechancanough could not have been the same man as Don Luis (Paquinquineo).

One last item about Powhatan's father. Robert Beverley wrote in 1705 that the native people of that time were saying that Opechancanough did not come from Virginia at all. Instead "he was a prince of a foreign nation and came to them a great way from the southwest."[12] Beverley and his contemporaries took that to mean the distant southwest, as in Mexico, which I find to be more than a little far-fetched. However, a closer southwestern origin is entirely possible for Opechancanough's (and perhaps Powhatan's) father.

The ceramics that archaeologists find along the Appomattox and the James below the falls (in Powhatan's original inheritance) are called Gaston-Cashie, named for places in the inner coastal plain region of North Carolina where they were first uncovered in modern times. As Randolph Turner has pointed out,[13] in the last few decades before Jamestown was founded, the people in a swath of territory from the Tuscarora area along the Roanoke River, through the Meherrin and Nottoway territories, and northward to the James River near its falls were all making the same kind of pottery, indicating alliances sealed by marriages. The Paspaheghs, on the other hand, had some of the same pottery as the people in the Carolina Sounds region, where the Paspahegh youth Paquinquineo/Don Luis went visiting.[14] Among the Virginia Algonquian speakers, at least, women went to live in their husbands' towns.[15] Intensive marriage back and forth would have meant an exchange of pottery-making women throughout the alliance and, after a generation or two elapsed, a common style of pottery. Given the ceramic finds and the oral tradition, Powhatan's mother may well have married a man from among those Virginia/Carolina Iroquoian speakers.

It is even possible, though unlikely because of their future position, that her children may have lived down south with their father's people until it was time for her—or the eldest of the boys—to become paramount chief of the six territories. In any case, the boys would have grown up speaking Powhatan as well as at least one Iroquoian language even if their father was not foreign. Bilingual people were as common in the native world back then, when completely different languages could be encountered a few dozen miles or kilometers away, as they are among Europeans today.[16]

The Extended Family

Powhatan's biological relatives were fairly numerous in his generation and abundant in his children's generation because of all the wives he and his brothers were allowed to marry. But seventeenth-century people's lack of interest in celebrities' private lives means they recorded limited personal information about Powhatan himself and even less about his relatives, including Pocahontas. Let us dispose of Powhatan's two sisters immediately, for the seventeenth-century writers say next to nothing about them: no names, no mention of husbands, and only one note about children: between the two of them, there were two daughters, who were also heirs to the position of paramount chief.[17] Nothing else is known about them.

Powhatan's immediate heir was his brother Opitchapam, who, like Opechancanough, may have been a half brother or a mother's sister's son. In 1607 Opitchapam ruled the populous and prestigious Pamunkeys as viceroy and was living in the Pamunkey River town of Menapacute, where John Smith was taken to meet him. After his brother's death in 1618, he came to rule under the name Otiotan or Itoyatin, and he appears to have died in late 1628 or early 1629. The number of his wives and children was never recorded, and we have the name of only one son: Wecuttanow, who was suspected of trying to poison John Smith in 1609.[18]

Opechancanough was the next heir, being paramount chief from 1628–29 until his death in 1646. That official reign was preceded by a period of de facto rule that began well before Powhatan's death. Officially, he presided as weroance over the Youghtanunds, strategically a more dangerous place to be on the Pamunkey River thanks to encounters with Monacan hunters from west of the fall line. But his influence was such that he was sometimes called the "king of Pamunkey" long before Opitchapam became mamanatowick and made him viceroy of that territory. His wives and children went unrecorded with two exceptions. He had at least one daughter, for one was sent to Werowocomoco in February 1608 to beg the English visitors there to come upriver to see her father.[19] He also lost a favorite wife: another district weroance, Pepiscunimah of Quiyoughcohannock, seduced her away and made her his favorite instead. In 1610–11 William Strachey met the woman, living with her new husband, and he found her only moderately good-looking but extremely stately in her bearing. Being the favorite of two powerful men in succession seems to have gone to her head. She is the only Virginia Algonquian dignitary who is recorded as having refused to get out of watercraft under her own power: she insisted on being carried ashore. Opechancanough apparently was powerless to get this siren to return, and they were considered to be divorced. He had other comforters, however, for by 1608 he had "his wife, women, and children."[20] As for the seducer, Powhatan was angry on his brother's behalf and had the culprit busted down in rank: he became the *tanx weroance* (minor chief; literally, "lesser commander") of a mere hamlet, with a brother of his as the Quiyoughcohannocks' regent, and a very young son of Powhatan's was made the official weroance of the district.[21] The only personal description of Opechancanough we have is one from oral tradition that Robert Beverley recorded: "This Opechancanough was a man of large stature, noble presence, and extraordinary parts. Though he had no advantage of literature [formal education], . . . yet he was perfectly skilled in the art of governing his rude countrymen."[22]

The last of Powhatan's "brothers" was Kekataugh, who was coruler of the Pamunkey heartland with Opitchapam in 1607. He may have been the brother of Powhatan who met the first English exploring party to go up the James River. Nothing more is known about him, and he disappeared from the records after 1612. Only if he had outlived Opechancanough could he ever have become the paramount chief.

Powhatan Himself

John Smith met Powhatan and described him thusly: "He is of personage a tall, well-proportioned man, with a sour look, his head somewhat gray, his beard so thin that it seems none at all, his age near 60; of a very able and hardy body to endure any labor."[23]

William Strachey, who never had a chance to meet Powhatan but who knew one of his brothers-in-law, added that he was

> a goodly [good-looking] old man, not yet shrinking, . . . of a tall stature and clean [lean] limbs, of a sad aspect, round fat visaged [round face with wide cheekbones], with gray hairs, but plain [i.e., unbraided] and thin, hanging upon his broad shoulders, some few hairs upon his chin and so on his upper lip [i.e., he did not pluck his beard, a privilege of age]. He hath been a strong and able [man], sinewy, active, and of a daring spirit, vigilant, ambitious, subtle to enlarge his dominions. Cruel hath he been and quarrelous as [much] with his own weroances for trifles . . . as also with his neighbors in his younger days, though now delighted in security and pleasure and therefore stands upon reasonable conditions of peace with all the great and absolute [foreign chiefs] about him, and is likewise more quietly settled among his own.[24]

The "sour look" or "sad aspect" probably stemmed from lines on his face developed while he was having to be constantly on his guard against foreign enemies and disobedience among the chiefdoms that he had recently added to his dominions. A great many self-made business people or people who have achieved great political power have less than friendly countenances when their faces are at rest. The leanness was something he shared with most, if not all, of his male subjects. It was not only the low-fat and low-sugar diet they ate. Virginia Algonquian men were built like cross-country runners because that is what they had to be as professional hunters. Few deer were killed at the first shot. Usually they were wounded and then had to be run down and finished off, however great a tract of wooded uplands that meant crossing. Men did not give up because a deer ran away. A man had to bring home carcasses back across all those miles, in order to help (note the word *help*) feed and clothe his family, or else he might face a divorce.[25] Chiefs were in that situation, too: the tribute they collected did not include venison to eat, sinew for sewing, bones for tools, etc. Even the mamanatowick himself hunted not only because he enjoyed doing it[26] but because he had to do it as long as he was physically able. Powhatan was still hunting for his family in 1607, hence his spare frame.

Powhatan, and also Opechancanough as a subject weroance, dressed the same way that ordinary men did when they had no important visitors to meet with. That means that his tall, lean figure was draped only in a deerskin apron when he was in town (there were mats upon which to place his bare bottom), and with a breechclout, leggings, and moccasins when he went into the forest. The latter ensemble was his basic hunting attire when chasing a deer. The stuffed deer head and skin that he wore when stalking and the deerskin mantle he wore in very cold weather had to be cast aside when chasing a wounded animal, to be retrieved later. Skimpy clothing allowed freedom of movement and easier passage through the forest; even VIPs were expected to acclimatize themselves accordingly.

Opechancanough and most other male subjects of the paramount chief did not wear their hair hanging down to their shoulders, as Powhatan did. And Powhatan probably did not do it when he was out hunting. Hair can get caught in bowstrings, with painful results. So the men's wives shaved the right-hand side of their heads for them (presumably left-handed fellows did the same, for conformity's sake), cut the hair front to back along the crown moderately short to make a roach, and let the left side grow long—"an ell [45 inches, or 1.14 meters] long." This hair was then braided up into an elaborate knot (which kept left-handed men from losing their hair to their bowstrings). On ceremonial occasions the knot was stuck through with various objects, feathers being only one of them. One man's wartime trophy, stuck onto this hair, was "the hand of their enemy, dried."[27] Both weroances and commoners used another body part for garish display: the ears. All men (and perhaps women) had multiple holes through the fleshy parts of the ear, the better to display whatever wealth they had in copper or chains of freshwater pearls or shell beads. One man chose to wear a young, live greensnake through one of his holes, letting the harmless creature "crawl about his neck [and] oftentimes he suffers [it] to kiss his lips."[28] With age and after bearing jewelry on many important occasions, the fleshy parts of Powhatan's and Opechancanough's ears probably drooped.

The name by which Powhatan is generally known was actually similar to what the British call a "throne name," the official name assumed when one ascends the throne and becomes a monarch. Powhatan came from the town of Powhatan near the falls of the James River. The town's name may have been taken from the falls just upstream, for William Strachey mentioned "that cataract, or fall of water, which the [native people] call Paquacowng." The paramount chief's personal name was Wahunsenacawh, the meaning of which is unknown, and that is what his people usually still called him after he became mamanatowick. He also had the name or title of Ottaniack, for which no translation was recorded. He got the name Powhatan because his "frontier neighbor princes" (such as those of the Monacans, Nottoways, etc.) called him by it in his early days in power, and the name stuck.[29]

The Paramount Chief's Ménage

The social unit of Powhatan, his wives, and his children, both in and out of residence, fluctuated from year to year, even from season to season, making it a ménage rather than a family. The reason for that fluctuation was the revolving-door policy he (and perhaps his weroances) had on wives, as well as the custom governing what to do with the resulting children.

According to writers who had a good interpreter, as well as the account of one interpreter himself,[30] Powhatan had (or, more likely had had) "many more th[a]n one hundred" wives by 1610. When he was ready for a new one, he would have his minions bring the best-looking marriageable girls (i.e., girls who had at least had their first menstrual period) to his capital town. He would look them over, choose the one he liked, and pay the bridewealth to her parents. The new wife would then be ensconced in his household, along with his other wives, until she bore a child. At that point she would be sent back to her own family, along with the child, and Powhatan would send "copper and beads" for their support. The wife would need that income, for she was still married to the paramount chief, and she had no on-the-spot husband to hunt and fish for her. Her brothers and male cousins could take up the slack, but it apparently was felt that they should be compensated. The child would go to live with Powhatan when "old enough," and the wife would either be "given" to one of Powhatan's councillors or else divorced, which freed her to remarry. Powhatan's strategy behind this system of marriages and divorces was to establish in-law relations with a very large number of people, both inside and outside his dominions, thus binding them to him by ties of kinship as well as politics. It is a strategy that has long been practiced by aspiring potentates elsewhere in the world.

Such a coming and going of wives each year implied something else: Powhatan could not afford to get emotionally close to any of those young women. If he did, it would lead to a wrenching separation when custom decreed that the wife and her new infant had to leave. Powhatan may have been in that condition in 1610–11. His favorite daughter, Pocahontas, had just married. Now his favorite wife, Winganuske ("good woman") had had a daughter, and she was supposed to leave. But when William Strachey was at Jamestown (mid-1610 to mid-1611), he heard that Winganuske was still Powhatan's favorite-in-residence, even though their daughter had been born sometime before. Regrettably, neither Strachey nor anyone else asked later just how much longer Powhatan had kept Winganuske with him before giving in to tradition. It may have been that particular "hedonistic" tradition (as Strachey viewed it), politically useful but potentially hard on the emotions, that led Powhatan to attach himself so strongly to a daughter like Pocahontas.

Besides that infant of Winganuske's, Powhatan was said in 1610–11 to have "then living 20 sons and 20 daughters."[31] Each of these children went through the process of being raised as an only child by his or her mother for a number of years, albeit within a gaggle of maternal cousins, because everyone lived clustered together in extended families. When the child had received enough individualized training in the skills needed by adults of her or his sex, she or he moved to Powhatan's household in the capital town. That household would be comprised of a welter of older half siblings, whom the child might have met on visits to Daddy, as well as numerous stepmothers-in-residence, some of them new to the capital themselves. No one would be required to undertake the training of a young arrival, so it made sense for Powhatan's children to rejoin him only when they had learned enough to be able to earn their keep on their own. Typical of Native American traditional societies, the move was made at no set age. Each child entered the next stage of life when ready to do so.

It was easy to get lost in that crowd around Powhatan, especially at times when the paramount chief was preoccupied with the incursions of enemies into his territories. In that, Powhatan resembled modern business tycoons and high-ranking military and political figures: at the best of times, he had limited attention to give to any one of his children. One way to get and keep such a father's attention was to prove oneself to be politically astute and therefore useful as a viceroy somewhere in his dominions. Several people are known to have taken that route. One was a wife, Oholasc, who was made the new weroansqua of Quiyoughcohannock after Pepiscunimah stole Opechancanough's favorite wife and lost his position as weroance in consequence.[32] Her having had Powhatan's son Tatahcoope, who would be her heir, probably helped. Nothing is known of her personal background, whether it was chiefly or otherwise, but it is unlikely that she would have been appointed weroansqua in Powhatan's dominions if the position had not unexpectedly opened up. She was probably assigned a regent because, like all Powhatan's wives, she was very young. Powhatan made two of his sons weroances as adults: Pochins at Kecoughtan and Parahunt at the town of Powhatan. Both of those were strategic frontier towns, which speaks volumes for the two sons' military and governing ability.

Several other children of the paramount chief appear in the historical record. The only other son to do so was Nantaquod (or Naukaquawis), who was one of the men who actually grabbed and held onto John Smith during his capture. Smith wrote later that he was "the most manliest, comeliest [handsomest], boldest spirit I ever saw in a [Powhatan man]."[33] Among the daughters, three are known by name and a fourth is known to have been married at the age of eleven to an important tribal leader "three days' journey" from Powhatan's then-capital on the upper Pamunkey River.[34] Matachanna was married to the priest Uttamatomakkin by 1616, when he (and perhaps she) accompanied Pocahontas to England. Another daughter, whose name was corrupted by the English into "Cleopatra," was still alive in 1641, when Pocahontas's son went to visit her. Nothing more is known of either woman. And then there was Pocahontas.

The Favorite Daughter

One daughter of Powhatan got and kept his attention—and ours—by sheer force of personality, and that was Pocahontas. Her mother's name and background were never recorded. If her English husband knew, he did not write it down, and no one else seems to have been interested at the time. However, if the girl had had a mother of exotic origin, John Smith would probably have said so in his 1624 *Generall Historie*, which had factual additions to his earlier works, as well as exaggerations. Smith uttered not a word about the mother, or about where Pocahontas had spent her early years.

She was probably born sometime during 1596. The several different estimates of what her age was in the late spring of 1608 range from ten to fourteen years.[35] The only figure we have directly from Pocahontas herself was the age she gave the engraver Simon van de Passe in January or February 1617: she was "*Aetatis suae 21 Anno*" ("in the 21st year of her age"), i.e., twenty but not yet twenty-one. Assuming she knew her own exact age—and not all non-Western peoples keep track of such a thing, birth order being more important—I am inclined to take the lady's word for it. She had turned twenty before January/February 1617, so she was most likely born in 1596. That would make her eleven when she first met the captive John Smith at the end of December 1607; by the time of her first visit to the fort at Jamestown, in the spring of 1608, she may have turned twelve. She apparently looked younger, judging by John Smith's earliest estimate of her being ten years old; perhaps it was because she was small.

No written description of Pocahontas has come down to us, other than John Smith's offhand remark in 1624 hinting that she was of short stature. However, we do have an engraved portrait of her that more than makes up the deficiency. Not surprisingly, it is an American Indian face, not the Europeanized one that appears in so many later portraits of her. Her face has high, wide cheekbones like her father's, with hollows beneath them. Her cleft chin is squarish, her mouth somewhat wide. The partial epicanthic folds over her eyes give her a somewhat almond-eyed look.[36]

Pocahontas, as well as her half sisters and stepmothers, would have looked like ordinary girls or women on ordinary days, for when no ceremonial or diplomatic occasion commanded their labor, they did the same work as everyone else in town.[37] That work was heavy physical work—getting firewood, carrying water, digging for edible roots, besides farming—so that the women and girls were heavily muscled. Their favorite leisure-time activity, dancing,[38] would have made them more so. A biological anthropologist once told me that the Late Woodland Indian women's skeletons she had examined had proved to be "more robust than that of the average man today."[39] That means that Pocahontas would have been not only short but stocky.

Ordinary dress for women was the same as it was for men, for both sexes were working parents. Around the town women wore a deerskin apron, or "semicinctum" as William Strachey put it.[40] When going into the woods for firewood or saplings for house building or into the marshes to gather reeds for mats, they would wear a breechclout and leggings to avoid getting scratched. Scratches could turn septic, especially in the warm months, and blood poisoning killed people. In colder weather women donned leather mantles, if they could afford them; the wealthier women also put on over-the-shoulder fringed deerskin dresses when meeting visitors. (The fringes were a conspicuous consumption feature as well as decoration, for they wasted hide that could otherwise provide warmth.)

That is how Pocahontas dressed after she reached puberty in about 1609–10.[41] Before that, like other girl children (no writer mentioned boys' dress), she wore nothing at all, except for a mantle in the very coldest weather. William Strachey was definite about Pocahontas's being prepubescent and "naked" when she visited Jamestown Fort, probably in 1608.[42] Not only that, but her hairstyle was the standard Powhatan girl's: "The forepart of their heads and sides [was] shaven close, the hinder part [left] very long, which they wind prettily and embroider in plaits, letting it hang so to the full length." Because the shaving was done by "grating" it off with a pair of mussel shells, the regrowing hair had to reach at least half an inch of length before the next "shave," which meant that usually much of Pocahontas's head was bristly rather than clean-shaven. When she married, she took on the married women's hairstyle, which was cut short all around, "as the Irish [do], by a dish."[43] At some point in her young life she would also have undergone the tattooing process that all Powhatan girls and women went through for beauty's sake. Strachey wrote that "the women have their arms, breasts, thighs, shoulders, and faces cunningly embroidered with divers works ... [by] pouncing or searing their skins with a kind of instrument heated in the fire. They figure therein flowers and fruits of sundry lively kinds, as also snakes, serpents, efts [salamanders], etc." Those designs contrast with the geometrical ones favored by Algonquian-speaking women in the Carolina Sounds region.[44] Pocahontas's tattoos do not appear in the only portrait we have of her, the engraving of 1617; in it the only visible parts of the lady, her face and hands, show no "embroidery."

Pocahontas's given name was Amonute, the meaning of which is unknown. She also had a secret, very personal name, Matoaka, which she would reveal only after her conversion to Christianity. But her best-known name was a nickname that she earned, probably after she arrived at her father's court. William Strachey, who heard it from Powhatan's brother-in-law,[45] recorded her given name and went on to say that "Pocahontas" meant "little wanton."[46] He was also told by compatriots in Jamestown, who had met her a couple of years before, that she was a "well-featured but wanton young girl."[47] "Wanton" is almost an obsolete word today, and by the nineteenth century it had come to have only the meaning "lewd." However, in the early 1600s, according to the *Oxford English Dictionary,* the word had several meanings: sportive, capricious, insolent, insensible to justice or pity, and (since the thirteenth century) lewd. Add in the sexual nature of much traditional Native American humor (when children but not strangers may be around),[48] and the reason for the child's nickname becomes apparent. She was trying to get her busy father's attention, amidst a welter of stepmothers and half siblings, and her father was such a formidable man that "at the least frown their greatest will tremble."[49] So she became a court jester, making him laugh in spite of himself, and at himself, until he protested that she was a cruel, bawdy, undisciplined little girl. The teasing nickname he gave her stuck. It would be wonderful to know what names she had been calling him.

The paramount chief had need of people who at the end of the day could take his mind off business, either by teasing him (Pocahontas) or seducing him (his wives). He may have had a fairly wealthy lifestyle and the loyal support of his relatives. But he was nonetheless a leader whose people were beset by new enemies, and who was building an "empire" in order to keep those enemies at bay. It is to Powhatan the nation builder that we now turn.

4

Expanding His Dominions

N O O N E K N O W S when Powhatan assumed the position of a (not yet "the")
paramount chief, but it could have been as early as the late 1560s. He inherited six district chiefdoms, each with its weroance who ruled over a lesser
weroance in each satellite town; any or all of these people could have been
cousins of his, though the historical record is silent about it. The districts
were: Powhatan town, three miles (5 km) downstream from the falls of the
James; Arrohateck, a bit farther downstream; Appamattuck, with its capital
town downstream from the falls of the Appomattox River and several satellite towns near the river's junction with the James; Pamunkey, along the lower
reaches of the river of the same name; Youghtanund, upstream from Pamunkey and reaching nearly to the river's splitting into the North and South
Anna; and Mattaponi, located all along the river of the same name below its
splitting into several heads.[1]

   All of these territories were just east of the fall line, that invisible line con-
necting the places in the rivers where rocks and rapids begin to occur as one
goes upstream (it is approximately followed today by Interstate 95 from Virginia northward). That means that whenever those districts' men went out
hunting, they ran the risk of encountering the neighbors, and the neighbors
were not friendly. Known as the Monacans, they spoke a language distantly
related to Sioux (hence their often being called Siouan speakers), and they
lived in towns along the James River in the piedmont province. They are
known to have been exchanging raids with the Powhatans every year in the
summer or "at the fall of the leaf" since at least 1570.[2]

The Powhatan paramount chiefdom in 1607

Downstream from Powhatan's inherited territories were fellow Algonquian speakers, ruled by district weroances who were independent of his family, although they may have been related in some way by marriage. The same was true of the people northward on the Rappahannock and Potomac Rivers, on the Eastern Shore, and southward on the Chowan River and the Carolina Sounds: Algonquian speakers ruled by chiefs, sometimes district chiefs with lesser chiefs under them. Two groups of people, however, were exceptions. One was the Piscataways and Nanticokes, who may already have developed paramount chiefs (governors of multiple districts, each with hamlets) by 1570. The Piscataways preserved an oral tradition, recorded in 1661, that their system had originated with the Nanticokes and that it had existed for thirteen "generations"[3]—probably meaning through thirteen rulers. The Powhatans had developed their paramount chiefs independently and perhaps a little later, because their word for such leaders was not a cognate with the northerners' terms: *mamanatowick* in Powhatan versus *tayac* in Piscataway and *tall'ak* (feminine: *tallakesk*) in Nanticoke.[4] The other exceptional group was the Chickahominies, who resisted putting themselves under the governance of any weroance at all, however able: they chose instead to be led by a council of eight elders. Their determinedly tribal government would resist joining Powhatan's organization until they absolutely had to, in the meantime remaining his allies. The Chickahominies' attitude toward Powhatan was shared by some of the chiefdoms near the Chesapeake Bay. They were generally friendly to Powhatan and very probably exchanged women as wives. But when Wahunsenacawh began expanding his dominions, he would have to conquer some of them rather than bringing them in peacefully.

Powhatan seems to have had good relations with other people: the Nottoways, Meherrins, and Tuscaroras, who all spoke languages distantly related to Iroquois (hence our calling them Iroquoian speakers). The historical and archaeological records both indicate that friendship, and no evidence indicates that either side tried to draw the other into a master-subject chiefdom situation. Instead, Powhatan traded with the Iroquoians for puccoon and other things. His major emissaries in the early days would have been the Appamattucks, who were to serve as guides to European explorers for the next century. By the early 1600s, when the Weyanocks had been incorporated into the paramount chiefdom, they were major middlemen, too, being sent to the "Anoegs" or Enoes.[5]

Lastly, a serious threat on the northwestern horizon was posed by people called either Massawomecks or Pocoughtraonacks. Their identity is uncertain, but they seem to have been Iroquoian speakers, probably a western branch of the Susquehannocks living in the Appalachian Mountains.[6] By the time Jamestown was settled, they were making regular raids on the Potomac River Algonquian speakers and scaring all the people living elsewhere in the Chesapeake region. They were more than usually fearsome at that time because they were wielding metal hatchets purchased from the French.[7] In 1570, though, they would have had only one military advantage: birchbark canoes. Paper birch does not grow outside the mountains at Virginia's latitude; that is why the native people had to use heavy dugouts for their water transport. Birchbark canoes are lighter and faster to paddle, so the Massawomecks could make lightning raids almost with impunity. When the victims tried to pursue their tormentors upstream, it was like chasing a Porsche in a pickup truck.

Enlarging the Domain

The very real annual threats from the Monacans, and the possibility if not the actuality of some raids down to the James by the Massawomecks, made the town of Powhatan a perilous place to live. Unlike most of Tsenacomoco's other towns, which were dispersed among fields and groves of trees, Powhatan town was a dense cluster of houses surrounded by a palisade. The palisade only worked, though, when people stayed inside it, and the mixed economy of farming and foraging demanded that men, women, and children range over their territory to get their food and fuel. The townspeople may have suffered repeated casualties from marauders, and they and the paramount chief based at the town must have been extremely sensitive to foreign threats. Powhatan once told John Smith during a conversation about war that he "had seen the death of all my people thrice, and not anyone living of those three generations but myself."[8] That statement has often been interpreted to mean epidemics of European diseases. But no archaeological evidence of epidemics has been found in the state, and that pronouncement from a man with Wahunsenacawh's background very likely has another meaning: he had seen three enemy attacks at Powhatan town that made for a very high death toll.[9]

Therefore if any chief in Tsenacomoco was going to follow the Piscataways' example (assuming they were the first to do it) and organize a paramount chiefdom, it would logically be the weroance at Powhatan town, a man eager to gain dominance over many subject warriors who could be sent on retaliatory raids meant to discourage more warfare. That didn't happen, of course; the warfare only escalated.

Powhatan's original inheritance shows signs of having been assembled with several useful functions in mind. The Powhatan townsmen, backed up by the Arrohatecks, were the point men for dealing with enemies. The Appamattucks were a conduit to luxury goods like puccoon, to make a paramount chief look wealthy and impressive. The Pamunkeys were the guardians of the holiest place in the region, Uttamussak, and therefore a conduit to supernatural power. And they, the Youghtanunds, and the Mattaponis could be a breadbasket of the organization if the James River groups lost their crops to the enemy. The Pamunkey River in particular has extensive, fertile farmland, and within its many meanders are huge marshes containing tuckahoe and wild rice.

By the same token, if any of Powhatan town's new mamanatowicks was going to expand the paramountcy by taking in neighboring chiefdoms, it was likely to be Wahunsenacawh. He came to power when the Massawomeck raids were well under way, and because he would have been in some kind of contact with friendly Algonquian speakers to the north,[10] he would have heard that the Iroquoian-speaking Susquehannocks were beginning to move southward and pressure the Patuxents and their neighbors—another threat on a more distant horizon. (The Susquehannocks would reach the Potomac River near what became Washington, D.C., in time to help spark Bacon's Rebellion in 1676.)

Another factor may have been in operation as well by 1570. From 1564 through 1569 a drought, of greater or lesser severity, had taken hold.[11] Even wild marsh plants like tuckahoe, dependent upon fresh water coming from rain runoff, will decrease when a drought goes on that long. Consequently the land had seen "famine and death."[12] The people lived in a prescientific culture, so like the Quiyoughcohannock chief Chawopo in 1609, they assumed that their gods were angry with them and were withholding rain.[13] Too many years of that kind of anxiety, not to mention hunger, can disrupt a political system. The drought may well have paved the way for a young paramount chief—with access to the very holy temple at Uttamussak—to begin wooing neighboring chiefdoms into his fold.

Powhatan's expansion took a downriver direction first. He added the York River towns, including the Chiskiacks and the people of what would later be called Werowocomoco ("chief's place"). He added the Weyanocks, with their useful trade connections, and the other James River groups, perhaps one at a time, perhaps in a clump. At some point he added the Accomac and Occohannock chiefdoms on the Eastern Shore, probably by negotiation, because they were less warlike than the people on the western shore. Their value was less for manpower in wars than for their access to whelk and hard-clam shells for jewelry, which would now flow copiously in Powhatan's direction and which he could use to hire warriors. It was probably after that coup that he changed his capital from Powhatan town—or perhaps Pamunkey, after he came to power—to Werowocomoco on the York River, because it was a more central location for receiving tribute. He went on to add the Rappahannock River chiefdoms, although their continuing distrust of him was shown by their having located most of their towns as of 1608 on the north bank of the river, well away from him. He used both intimidation—easier as his paramountcy became larger, with more warriors in it—and outright force, but which he used on whom is usually unclear.[14] It is impossible to reconstruct the dates for his successes from the limited records made by the Jamestown settlers. One can, however, estimate the dates that he converted long-term failures into final successes, for records did get made about those.

William Strachey heard in 1610–11 that "some 15 or 16 years since" (i.e., between 1594 and 1596), Kecoughtan had been taken over. That chiefdom had closer ties with the Nansemond-Chesapeake groups and the Roanoke Island chiefdoms than with anyone upriver, judging by the pottery style (Roanoke simple-stamped) that was common to all of them. The elderly Kecoughtan weroance was an able man, fully capable of stalling Powhatan's plans for expansion. But finally the old chief died in 1594–96, and Powhatan made his move. The new weroance was either less able or ill prepared, for the mamanatowick was able to have his forces swoop down on Kecoughtan town, "killing the [new] chief and most of them." He had the survivors "transported over the river, craftily changing their seat and quartering them amongst his own people," probably in his capital, where they could be put to work under close scrutiny by his bodyguard (a readily available labor force for the job). In the empty town, with its strategic view of shipping in the lower Chesapeake Bay, he installed his son Pochins and a hundred or so loyalists.[15] These were the "Kecoughtans" that Europeans met in the early 1600s.

The real Kecoughtans were sufficiently integrated into Powhatan's organization by 1608 that he permitted them to leave their captivity after the fall

of that year. The territory of the Piankatanks had become available for oc-
cupation, so that is where the Kecoughtans ended up, being joined by the
Chiskiacks in the 1620s. William Strachey's description of the annihilation of
the original Piankatanks as a tribe tells in detail how Powhatan could orches-
trate the takeover of a small chiefdom in one day. Strachey claimed that the
people's offense was "unknown," but they had met John Smith during his explorations in cohattayough and promised to share their harvest with the foreigners.[16] That would have been enough for the paramount chief to take
offense. He waited until taquitock, the season of communal hunts, and then
he sent a party of loyalists "to lodge amongst them one night," preparatory
to going on "a general hunt" the next day. Waiting outside the town was a
much larger force. When the men in the houses gave the signal "at the hour
appointed," the attack was on; "24 men they kill'd outright, the rest escaping
by fortune and their swift footmanship." The dead men's scalps were taken as
trophies to Werowocomoco, where they were shown off to foreign visitors
including John Smith "not long after." The Piankatank women and children
and also the weroance were also taken to Werowocomoco, as the Kecoughtans had been.[17] There they would have been put to work: chiefs were supposed to be kept alive if possible, and the Virginia Algonquians did not believe in wasting laborers.[18]

The other conquest mentioned in the historical records is that of the
Chesapeakes, who lived in the Lynnhaven area of Virginia Beach in the 1580s
and by the early 1600s along the Elizabeth River in what is now Norfolk and
Portsmouth. They, too, had closer ties with the Roanoke Island people than
with Powhatan, and they, too, had held out against joining Powhatan's bur-
geoning organization. For that staunch refusal the mamanatowick and his subject chiefdoms considered the Chesapeakes to be bitter enemies by 1607,
rather than autonomous potential allies. Some of the animosity came from a
prophecy made by the priests, whom Powhatan trusted, stating that "from the
Chesapeake Bay a nation should arise which should dissolve and give end to
his empire." Although there were "divers [several] understanding[s]" of who
the culprits might be, Powhatan concluded that the Chesapeakes were meant,
and accordingly he "destroyed and put to sword all such who might lie under
any doubtful construction of the same prophecy, as all the inhabitants, the
weroance, and his subjects of that province." The territory was then repeopled
by others, apparently some of the Nansemonds. If the Chesapeake chief was
killed deliberately, rather than accidentally in action, then the virulence of the

attack shows how afraid Powhatan had become of the holdouts. The timing of the attack is regrettably vague: Strachey says only that it happened "not long since." It could have happened either before or after Jamestown was founded, but what concerned Powhatan himself was that this last chunk of land in southeastern Virginia was now controllable.[19]

Powhatan's ultimate dominions—they ceased growing once the English arrived—were all of the Virginia coastal plain [i.e., east of the fall line] except for the territories of the Chickahominies[20] and the Iroquoian-speaking Nottoways and Meherrins. He took care to be an ally of all those tribes. However, the term *dominion* used here does not mean that Powhatan's grip on all of his districts was equally strong. Rather like his allies, the chiefdoms on the Eastern Shore and the south bank of the Potomac River were more under his influence than under his domination, which is why I have called them a "fringe" of his organization in my other books.[21] Only well-developed states have the power to dictate who is and who is not part of their citizenry. Chiefdoms do not. People claimed by a chief may or may not act like subjects at various times, especially if they are far enough removed geographically that they can avoid retaliation for disobedience. Significantly, those fringe territories would be the first ones detached from Powhatan's organization (after 1610).

Some English writers claimed a much larger domain for Powhatan than even eastern Virginia: they extended his rule north to the Tockwoghs at the head of the Chesapeake Bay and south to the Chowanocks and Nottoways in the south.[22] This was unrealistic, for the distances were too great to keep up the kind of fairly frequent, usually face-to-face communication that chiefs need to stay in power. It is more likely that the English were engaging in wishful thinking: if Powhatan ruled that much territory, and ruled it as absolutely as they (erroneously) believed he did, then making him a subject of King James made all those more distant territories the king's subjects as well. No further negotiations or military maneuvers would be needed.

The Role of Europeans

It is significant that when Powhatan heard the prophecy about someone coming from the east to conquer him and his people, he discounted Europeans as the enemies to fight. It is with only hindsight that we know he was wrong. In 1607, amid all the threats from native enemies to the west and northwest and after all the onerous efforts to marshal subject chiefdoms to cover his back against them, Powhatan must have seen the activities of Europeans heretofore as once-in-a-decade pinpricks. For the intruders had not come often, and most of them had landed in places which were—at the time they arrived—outside of Powhatan's dominions. The mamanatowick would have received news of them, of course, because their coming was definitely newsworthy, but the reports probably lacked the detail in the Europeans' own written accounts. The point of view in them would also have been from the opposite, non-European side.

Most of the rest of this chapter—and much of the rest of the book—presents things through the reconstructed views (plural) of the native people.

During nepinough (harvest season, specifically September 1570), when Powhatan was either a new paramount chief or else getting ready to become one, he and his relatives heard that Tassantassas (meaning Strangers, or Foreigners) had landed in the country of the Paspaheghs, after which they had crossed the peninsula (whatever for?) and settled in the territory of the Chiskiacks. They had brought a Paspahegh man (Don Luis) with them after a years-long sojourn among them, and that man was telling his overjoyed relatives tales of some very strange sights he had seen. He said he had come back with the intention not only of returning home but also of teaching his people about a new and better religion. However, he was already losing his interest in proselytizing, while his locally powerful family welcomed him back into their lives.[23]

It was a poor time for outlanders to try settling in Tsenacomoco. Although the rainfall in 1570 was nearly average, the six years of drought before that year meant that no one was in the mood to promise to feed foreigners who would not support themselves. During the cold season of popanow (specifically, February 1571), word trickled up the James that the Paspaheghs had disposed of the aliens (Jesuit missionaries), who had thoroughly worn out their welcome by their pushiness and their demands for food.[24] Just as well, Powhatan and Opechancanough would probably have thought, and then they would have gone on with their own business. However, they may not have been surprised to hear the next summer that an alien ship came nosing around the Kecoughtan area and took a couple of prisoners. Retribution could be expected after that, though not directed toward themselves. And sure enough, the following year (1572) the aliens returned, this time with mysterious and powerful weapons (firearms). They retrieved the one survivor of the mission, whom the Paspaheghs had spared because of the custom of not killing children. Then they took Paspahegh hostages, killing others in a sudden attack, and as ransom for the prisoners, they demanded that the man who had lived among them so many years be brought to them. They knew somehow that he had led the killing of the missionaries, and they wanted to punish him. When the Paspaheghs very properly refused to give up a member of their chief's family for hanging, the foreigners killed some of the hostages, and then released the rest and sailed away.[25]

It was a very nasty encounter. The outlanders who stayed and preached had made such pests of themselves that they deserved killing, didn't they? The aliens who came after them had proved to be both short-tempered and violent. From the Paspahegh chief's relative, who had lived among them so long, the word went out that they were called "Spaniards."[26] He had many tall tales to tell about them, but that's all it amounted to: tall tales. No place and no people could possibly be as strange as that. (Thus the near absence of oral tradition about the Spanish among the early seventeenth-century Powhatans.)

The ghastly "Spanish" returned briefly to the Chesapeake Bay some years later (1588)]; they took young people as prisoners (to make them interpreters) in the Potomac River area, before sailing away.[27] The stolen children were never heard from again. Powhatan's paramount chiefdom may have reached the bay by that time, but it is doubtful that he had the same personal feelings of outrage as the Potomac River people did. Nevertheless, news of another visit by outlanders was somewhat disquieting.

Shortly before the abductions up on the Potomac, the "moccasin telegraph" had informed Powhatan that Tassantassas were intruding themselves among the people of the Carolina Sounds (in 1584–87). Some of them stayed for part of the cold season (1585–86) with the Chesapeakes,[28] whose enmity to Powhatan's importunities was growing. Naturally, native people from miles around flocked to gawk at the Strangers, who indicated that they were not called "Spaniards" but "Englishmen," whatever that meant. They were just as foreign in speech, just as hairy, just as dirty and smelly—didn't they ever wash?—but much more friendly. They had a peculiar substance with them that they unrolled and made mysterious markings on; one of them in particular (John White) tried to ask a lot of questions through the language barrier about who lived in the surrounding districts. (Either he did not ask, or people did not tell him, about the paramount chief whose dominions had been expanding down the James, for his map stops short even of the Paspaheghs.)[29] No one remotely like Powhatan appears in any of the English accounts from the Carolina Sounds. It is possible that from Powhatan's point of view, that region and the intruders into it seemed equally irrelevant.

The mamanatowick probably would have heard, though, that this set of foreigners eventually alienated most of the native people round about. He may also have heard things about what became of the foreigners left behind by their leader, rumors that the aliens had been attacked and dispersed.[30] However, after 1607 Powhatan and his subordinates made no move to pass that word to the Jamestowners who asked about them. Instead they allowed them to stew about it, or else let them slog their way southward—with loyal guides, of course—to ask people like the Chowanocks.

After leaving Roanoke Island, most of the "Lost Colonists" probably headed to the North Carolina mainland, for that is where most of the inquiries were made for them in 1608–9. However, it has been suggested that some of them may have fled northward and come to rest among the still-friendly Chesapeakes, where any of them who survived for twenty years would have been exterminated along with their hosts when Powhatan took over that territory.[31] If that did happen, then it is the closest Powhatan ever came to doing what the English king later accused him of doing: wiping out the entire "Lost Colony" in order to eliminate English people from "his" (grossly overestimated) territories.[32] With the "Lost Colony," as well as with the Spanish in the early 1570s, the foreign intrusion took place in areas then out of Powhatan's purview, and the visitors were handled by local people known to Powhatan but not ruled by him.

The experiences of all those other people apparently did not show Powhatan that he should fear Europeans, so that when they began to push into territories that really were his in 1607, he did not go on the defensive for a long time. He appeared to believe that small-scale raids would be as effective against the Jamestown aliens as they had been in the 1570s and 1580s. After all, how could a relative handful of foreigners, who had proved that they could not live off the land even in good years, hold out for long against much greater numbers of seasoned warriors?

On the Eve of Invasion

Let us shift away from the native people's point of view for one last moment. In the spring of 1607 the Powhatans and the English were in opposite positions from the way many people see them today. With hindsight (especially if you believe John Smith), it is easy to think of powerful, confident Englishmen taking control of the land from a small flock of primitives. That's not at all how things looked in 1607. The Powhatans were a political and military organization that had just finished spreading successfully over nearly all of the Virginia coastal plain. They did not know that 1606 had been the first of seven consecutive drought years; they hoped that the bad year had been a fluke and food soon would be plentiful again. They had met or heard of a very few parties of Europeans in the previous thirty-seven years, and none of those lasted long. Nothing much to worry about! Perhaps the next batch of touring Tassantassas could be made into allies, as it was rumored the Chesapeakes had done with their visitors two decades before.

The English, on the other hand, were not nearly so confident as their outward bravado indicated; close examination of their writings shows how insecure they really felt. In 1607 their nation had not yet managed to establish a North American settlement that "stuck." They hoped their supply lines across the Atlantic would keep them fed, for if those lines failed, they had no idea how to live off the land. Though the country looked nearly empty to them, their own numbers in Virginia were much, much smaller than those of the native people. And if they had to fight, which many of them were not trained to do, they had to go up against an enemy whose methods were unfamiliar and, once known, hard to combat.

The English records make it easy to assume that their firearms gave them an advantage over the native people at all times. That was not so, and within a year the residents of Tsenacomoco showed that they knew it. The records of their earliest encounters with firearms indicate that it was the noise as much as the destructive power that frightened people. But almost immediately it became apparent that while the Tassantassas' guns could do great harm when fired straight at a target, all the guns took a long time (and both hands) to reload, during which a warrior could loose about five arrows at the same target. How far those guns could shoot accurately was another matter. For the first year or so, the Powhatans yearned to know that, and they engaged in a number of subterfuges to find out. The answer was that while a bow could shoot an arrow "forty yards . . . very near the mark, and 120 yards . . . at random," English pistols of the time (at .40 to .50 caliber) could only shoot accurately up to about 25 feet, after which both aim and impact were lessened. Muskets of .69 caliber were effective up to 70 yards, while .90-caliber ones could do great damage at 100 yards and less accurate damage at 300 yards.[33] Larger ordnance, of course, like that carried on board the ships, could shoot much farther still, and the Powhatans never challenged it. Muskets threatened the native people the most, but in those days long-barreled guns were very heavy and hard to aim without setting them on a fork rest first. They also, as of 1600, were matchlock affairs, so that a "match" (wick) had to be kept alight—somehow!—if the soldier wanted to fire the gun anytime soon.

Weapons like those were useful enough in open-field fighting. But the Powhatan method of warfare was guerrilla tactics: strike hard, run fast, and use any woodland cover you possibly can. Powerful but ponderous weaponry was not much help against such targets. Add to that the fact that many of the first foreigners to come from England, and most of the would-be farmers later, were not trained as soldiers. They were not experts in weaponry from childhood, as Powhatan men were, and they were not used to going about warily, as good predators do. John Smith once wrote in despair that "no punishment will prevent [their strolling around outside the fort] but hanging."[34] Native men who kept an eye on the foreigners' doings probably marveled at how naive the newcomers were, for all their bragging about the superiority of their weapons and their culture in general. Instead of strutting about the landscape with impunity, the campers in Jamestown Fort would prove again and again to be the perfect sitting ducks for snipers.

Powhatan men's eagerness to learn about the outlanders' weapons and tools, coupled with the language barrier, left a less than complimentary impression of the locals in the newcomers' minds. Seeing the native people reacting to their own behavior, they concluded that the inhabitants

are inconstant in everything but what fear constraineth them to keep—crafty timorous, quick of apprehension, ingenious enough in their own works. . . .

Some of them are of disposition fearful . . . and not easily wrought to trust us or come into our forts. Others again of them are so bold and audacious as they dare come into our forts, truck and trade with us, and look us in the face crying "All friends!" when they have but new done us a mischief and when they intend presently again if it lie in their power to do the like. They are generally covetous of our commodities, as copper, white beads for their women, hatchets, of which we make them poor ones of iron, hoes to pare their corn ground, knives, and such like.

They are soon moved to anger, and so malicious that they seldom forget an injury. They are very thievish and will as closely as they can convey anything away from us, howbeit they seldom steal one from another, lest their conjurers should reveal it, and so they be pursued and punished.[35]

The newcomers left no better impressions on the native people. William Strachey learned from one of Powhatan's brothers-in-law (Machumps), through his fluency and that of the decent Jamestown interpreters available by 1610–11 (Henry Spelman and Thomas Savage), that the Real People of Tsenacomoco had long resented, feared, and wanted the foreigners' firearms and steel swords.[36] It sounds rather like modern local people's dealings with money-bearing tourists. The difference was that in the early 1600s the foreigners stayed on long after they should have left. Strachey may not have fully realized it, but whenever sniping incidents, never mind larger-scale attacks, occurred, that was not the neighbors being "savages as usual"; that was some of the legitimate citizenry expressing a negative opinion about squatters.

Ironically, from the very beginning the English had fully expected to fight the native people sooner or later. They had orders from London to try to settle in the region and assimilate the residents there, creating "England in America." With this purpose in mind, they expected to encounter some immediate resistance, which made them downright paranoid. Powhatan's people knew nothing of the Virginia Company's plans, though in time they began to guess. But in the early days they made hospitable overtures, hoping to create allies against their enemies to the west and northwest. Instead they found themselves presented with the spectacle of "visitors" who were simultaneously friendly and quick to grab their guns at the least little thing. Peculiar specimens! It also means, for us who read what those Strangers wrote, that on many early occasions when a writer expected the worst, the native people would have had no hostile intentions at all—yet.

5

Watching from a Distance

FOR THE FIRST several months that the Strangers were in his land, Powhatan remained in and around his capital, letting his subject chiefs meet them, treat them as they would, and then report back to him. He did not rely solely on the moccasin telegraph, which spread news rapidly among all the towns. He expected, as was his right as a regional potentate, to receive direct communication from his "trusty scouts and careful sentinels . . . which reach even from his own court down almost to our palisado gates."[1] Given the prevailing uncertainty about why the Tassantassas acted the way they did, careful surveillance was the only sensible proceeding. However, that hands-off policy led to a dizzying variety of encounters in the first few months, ranging from friendly to vicious.

Choosing a "Wrong" Place

Powhatan received word that peculiar watercraft, rather like those of the Strangers of three-and-a-half decades ago, had entered the Capes (on April 26, 1607) and dawdled around for a while. The residents of the area, who could have been either loyalist Nansemonds or still-independent Chesapeakes, attacked them almost as soon as they went ashore to explore.[2] Whichever chiefdom it was, the assault shows that foreigners were not popular in the area.

The Strangers then crossed over to Kecoughtan, where they met Powhatan's son Pochins and received a warm welcome (on April 30). Pochins was able to report that the Strangers were not dressed as the Spanish missionaries were said to have been and they were capable of acting friendly when well

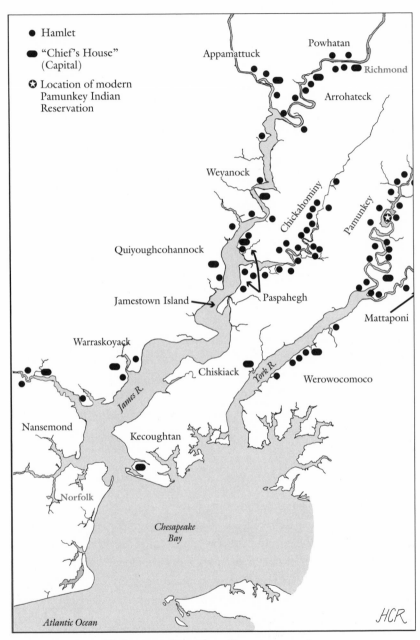

Hamlet

"Chief's House" (Capital)

Location of modern Pamunkey Indian Reservation

Powhatan

Appamattuck

Richmond

Arrohateck

Weyanock

Chickahominy

Pamunkey

Quiyoughcohannock

Paspahegh

Jamestown Island

Mattaponi

Warraskoyack

Chiskiack

York R.

Werowocomoco

Nansemond

Kecoughtan

James R.

Norfolk

Chesapeake Bay

Atlantic Ocean

HCR

Native towns in southern Tsenacomoco, 1607

treated.[3] The foreigners then began trying to sail up the James River, which has some mighty turns in it just upstream. Their ships could not sail nearly as close to the wind as ours can today, so unless the wind was favorable, the mariners would have had to tack in a zigzag up the river. Too little wind meant moving slowly or not at all, for the ships were not equipped for being rowed, as galleys were. That explains why they did not reach Paspahegh territory, about forty miles (ca. 65 km) upstream, until four or five days later. The spectacle very likely prompted endless speculation and amusement among the inevitable onshore watchers who knew nothing of sailing ships.(Why are the nitwits heading for that shore, now?)

The weroance of Paspahegh, Wowinchopunck, met the visitors somewhere along the shoreline near Jamestown Island and honored them with a long oration. Before long, though, he had competition. The Rappahannock weroance, who was a guest of the Quiyoughcohannock regent, Chopoke, and his retinue came paddling across the river to insist that the Strangers visit them, too. That offer was declined at first, but when he repeated it the next day, it was accepted. He met the visitors at the waterside and led them along the path up the bluff and through the cornfields to his town, where he, too, entertained his guests lavishly.[4] The popularity of the Strangers, due in large part to curiosity, was enhanced because when they were given food, they reciprocated with glass beads and metal trinkets. The native people were unaware that the givers considered these things to be "trash." The foreigners would find out later another motive for their cordial reception: the Rappahannocks were looking them over carefully, for they had lost people to European firearms a few years before and wanted to find and punish the culprits.[5] No one in this group matched up, so the weroance and his men went home to their own river, to await another day.[6]

The ships carrying these odd but "rich" people continued upriver, so that Powhatan would have received reports from a succession of chiefdoms. They reached the mouth of the Appomattox River (on May 8), apparently sailing past the Weyanocks. Their first encounter with the Appamattucks was uneasy. A man stood at the waterside with a tobacco pipe in one hand and a bow in the other, in a gestural demand about whether the Tassantassas intended peace or war. The Strangers indicated the pipe and were allowed to land, after which they stayed in the vicinity for several days. Returning downriver, again giving the Weyanocks a miss, they stopped (on May 13) at a long, low island, and next day they began off-loading things, making themselves at home. Settling in included starting to build a wooden palisade around their camp.[7] To the local people this construction indicated that these visitors expected trouble of some kind. The island (Jamestown Island) was in Wowinchopunck's territory, but nothing in the records indicates that his permission was sought first.

Wowinchopunck was naturally curious, not to say suspicious, about what the foreigners were doing there; he also had his superior, Powhatan, to satisfy. He may further have wanted to give these weird aliens a chance to do the proper thing and make it right with himself, the Paspahegh weroance, the steward (not the owner) of that island. What the Strangers were really doing would not have occurred to him: claiming permanent and absolute ownership of the property (land being a commodity) for some overlord who lived thousands of miles away. That king's feelings of entitlement would have left Wowinchopunck gaping. He must have wondered why, if these outlanders intended to stay a while, didn't they get some good advice, instead of choosing that mosquito-infested place where the river water was brackish and undrinkable for part of the year? A deepwater anchorage close to shore (which was the English motive) meant nothing to a man whose normal means of transport was a dugout canoe.

Wowinchopunck sent a canoe of men to look at the Strangers' camp that very first night. The Strangers saw them, took fright, and grabbed their weapons. Seeing this panicky behavior, the men returned home and reported in. Next day, the chief sent several of his councillors to give the foreigners a polite message that he was going to visit them, bringing a "fat deer" for a meal. The councillors would have noticed, as other Paspahegh men had done from the edge of the woods, that the logs for the visitors' palisade were somewhat thicker than the ones used in some native towns. They were also placed side by side, rather than spaced apart for bark to be tied on or branches to be woven between them.[8] Bigger poles, and many more of them, to surround a camp! What kind of fabulous tree-cutting tools did the aliens have? How can we get some of those?

The meeting took place (on May 18), and far from allaying the suspicions of the local people, it raised them higher.[9] The chief arrived, most likely by canoe, along with a large crowd of his people. Because he planned to have a meal there, he may well have had women along, bringing a stewpot in which to cook the venison.[10] Also present were men, one hundred of them according to one writer, all of them armed to the teeth and "guarding" their chief. The aliens were heavily armed, too.

Wowinchopunck made signs asking his hosts to disarm, and they would not. Then "he . . . made signs that he would give us as much land as we would desire to take"—which is how George Percy read it but probably not what the weroance intended. It is more likely that he was telling his hosts that they were in his territory and they had better behave. Then a nasty incident occurred that broke up the gathering. One of the chief's retinue "stole" a hatchet, perhaps to keep it, perhaps just to get a close look at what the cutting edge was made of. The Tassantassa owner took offense at the "theft" and snatched it back, slapping the man's arm for good measure. Another Paspahegh man, seeing the foreigner slap his countryman, went at him with his "wooden sword." The Strangers immediately took up a defensive posture, at which point Wowinchopunck disgustedly called his people together and left. It would be interesting to know if he later reprimanded the thief, or whether he and his people considered taking things from nonnatives to be a neutral or even "good" act (which is the case in some non-Western societies).

More uncomfortable incidents soon followed. The very next day, some newcomers out walking blundered into a Paspahegh village.[11] It was cohattayough, and most of the townspeople were out foraging for food. The town's weroance, Wowinchopunck's subordinate, was among the foragers and therefore was out of town, unable to greet guests. When one of the people remaining behind went running out to notify him, the Strangers took fright and left hurriedly, in effect refusing the meet the chief. Another man courteously guided them back to their fort, on the way picking some of the town's growing tobacco as a special gift. The Strangers made little of it, not knowing its value. Then, the day after that, Wowinchopunck himself sent forty men to the foreigners' camp, very likely in canoes, along with a deer to cook that night. That many men probably meant a test: friend or foe? The Strangers would not let the men stay overnight, and worse, they "won" an archery demonstration. A man was invited to shoot his arrow at a Tassantassa's wooden shield, which he did—clear through it, in fact, which was more than a pistol could do. Worried at this sign of native power to injure, the foreigner set up another shield, this one made of steel. When the man shot it, his arrow shattered, and he left immediately, in high dudgeon.[12]

Within a week of the aliens' arrival, then, Wowinchopunck would have been able to make a report to Powhatan: Some very peculiar people had plunked themselves down on an island in his country, without a by-your-leave, and they were fortifying their camp. The absence of women or children was more evidence that their purpose was war making. Whenever they met any of Our People, they either ran away or reached for their weapons. They were rich but thoroughly untrustworthy—not to mention olfactorily objectionable—and he, personally, would like to be rid of them. Shortly after that, a coalition of chiefdoms began to organize for war.

Meeting the Strangers Upriver

Oblivious to the fact that their popularity with the local people was fading, a large party of the foreigners made an expedition (May 21–27) up to the falls of the James River, asking questions of the people they met along the way.[13] Powhatan heard about it, of course. And he heard that the Tassantassas were most insistent on learning what lands lay to the west, where his enemies the Monacans lived. The Strangers reached the town of Powhatan, the birthplace and namesake of the mamanatowick, just three miles (5 km) from the falls. There they met his son Parahunt, the chief of the district, and while mistaking him for the "great king Pawatah," they tried to induce him to take them westward. Suspicious of their avidity to go, Parahunt sensibly declined to accompany them beyond the falls without notifying his father, even though they had assured him by signs that they considered the Monacans to be their enemies, too. Part of his hesitancy probably stemmed from the cock-and-bull story the foreigners told about Monacans living on a salt sea and killing one of their number; sensible Real People knew the Monacans lived along inland streams. Parahunt's unwillingness to supply guides caused his visitors to desist and erect a cross instead. They answered his question about its meaning with a lie: the two arms stood for Powhatan and their king, and the fastening in the center signified their alliance.

The foreigners also made contact with the Arrohatecks, with a satellite town of Appamattucks, and with the Weyanocks during their trip. The Arrohatecks, one of Powhatan's original chiefdoms, were extremely hospitable to the visitors as they made their way up and back down the river. The others, who were visited only on the downriver leg, were not. At the request of the Arrohateck and Appamattuck chiefs, the outlanders had shot off their guns, and the noise was horrible. Nothing in the Powhatan world sounded quite like gunpowder suddenly going off. But Opossunoquonuske, the Appamattuck weroansqua, who had given grudging hospitality to the visitors, staunchly showed little fear of the racket.

There were probably two reasons for the less than enthusiastic reception the Appamattucks and Weyanocks gave the exploring party. First, they may have felt insulted that the outlanders did not pay them a call on the way up-river; the Weyanocks had also been ignored the month before, a serious breach of protocol. Second, both of these chiefdoms were in regular contact with Algonquian- and Iroquoian-speaking people to the south,[14] which included the Chowanocks who had met Europeans from the Roanoke colonies and perhaps harbored some of the "Lost Colonists" after 1587. No Appamattucks or Weyanocks knew (in May 1607) just how the current intruders, who came from the same country, would take the news that their hosts were friends of those Chowanocks, and the language barrier prevented them from probing delicately to find out. Meanwhile, it was awkward about the boy; hadn't anyone told him to stay out of sight? There he was, in the Appamattuck satellite town that day, "a . . . boy about the age of ten years, which had a head of hair of a perfect yellow and a reasonable white skin, which is a miracle amongst all savages."[15] Well, if the visitors were asking about his origin during their babblings, the language barrier could be used to foil them.

One other luminary met the Strangers (on May 26), one who came from the next river north especially to see them: the "king of Pamunkey." The title indicates that it was one of Powhatan's three younger brothers. Which brother the visiting chief was is uncertain, but Opechancanough can be eliminated at the outset. Gabriel Archer wrote that this man, "sitting in manner of the rest, so set his countenance striving to be stately as to our seeming he became [a] fool."[16] No one who met Opechancanough ever indicated that he was anything but a polished performer on public occasions like this one. John Smith, who had met all Powhatan's brothers before he wrote his first account, did not mention this meeting at all, but he did refer in passing to a meeting—supposedly at Jamestown Fort—with Kekataugh that occurred sometime before December 1607.[17] Smith may have been transposing a May encounter with Kekataugh to a Jamestown setting.

The weroance, whom we may assume to be Kekataugh, probably was sent by Powhatan to intercept the aliens and then report back. The result would have been amusing at first. The Tassantassas now claimed to have become allies with several of his subject chiefdoms, as well as with the mamanatowick himself (due to their mistake about Parahunt). Further, they had indicated to Kekataugh by signs that they were able to help in conquering all of the Monacans. An entertaining idea, though a dubious one for the time being, unless those firearms proved to be lethal as well as noisy. Then the reporter would have come to a disillusioning experience, similar to what Wowinchopunck of Paspahegh had gone through. Upon greeting his guests, Kekataugh had the women of "his" town (actually a Weyanock town) start working on a feast, as protocol demanded, and he tried to get the Strangers to stay long enough to be entertained properly. They, assuming (perhaps correctly) that it meant staying the night ashore, refused. Not only that, but they acted unnecessarily suspicious of their host. Their leader (Christopher Newport) was affable, giving the chief gifts with a generous hand, and he had been willing to walk together with him, well away from his soldiers, as though he trusted a native leader. But the soldiers followed along at a distance, armed and ready for trouble. Kekataugh took offense: canceling the feast, he escorted the aliens to their boat and sent them on their way. He probably felt unjustly suspected of an ambush, when in fact—at that time—he could learn far more about them by friendliness than by hostility.

First Warnings

Two days before the explorers returned, and less than two weeks after they had begun off-loading supplies, the squatters on the island were attacked for the first time. Some 200 men, led by "their king," made a serious attempt to discourage the foreigners from staying. The skirmish "endured hot about an hour," with warriors coming "up almost into the fort"—whose palisade was not finished yet—and shooting "through the tents." Many muskets and pistols had not been unpacked yet, so that it was up to the "gentlemen" to use their personal firearms, but even so, several people on both sides died in the fray. Only when the ships, anchored close by, opened up their big guns did the attackers leave.[18]

The "king" was probably Wowinchopunck, but the size of his forces indicates a multitribal effort. Several weeks later a still-friendly Arrohateck visitor would inform the Tassantassas of what Powhatan already knew: the

Strangers' "friends" were the Arrohatecks, the Pamunkeys, the Youghta-nunds, and the Mattaponis, while their "contracted enemies"—and the logi-cal sources for the attackers—were the Paspaheghs, the Quiyoughcohan-nocks, the Weyanocks, the Appamattucks, and the Chiskiacks.[19] Significantly, the hostile chiefdoms were those closest to Jamestown Island; additionally, the Paspaheghs and Chiskiacks had had face-to-face trouble with the Span-ish thirty-five years before. The Arrohateck informant may also have tipped the Strangers off to the unsettling fact that though they had supposedly befriended Parahunt at Powhatan town, they had not met Powhatan the mamanatowick.

Did Powhatan instigate the assault? Probably not. Given Wowincho-punck's distaste for his new neighbors and his reputation as an outstanding warrior-leader,[20] he could easily have organized the assault himself. The re-cruiting of other chiefdoms' men would have taken a few days after his final disillusionment (on May 20), so the timing of the engagement is about right. Wowinchopunck must have notified Powhatan, though, of what he intended to do. Removed from the scene and ostensibly detached as he was, the ma-manatowick still had the ultimate right to declare peace or war—or to give his subordinates their heads, play both ends against the middle, and see what the outcome would be. Wowinchopunck's attack certainly served the purpose of establishing what a ship's big guns could do. But remove the ships, and how effective were the smaller handheld weapons? Better to let some of his sub-ject chiefs test the newcomers a bit longer, while his younger brothers could befriend them if they wanted to. Kekataugh's meeting with the outlanders may have served another purpose besides gathering intelligence: it helped delay the exploring party so that its soldiers would be absent during Wowin-chopunck's "test."

The squatters did not leave. Instead they completed their fort (by June 15) and watched the corn, from kernels probably donated by the Arrohatecks, grow to "a man's height." It would not grow well much longer, though, for the rest of the summer proved to be a continuation of the dry spell that had begun in 1606. The Quiyoughcohannocks across the river remained inimi-cal for a time, taunting the newcomers when chances arose. However, around the time that the ships departed (June 22, 1607), leaving altogether too many Smelly Ones behind, Powhatan and one of his brothers (name not recorded) both made overtures to the Tassantassas. Their messengers said that they wanted friendship and that the mamanatowick had ordered the Paspaheghs and Quiyoughcohannocks to cease their hostilities. The latter chiefdom grudgingly made friends (on July 7), when Chopoke promised to sell some of his corn when it became ripe enough; a real truce came (on July 27) when some foreigners returned a canoe to him that had drifted across the river.[21]

Why did Powhatan decide to involve himself personally with the new-comers only a month after letting his subordinates attack them? He probably had found out that the Arrohateck man had told them about him, so that it would be counterproductive not to begin dealing with them directly. His change in policy may also have had to do with the ships' leaving. Now that it seemed somewhat less dangerous for native people to approach the Strangers' fort, his emissaries could visit there and learn more about these touchy aliens. He did not know how soon his plan would fail.

As the weather stayed dry and cohattayough became prolonged, the corn began to wither all over Powhatan's dominions. Families remained in a for-aging mode in order to eat, and Powhatan and his brothers knew that the trib-ute corn would be limited this year. The records made by the Strangers at Jamestown hint that no corn was ripe enough to give to allies until the second week in September, which is a month late for the first and probably only crop of that year. Even then, it was green corn, palatable to the Real People but not to the Tassantassas.[22] If the native people offered their guests wild foods such as tuckahoe bread, there is no record of it; perhaps they felt that only high-status corn was appropriate for foreigners.

Those foreigners began to run low on the familiar, more palatable food they had brought from home, and they assumed that the local people were hostile and withholding sustenance from them. They did not see the imma-ture corn in the fields across the river because they stopped moving around. They still had not dug a well where they lived (it would be nearly two years before they did!), and they had not put their fort next to a spring, so they got their drinking water from the river. Fools! The Paspaheghs and Quiyough-cohannocks knew that that was a bad idea in the summertime. The water made them all sick, both from its brackishness and from the human pollution that found its way into the river from the fort, where sanitation was primitive. Feeling not only sick but extremely vulnerable, they shut themselves up in their fort. However, several of them broke out and went to live with the neighboring chiefdoms.[23] From such runaways, Powhatan and his subordinates learned in August that their "friends," these unwanted guests, were now slowly starving.[24]

Thick-headed, feckless specimens! Wild food grew all around, even during a drought, and people were willing to help them get it if they would only ask, but they stubbornly wanted what was familiar. Anyone approaching the aliens found that their tempers were not improved by the brackishness of the water they were stupidly drinking, for salt poisoning makes people ornery as well as sick. They would not let in any of the Real People who came around their fort, preferring to keep their weakness to themselves—they hoped!

Finally the corn became ripe enough—by local standards—that the Quiyoughcohannocks could take some of it to the newcomers as they had promised. It was accepted, apparently with gratitude (though the bestowers could not know that the Strangers actually assumed that their God had changed the "savages'" stony hearts).[25] The weroances harboring runaways sent them back to the fort. Soon some of the foreigners began moving about again, though now they seemed fewer than before (about half had died of typhoid and dysentery).[26] Unfortunately, the ones who were still there were about to wear down the neighbors' patience once more.

The Strangers Became Pesky

A few baskets of green corn only seemed to whet the appetite of the Tassantassas. Their own crop had failed, of course, for lack of weeding as well as lack of rain. Their compatriots across the ocean did not come back to help them or take them away, and they were closemouthed about the matter. (Actually, they were anxious, and for good reason. Christopher Newport's ships had left them short of food and had promised to return by mid-November. But Newport would not come back until after New Year's, and one of his ships, lost in a fog, would arrive even later.)[27] They began to act as if they expected the native people to provide for them, albeit in exchange for inedible beads and metal items. Some of those metal items might be useful in gardening—next year, if another drought didn't come.

The Strangers did not understand that a certain amount of corn, even in a poor year like this one, had to be reserved not just for seed for another crop but also for the tribute needed in chiefly hospitality, especially at Werowocomoco. It would be unthinkable for the mamanatowick to put on a feast for a

VIP without any corn at all, especially just after harvesttime. Word of his poverty would spread via the moccasin telegraph, not only throughout his domain but out into the ears of friendly neighbors like the Chowanocks and the Piscataways, and he and his all people would become a laughingstock. Horrible to contemplate! However, once a certain amount of corn had been set aside,[28] it was up to the local people, meaning the women who did the farming, to decide whether to hold onto their supply or trade it away for inedible goods. If they did the latter, they would have to spend the bitter cold winter digging tuckahoe out in the marshes. That was a hard enough job in nice weather, the plant's tubers being so far below the surface; in the freezing cold, it would be well nigh unendurable.

Before long, the native people's "gifts" of food began to slack off. Simultaneously, the foreigners were about to run out of the very last of their supplies from home. To fill that gap, one of the most aggressive of the aliens (John Smith) went out with a party of compatriots to try to buy corn. Thus a series of Powhatan's subject towns received uncomfortable visits that must have been disquieting to the mamanatowick.

The Kecoughtans were first. Pochins and his people had not interacted with the Tassantassas since the previous April, when they first arrived in Powhatan's territories. But Pochins was in his father's councils, and he must have heard plenty. These Arrogant Ones had been near famished only a short while ago. They had been revived through the good offices of several upriver chiefdoms, and now here they came, expecting to get more food. Pochins's people did not have tuckahoe growing in their district; it is a freshwater plant. The food they fell back on in really awful years was oysters and clams, another ghastly uncomfortable food to gather in the depth of winter. So it was more needful than usual, being a poor crop year, to hold onto as much corn as possible.

The townsmen's initial reception of the would-be traders was scornful: the price they demanded was a hatchet or piece of copper for some small pieces of bread or a few beans. Smith waited them out, and the next day he was able to buy a few bushels. On the way upriver, he happened to meet Warraskoyacks, who invited him to trade at their town as well (it being their first encounter with Tassantassas).[29]

The next chiefdoms to receive a visit were the Quiyoughcohannocks and the Paspaheghs. The Quiyoughcohannock men were not in evidence, which indicates that they were out hunting that day. The women and children, whose presence in town indicates that the communal fall hunt had not yet started, initially fled rather than get into a tiff. When they returned, they were still uncooperative, though it was probably their own idea rather than their husbands' preference: "Truck they durst not, corn they had plenty, and to spoil I had no commission," wrote Smith a few months later. So the intruders went away empty-handed. The Paspaheghs gave up only ten bushels of corn, and their men first attempted to "liberate" the foreigners' weapons and then to draw them back onshore as they went downriver, supposedly to trade. Night was falling, and the aliens decided to avoid a confrontation.[30]

The Tassantassas did not try their luck with any of Powhatan's people farther up the James River. Instead they chose to contact the Chickahominies for the first time, which probably did not please Powhatan at all. Those tribesmen were not his enemies, but they were not exactly his friends, either. An alliance between them and the Strangers, both living inside his dominions, could be threatening. Powhatan need not have worried, though, for the ravenous traders soon wore out their welcome.[31]

The lower Chickahominy towns seemed to be almost ecstatic at finally being able to lay hands on the exotic trade goods presented to them. They filled the outlanders' "barge" (a large rowboat) with seven hogsheads of corn. After taking their load back to Jamestown, the traders returned to Mamanahunt, where they had done an especially brisk trade already, and they acquired seven more hogsheads, which they carried off. In a couple of days they came back yet again, this time trading exhaustively with the upriver towns. If matters had rested there, the Chickahominies and the foreigners would have been reasonably content with one another.

But the leader of the traders (John Smith) was not satisfied: he came back up the river a fourth time. His writings do not say whether or not he tried to buy any more corn, but the local people most likely assumed that was his intention. If he had had an interpreter to tell them that he only wanted to explore on this trip, it is doubtful they would have believed him. They knew their river did not go very far into the piedmont, much less approach the mountains. So in their minds, here he was, back on their doorsteps, hoping to buy more food with trinkets of which they now had enough samples, thank you. The honeymoon was over. When emissaries from Powhatan invited them to help capture the leading intruder so that he could be really interrogated, they were agreeable.

The boatful of foreigners went to the town farthest upriver, Apocant, near the mouth of Schiminoe Creek, a mile or two (2–3 km) upstream from modern Providence Forge.[32] By now it was late in taquitock (specifically, early December), the season for laying in large amounts of venison for the winter. The hunting was done communally, by large numbers of men and boys who surrounded an area containing deer, set fire to the woods in a ring moving inward, and drove the deer into a small area where they could be slaughtered. Whole families went on these trips, for the carcasses from one day's hunt had to be processed by the women and girls while the next day's hunt went on. In order to find enough deer to be worthwhile, these communal hunts were conducted up near the fall line, because the lower parts of the necks between rivers were overhunted.[33]

John Smith wrote in his 1624 book that Opechancanough had found out his intention to explore upriver and deliberately set out with a large force to capture him. In his 1608 letter he did not speculate on what brought Powhatan's brother to the area, but he noted the "abundance of fires in the woods."[34] A runner from Apocant probably did inform the chief of Smith's movements, and the nabbing of Smith was probably deliberate. But it took a communal hunt to bring that many men out into the deep woods together. Far from tracking down Smith, the people were simply out there going about their annual business. In that year Chickahominy families joined those of several neighboring chiefdoms in the hunt: Paspaheghs, Chiskiacks, Mattaponis, Pamunkeys, and Youghtanunds (as John Smith would learn later from a captured Paspahegh councillor). The chief of the last-named group, Opechancanough, happened to be among the hunters.[35]

Opechancanough and his companions began angling their operations over toward the Chickahominy River's headwaters. The aliens had attempted to explore farther up from Apocant, but they found within ten miles (16 km) that it became a swamp of braided shallow-water streams that their boat could not navigate. They therefore returned to Apocant, and their leader made other arrangements, which played right into Opechancanough's hands.

6

Meeting a Captive Englishman

THE FOREIGN INTRUDER could scarcely do a better job of leaving himself open to capture than what he did now. Taking two men with him, he left the rest of his men in the boat moored at Apocant, telling them to stay on board. Unknown to him but known very soon to the native people for miles around, the townspeople succeeded in capturing one of the outlanders (George Cassen) and showing him what they now thought of greedy, prying aliens: they tortured him to death. He did not die stoically, as a "real man" should. Those remaining in the boat, who were not "real men" either, turned tail and scuttled back to Jamestown.

The Tassantassas' captain and his two henchmen were now alone in Chickahominy territory, probing upstream in a canoe with two Apocant men as guides. They reached a point about twenty miles (30–35 km) from the town, and the captain proceeded to separate himself from his remaining men.[1] Taking one Apocant guide with him, he went out on foot. He was now probably about two miles (3–4 km) above modern Bottom's Bridge, which is where U.S. 60 and Interstate 64 cross the swampy headwaters of the Chickahominy River.[2]

Interception

Suddenly the foreigner found himself beset by men who were intent upon taking him prisoner. All the accounts indicate that he was taken unawares, an unusual situation for the canny captain. Being an experienced soldier, of course, he put up a good fight, though predictably he gave it a more heroic slant in later versions of the story.[3] A few men found him and held him at bay until all the other hunters arrived and closed in on him.

Once subdued, the prisoner immediately set about charming Opechan-canough—who was perfectly willing to be charmed. The great weroance may have been wary of the Tassantassas, but he and his sovereign brother were also still intensely curious about them. Under those circumstances it would have made no sense whatever to harm this potential informant, much less kill him. (Only Smith's 1624 version adds a sudden attempt on his life; it was something he anticipated, not something he experienced. Smith admitted in his 1608 letter that he was afraid for his life every day he was a prisoner; among other things, the English were uncertain about whether the Powhatans were cannibals; as it turned out, they were not.) Opechancanough undoubtedly sensed that his captive's efforts were strongly motivated by fear. So he listened politely, while being presented with a foreign gadget (a compass) and treated, without benefit of interpreter, to a description of the world as a sphere and the movements of sun and moon. It probably made little sense to him, because he came from a people who believed firmly in a flat earth,[4] but attentive listening was a hallmark of good manners in his world. After that, he answered properly with "kind speeches," which the captive in turn couldn't understand.

After this initial and scarcely satisfactory interview, Opechancanough and the hunting party led their prize some six miles (ca. 10 km) through the woods to the "town," actually a hunting camp where they and their families were spending their nights.[5] The European, the first one that most of the people had ever seen, was paraded into camp under guard as the women and children watched avidly. The hunters had put on facepaint for the occasion, either to honor the foreign captive or to signify a military exploit, and they moved in a file, brandishing the weapons taken from Smith and his two dead companions. Once all the men were in the camp, they began to dance in a circle.[6] It could have been either a victory dance or a welcome dance, because Smith's descriptions of the movements resemble the welcome dance the Kecoughtans had put on for the newcomers the previous April.[7]

Opechancanough treated his prisoner from the beginning as an honored, though carefully watched, guest. Smith's writings mention no physical mal-treatment at Rasawek, such as being made to run the gauntlet. Instead he was presented with immense amounts of food, which sounds like the aggressive hospitality normally shown to VIPs. In 1608, when his memory was fresher,

Smith wrote: "A quarter of venison and some ten pound of bread I had for supper. What I left was reserved for me and sent with me to my lodging. Each morning 3 women presented me three great platters of fine bread; more venison than ten men could devour I had. My gown, points and garters, my compass, and a tablet they gave me again."[8] His 1624 *Generall Historie* has more details about the handling of leftovers, and he must have left plenty of them, because he could hardly touch any of the food for fear that the locals were fattening him up for eating.[9]

While still in Rasawek, Opechancanough again tried to interview this interesting foreigner, though the language barrier must have made it a frustrating endeavor for both parties. One thing he would have tried to learn was the captive's name, which, when told, he probably have pronounced in a run-together way as "Chawnzmit." Opechancanough also wanted to know more about his prisoner's background, so the two attempted more conversation. Smith's 1608 report of it, with his learning about the Chowanock town of Ocanahonan, shows that he was pushing for information, too. Matters were friendly enough that the great weroance allowed Chawnzmit to use his notebook to write a letter to Jamestown. What harm could a few pictograms on that woody substance possibly do? (Unknown to him, Smith was also writing that the people who captured him, who he knew included Paspaheghs, wanted to attack the fort, an idea he was trying to discourage.)[10]

Divining His Intentions

Without an interpreter, Opechancanough could not ask his captive the question that was uppermost in his and his brother's minds: Why had the Tassantassas come to Tsenacomoco? He also knew that the man might lie, even if an interpreter was available, so he took the standard route that the native people used to find out the "real truth." In the Powhatan world priests were believed to be able to read minds, through the power of the deity they called upon, and therefore priests' advice carried tremendous weight in chiefly decision making.[11] With so rare and important a person as this detainee was, it only made sense that Opechancanough would enlist the best priests of his brother's realm to find out what the Strangers were about and what they intended toward the Inhabitants. He needed to be about it soon, too, for his guest's life was in danger.

The captain had killed a man while he was being subdued out in the swamp. That man's father was among the participants on the fall hunt that year. Powhatan people took their kin relations seriously, and the bond between parent and child was an especially warm one.[12] Thus the father's grief at losing his son was boundless, and in Powhatan culture a wronged person took his own revenge. Thus from the beginning of Smith's captivity, it was very possible that this bereaved father would try to make him pay for the "murder" he had committed—a prospect which came to pass not long after.

When the language barrier proved too much, Opechancanough promptly sent for priests to come to Rasawek. Seven of them came now, probably by canoe and on foot from Uttamussak.[13] Opechancanough went out with the hunters, letting the priests do their job in peace. It is entirely possible that weroance though he was, he would not have been permitted to attend the divination, so that Smith's accounts of being conjured[14] are, in fact, a privileged view.

Smith did not specify the result of the divination, but his subsequent history among the native people indicates it: the priests declared the Strangers' intentions to be friendly ones. The captive was therefore to continue as an honored guest, albeit a closely guarded one, and protocol demanded that he be taken to Werowocomoco to meet the paramount chief, who must have been kept apprised of developments all along. However, Opechancanough may have received a message from his elder brother to take Chawnzmit northward first, to settle a second revenge question. The timing of the departure was due to the first vengeance matter.

Shortly after the priests gave their verdict, the grieving father made his move and attacked the foreigner. He would have succeeded had not the guards in the house intercepted him.[15] At that point Smith's accounts diverge, and as before, it is the earlier one in which the native people's behavior—not to mention Smith's own—is more plausible. Opechancanough had the would-be assassin brought to him and questioned, after which he enlightened his guest. Unable, under customary law, to order the angry father to desist, he took Chawnzmit out of his reach geographically.

Taking Him on Tour

Opechancanough's ultimate goal in trundling Chawnzmit around part of Powhatan's dominions was to visit the Rappahannock capital, which was located near modern Tappahannock. The people of that town had been seriously wronged by the captain of a European ship a year or two earlier. The ship's captain had, at the least, kidnapped some people from there. Smith understood that the Rappahannock weroance had been suddenly fired upon and killed, after giving the foreigners a feast. And that occurred after Powhatan himself had feasted the strangers as guests at Werowocomoco.[16] To the people of Tsenacomoco, Europeans were just as inexplicable and treacherous as were the "savages" of Smith's *Generall Historie*. Justice demanded that if Opechancanough's guest proved to be the guilty European, he would have to be handed over to the Rappahannocks for an unspeakable death.

Smith would write in his 1624 book that he was taken as far north as the Potomac River chiefdoms, where they entertained him with "most strange and fearful conjurations." His fresher memories in the 1608 letter indicate that the journey covered a smaller area but was exceedingly roundabout.[17] First Opechancanough's party went north to Youghtanund,[18] where the guest was stuffed with more venison. Then they proceeded to the Mattaponi district and two other "hunting towns" of Powhatan's, perhaps hoping to intercept him during this season of intensive hunting. That would explain why the party traveled on foot across the necks of land, rather than simply going down the Pamunkey and then the York to Werowocomoco by canoe. Then, after "four or five days' march," the party walked all the way back to Rasawek, where apparently the communal hunt was still going on. The town was dismantled, and "binding the mats in bundles they marched two days' journey and crossed the River of Youghtanan where it was as broad as Thames, so conducting me to a place called Menapacute in Pamaunke, where the king inhabited."[19] This description indicates that instead of cutting across to the Pamunkey River and then boarding canoes, once again Opechancanough opted for an overland journey, this time down the main peninsula and then across the river (on December 10, 1607).[20] The reason may have been protocol-related. That inland route would not pass any more towns, where townspeople would cause inevitable delays by coming to gawk at the foreigner and lesser chiefs would want to play a part. Taking a land route to Menapacute meant a fast trip and also kept Smith as the protégé of the ruling family for the time being.

The town was not far from modern West Point, at or near a place later called Romancoke, which in turn was located within a mile or so of the temple at Uttamussak. It was probably during his visit to Menapacute that Smith

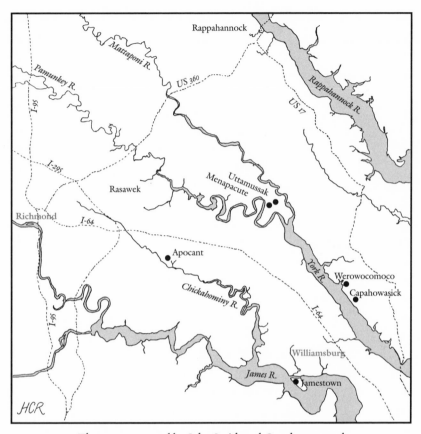

The country toured by John Smith and Opechancanough

learned what little we know about that temple. The town was at the brow of a high terrace, with a panoramic view over the meandering Pamunkey River.

The "king" in Menapacute (or Menapacunt) was still not the "great king," or mamanatowick, but instead was Powhatan's youngest brother, Kekataugh, who next day invited Opechancanough's guest to a feast at his house in the town. Not surprisingly, people came from far and wide to see the outlander. Part of the entertainment was to give the foreigner back his pistol, while "forty men" guarded him to prevent an escape, and then have him shoot at a target. The target they optimistically placed 120 feet away. But strange to say, the little gun wouldn't work. The people were disappointed, for the Tassantassa convinced them (via "body English," of course) that he had "accidentally" broken the exotic gadget.

Festivities over, and checking-in completed with a fellow royal, Opechancanough then conducted his guest northward to the Rappahannock capital. Here the people looked him over carefully and pronounced him too short to have been the murderous ship's captain. (Neither the identity of the captain nor the nationality of the ship has ever been established.) So after a night's stay, with full hospitality laid on by the Rappahannocks for the now-prestigious (rather than criminal) European, not to mention their paramount chief's brother, the party headed south again. The time had been far from wasted for Chawnzmit, who had been able to find out the names of the major districts along the river, all the way to the "Mahocks" (Mannahoacs) beyond the fall line.

Opechancanough moved very rapidly now, passing by the head of the Piankatank River to miss that chiefdom's residents, and after one overnight rest in a "hunting house," he brought his guest to his eldest brother and sovereign at last, probably on December 30.[21]

Arrival at Werowocomoco

Powhatan's capital was located on a wide, shallow bay along the north bank of the York River. Even today, the fishing in that bay is extraordinarily good,[22] so that one or more arrow-shaped weirs would have provided the townspeople with ample seafood for much of the year. Back beyond the town was a huge expanse of forest, covering all of modern Gloucester, Mathews, and Middlesex Counties. Aside from the several satellite towns of Werowocomoco, only one other town, the Piankatank district capital, shared all that underhunted foraging territory with Powhatan. The land of the lower Middle Peninsula is flat, and much of it is good for raising corn, though it is not naturally fertile like the alluvial soils deposited along the rivers of the inner coastal plain. Powhatan's wives and daughters raised ample corn for him in good years, and so did those of the other towns that paid him tribute. By the standards of Tsenacomoco, in which "victuals, you must know, is all their wealth,"[23] Powhatan was a truly rich man.

Most of the town proper was located on one of two necks, formed by three small creeks flowing into the bay. The two necks were connected by a bridge consisting of Y-shaped stakes driven into the mud and poles laid in the crotches to make a walking surface. Crossing either barefoot or in moccasined feet required good balance. If people had large burdens to transport, they would use the canoes that were an integral part of their daily life. Chawnzmit probably paid no attention to the bridge on this visit, because he arrived by land at the back door of the town, so to speak. However, he would get to know the "dreadful bridge" very well a couple of months later.[24]

Powhatan's chief's house, where he received visitors, lay about a third of a mile back from the waterfront.[25] Allowing for four centuries' erosion of the bluff at the water's edge, that would put the house on a slight rise of ground running parallel with the river. Although the rise is not so high that one could see over Indian-built houses, with their high-vaulted, rounded roofs, it would still give the distinct feeling that the mamanatowick's house was as elevated as his social position.

Because no early seventeenth-century account mentions a palisade, it seems that Werowocomoco was a typical eastern Virginia town: a scatter of interspersed houses, fields, and stands of trees or thickets. In the eyes of the men who went out to hunt and fish for its denizens, it was the premier capital because the highest military and political councils took place there. In the eyes of the women, it was a farming town—hence the fields in it—that happened to have a very exalted weroance who was the husband of some of them. The town was not readily visible from the water, which was true of other dispersed-settlement towns in the region. Scattered loaf-shaped houses, covered with gray bark or grayish-beige reed mats, blended readily with groves and thickets even in the leafless winter. In summer, sighting a town through the foliage and the small-sized cornfields the people preferred (an acre or less in size)[26] would have been even harder.

Powhatan had had advance notice, of course, of the coming of the foreign guest: there had to be a feast, and any feast took a great deal of preparation. Pocahontas would have been deeply involved in the operation, though probably not in the eating of the feast with the guest. Women and girls had to collect enough extra firewood from the forest for all the cooking ahead. Then they had to begin pounding tremendous amounts of corn into cornmeal to make corn cakes and pounding up nuts to mix with water to make the nut milk that was considered such a delicacy. Both the nut milk and the stewed meats of a feast required a large quantity of cooking water. Because Werowocomoco was in the brackish part of the York River, the women and girls had to

The site of Werowocomoco, looking toward the river. (Photo by the author)

begin early on to collect water from local springs, which in that area are seeps, not fountains. Men and boys rested up and carefully checked the condition of their hunting gear, because on the morning of Arrival Day they would have to go out and begin producing a large quantity of fresh deer and turkey carcasses for the women to butcher and cook. A genuine feast, with lavish amounts of food that had to be "made from scratch," took most of a day to produce. By bedtime there would be "scarce a bone to be seen," since the people's custom was to eat up each day's meat completely.[27] The next day Powhatan's household and their fellow townsmen expected to do it all over again, day after day after day for as long as the guest stayed.

Because the background labor for Powhatan's "effortless" grand occasions was actually so immense, advance notice was a necessity. Opechancanough probably sent a runner from Rappahannock as soon as the people there exonerated his companion ("they're not killing him after all, so get ready to feed him!").

Chawnzmit was led through the town to Powhatan's house, while every-one had a good look at him. Smith never mentioned what time of day he first met Powhatan, though it was probably in the late afternoon or early evening, but all his accounts agree that he was extremely impressed. He was led to what was by far the largest house in the town and then escorted through "many dark windings and turnings before any come where the King is."[28] There, at the far end of the house, he saw the Powhatan equivalent of a European monarch on a throne, surrounded by courtiers. Powhatan's demeanor was es-pecially striking: he had "such a grave and majestical countenance as drave me into admiration."[29]

Powhatan greeted Chawnzmit with the stately formality in which he was so practiced. They may have smoked a pipe of tobacco together, as was cus-tomary with guests, though none of Smith's accounts mention it; Powhatan was to extend that courtesy to Ralph Hamor six years later when he came to visit.[30] A feast was then laid on for the guest.

Powhatan would have engaged in polite conversation with his guest after the meal, as was normal with the entertainment of foreign emissaries, albeit captured ones lacking an interpreter. Smith's 1608 letter describes precisely that, implying the forging of a personal relationship with Powhatan on the first evening and the few subsequent days before he was escorted back to Jamestown.[31]

Smith's *Generall Historie,* on the other hand, reflects the book's being writ-ten during a war with Powhatan's successors. There is no conversation. In-stead, after Smith is fed lavishly, Powhatan held "a consultation" with un-known persons, which was followed by another sudden, inexplicable attempt on Smith's life that was foiled by Pocahontas.[32] This 1624 account, in which so many things ring false, is our one and only eyewitness source for the leg-end of Pocahontas saving John Smith's life, the act that made her a legend herself. Here I must leave off reconstructing the Powhatan side of things for a while and turn to analyzing Smith's famous story. It is wonderful drama, but it may not be historical fact.

The Rescue That May Not Have Happened

Where had Pocahontas been up till then? Most probably she was nowhere to be seen, for she had been helping her half sisters and stepmothers in prepar-

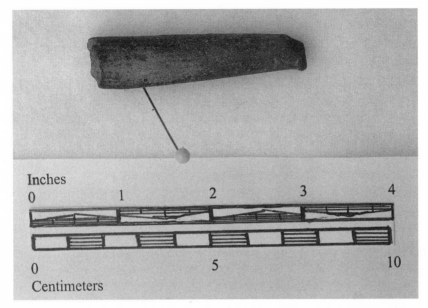

Native ceramic pipestem found at the site of Werowocomoco. The piece is oval in cross section, and part of the lip is still present, on the right. (Photo by the author)

ing the feast. Eleven-year-old girls (and boys, for that matter) were not very important on diplomatic occasions, and no historical account mentions any children at any formal Powhatan reception that preceded a feast. In patrilineal Europe princes and princesses might be present, because the boys were heirs to the throne and the girls, the future sisters of kings, were useful diplomatic pawns all their lives. But the Powhatan system was a matrilineal one. Pocahontas's brothers were not Powhatan's heirs, and she herself would lose whatever prominence she had among the multitude of her father's offspring when her father died. So no diplomatic reason would cause Powhatan to admit any of his children to the reception, except for the handful of sons whom he had made district chiefs. The foreigner was going to remain in town for several days, so Pocahontas and her half siblings would have plenty of chances to meet him later on. Given the lavishness of the meal about to be presented to the foreign captive, Pocahontas's hands were required instead to knead the cornbread, feed the cooking fires, stack the wooden platters, and so on—out in the town, away from the reception.

Once the feast began, she may or may not—probably the latter—have been allowed to be one of the servers of food and water. The feast was most likely held indoors, because it was the next-to-last day of December 1607, and indoors meant limited space. Judging by archaeological finds in eastern Virginia, a chief's house would be twenty feet wide at most, with a reception room not much longer than that. Limited space meant limited admittance to that high-powered occasion. Powhatan's heirs, who were his three brothers and two sisters, and his councillors and priests, and any visiting subject chiefs would have been entitled to be participants or observers, for their advice would be sought in future about the foreigner and his compatriots. Powhatan's loveliest wives would have been the next to have a chance to sit down at the meal. His other wives and those of any subject chiefs present would have been admitted to the room as servers. A chief of Powhatan's importance would want his guest to be aware that many of the decorative, nubile ladies he saw were his host's wives. Gratuitously including an eleven-year-old prepubescent girl would not add one whit to Powhatan's mystique in his own eyes (which were the ones that counted), no matter how witty and intelligent that child was. Establishing his own high status and power was the mamanatowick's (and his subjects') major concern in this first and very formal meal taken with the outlander. Meanwhile, a good many female hands were required to do the washing-up of cooking pots during the meal and of the serving platters and drinking shells after it. The women and girls also had to feed and wash up after the members of Opechancanough's traveling entourage, not to mention the less important people of the town, including themselves. So it is highly unlikely that Pocahontas was even inside the building, either while Powhatan feasted John Smith or later when the two sat and tried to converse through the language barrier. What transpired after the meal between Pocahontas's father and the Tassantassa prisoner was no business of hers, nor could she have expected to be told any of it until later, when the meeting was over. So Pocahontas was probably nowhere near her father and his guest when the "rescue" is supposed to have happened.

The "rescue" is part of a sequence of events that would be farcical if so many people did not take it seriously as "Virginia history." Here is the sum total of Smith's account, with all its abrupt changes of course: "Having feasted him after their best barbarous manner they could, a long consultation was held, but the conclusion was two great stones were brought before

Powhatan. Then as many as could laid hands upon him [Smith], dragged him to them, and thereon laid his head; and being ready with their clubs to beat out his brains, Pocahontas, the king's dearest daughter, when no entreaty could prevail, got his head in her arms and laid her own upon his to save him from death; whereat the emperor was contented he should live to make him hatchets, and her bells, beads, and copper."[33] Upon these few lines, written a decade and a half later, hangs much of the "legend of Pocahontas."

Aside from the redundancy of bringing two "great stones" when one would have been sufficient for the task at hand, the method of killing a foreigner is all wrong here. Smith himself made it plain in his ethnographic work, the 1612 *Map of Virginia*, that disobedient subjects were clubbed to death, while enemy prisoners were slowly tortured. Other early Jamestown writers, like George Percy and William Strachey, who had interviewed some native people with the help of an interpreter, corroborate that dichotomy. But Smith was neither a subject nor an enemy yet. Moreover, the priests, to whose advice the paramount chief and his councillors listened so carefully, had declared the prisoner and his cohorts to be well intentioned toward the native people. Powhatan was not at all likely to disregard their opinion, especially when the Strangers at Jamestown had not as yet done very much to threaten him. The threats seem obvious to us because the English wrote about their own intentions and we have four hundred years' hindsight. But Powhatan had no way of knowing such things at that juncture. Therefore, aside from the fact that he had just laid out an enormous amount of food to impress a foreigner, it simply does not make sense for the mamanatowick suddenly to ignore his supernaturally powerful advisers and order a potential source of information killed, especially in a culturally inappropriate way. John Smith was not in any danger.

William Rasmussen and Robert Tilton have suggested that the episode really happened and was a violent testing of Smith's courage before taking him on as an ally.[34] That idea is intriguing, but the timing is off. In other Woodland Indian tribes where prisoners were thus tested, the trial (usually running the gauntlet) occurred immediately upon the captives' arrival in town. But the attempt on Smith's life supposedly happened after a feast. Why would Powhatan feed a prisoner until he was comatose and then test his courage?

Philip Barbour has suggested that Powhatan seems to have adopted Smith afterward, so he speculates that the rescue incident was part of an adoption ritual among the Virginia native people.[35] However, the behaviors described by Smith (feast him, pretend to murder him, pretend to rescue him) do not correspond with the adoption procedures recorded for any other Woodland Indian tribe. And no adoption procedure at all among the people of Tsenacomoco was ever described, although they very probably had one. Instead the sequence of actions echoes the public phase of the *huskanaw,* or initiation of boys into manhood. But even then, things are out of place. In the huskanaw the candidates (who would be Pocahontas's age) ran a gauntlet thrice with older boys protecting them, partook of a feast, ran the gauntlet a fourth time and were "killed," and then spent several months in seclusion before returning to their towns as "men."[36] John Smith was not tested before being fed, and the age and gender of his savior are all wrong. And anyhow, why huskanaw that foreigner? No other seventeenth-century European account mentions any kind endurance test inflicted upon a visiting diplomat before making an alliance. And Smith's position, on the evening of December 30, 1607, was that of a representative of his country.

Other problems exist with the believability of the "rescue incident." For one thing, it is one more example of Smith's tendency in 1624 to portray the native people of Virginia as being prone to sudden, murderous treachery. That is how the English in Virginia and England had perceived the Great Assault of 1622, and Smith was preparing the ground in the book for his readers to see the Assault as the ordinary Powhatan Indian way of doing business, without any provocation from the "innocent" English. Another hindrance to credibility is the fact that in his writings throughout his life, Smith tells a similar story on other occasions. Indeed, he seems to have had a knack for getting into drastic situations and then being rescued by high-ranking females. He claimed it happened him not only in Virginia but also in Turkey and the Russian steppes.[37]

Smith claimed in his *Generall Historie* that he wrote a letter to Queen Anne of England in 1617, introducing Pocahontas, who was then in London, and claiming her as his rescuer. Conveniently, he quotes the entire letter in that 1624 book. The letter could be a partial corroboration, because of its somewhat earlier date, for the authenticity of the rescue incident—if, that is, any historian had ever found the original of the letter in any archive. But no one has. Instead, modern historians point out that inventing dialogue, letters, and other material was an accepted literary device that writers used in those days to make their stories more interesting. The seventeenth century drew no firm line, as there is today, between history and literature. Smith was writing both, and the rescue incident was very probably an example of the latter.

What did Smith's contemporaries say about the rescue incident in his book? Nothing—primarily because most of the people who had been with him at Jamestown were dead by 1624.[38] The deceased included the scholarly William Strachey and Pocahontas's second husband, John Rolfe.

Of the original arrivals in Virginia who were there when Smith was captured, only two, John Martin and George Percy, were known to be still alive in 1624. Martin was embroiled in a dispute with the Virginia Company and probably did not care what Smith wrote about "ancient history." Percy and Smith detested each other, and Percy was outraged by Smith's portrayal of him in his book. Philip Barbour has suggested that Percy's *True Relation,* which ends in 1612 when Percy left the colony, may in fact have been written in 1625 to refute the incompetence with which Smith had charged him.[39] Unfortunately, Percy was interested only in defending his own actions, and he did nothing to correct anything else in Smith's writings.

Of the people who arrived with the First Supply the day after Smith's return from Werowocomoco, and who might have heard immediately about a rescue if it had happened, the only documented survivors in 1624 were Nathaniel Causey and Thomas Savage. Neither left any writings at all, which is doubly unfortunate in Savage's case because he went to live with Powhatan for a time and later became an interpreter.

Several important Englishmen from subsequent arrivals in Virginia still survived in 1624, among them Samuel Argall and George Yeardley. Both men served as governors and dealt with the native people themselves. Ralph Hamor had met Powhatan himself in 1614 and was still alive, although because he lived in Virginia, he may not have seen the book before he died in 1626. If any of these people heard about a rescue from earlier colonists, they say nothing about it in their writings.

In fact, English people in Tsenacomoco seem to have cared little about Pocahontas personally, much less about how she first met John Smith. It is easy for us moderns to forget that Pocahontas was not a celebrity during her lifetime; instead she was thoroughly overshadowed by her father and uncle, who had the power to make English lives miserable. And seventeenth-century English society lacked the "cult of personality" that makes present-day

Western people focus so obsessively and intrusively upon the lives of the famous. This lack of interest is exemplified by the eighteenth-century Virginia historian Robert Beverley. His history of the early colony[40] does not even say much about John Smith, much less mention his captivity. Instead Beverley took an interest in Pocahontas's career in England and mentioned the "rescue" based upon the letter Smith claimed to have written. Beverley, too, may have regarded it as a literary device.

The logical conclusion, then, is that Pocahontas did not rescue John Smith. Even if she had been inside the house at the time, he would not have needed rescuing from anything other than overeating.

Forging an Alliance

In contradistinction to the suspect account in the *Generall Historie,* Smith's letter of 1608—written closer to the time and not intended for public consumption—feels much more authentic. In that version Powhatan talked at length with Chawnzmit the first evening and the next day, until he thought he knew enough about the newcomers to make them an offer. The details in that text hang together well, too.

On the first night Powhatan was "delighted" (more likely fascinated) when Opechancanough related what (he thought) Chawnzmit had told him about the solar system and the countries of the Old World. He wanted to hear them again and again. He also asked his guest the question uppermost on his mind, namely, why the Strangers had come to his country. He probably suspected that the answer would be a lie, and it was: the English had been attacked by the wicked Spanish and then helplessly driven by a storm into Chesapeake Bay. Now they were repairing one of their boats and waiting for the ships of Chawnzmit's "father," (Christopher Newport) to come and take them home. Powhatan probably enjoyed the signs and "body English" by which this tale was conveyed. The tale, of course, did not explain why the aliens had made a fortified settlement on Jamestown Island, but Powhatan passed over that and asked why, then, had they probed upriver? The answer was (another lie) that his "father" had had "a child slain" on the western sea, and the Strangers assumed the Monacans had done it. Powhatan mulled over whether or not he should correct this mistake, as he took it to be, and thereby give the foreigner the information he obviously wanted, and then he decided to cooperate. A long discussion of geography, North American and European, followed.[41] The guest, getting the impression that his host claimed to rule most of the distant territories he mentioned, claimed that his own king (James I) ruled all the European countries that he had described.

Finally Powhatan concluded that the Strangers were worth gathering in as allies against his inland enemies. However, they were also well worth keeping a close watch upon. So he offered the town of Capahowasick and its environs, just downriver from his capital, to the guest and his compatriots. He also "promised to give me corn, venison, or what I wanted to feed us; hatchets and copper we should make him, and none should disturb us. This request I promised to perform."[42] It is unlikely that the guest realized to what extent the alliance was taken seriously by Powhatan; Smith's writings show that though he admired the mamanatowick, he always distrusted his intention— which, in all fairness, was to assimilate the Strangers, not vice versa. It is also unlikely that he understood the extent to which the alliance was a personal one, between two leaders, in Powhatan's mind.

Chawnzmit had arrived at Werowocomoco on December 30, probably late in the day, and he left for Jamestown on January 1. Not all of that time may have been spent in official conversation with Powhatan (and, probably, Opechancanough). Time probably had to be made to satisfy the curiosity of the townspeople about the exotic visitor. Most had never have seen a European before. He would have appeared unearthly pale to them, and they probably wondered if he was white all over.[43] His face was hairier than any native man's could ever be. His clothing was most peculiar and decidedly impractical for the life a "real man" led. His body odor must have been awful, for it is unlikely that he would have been forced to bathe in the icy York River, as the townspeople did each morning. But his value as a curiosity was inestimable, and he must have been surrounded by a welter of people when he was not visiting with Powhatan.

It would have been during these more relaxed times that Pocahontas made his acquaintance. And as she had charmed her father, so she seems ultimately to have made more of an impression upon Chawnzmit than anyone else in the town. How much of that impression stemmed from their first meeting at Werowocomoco is impossible to say. The only contemporary evidence at all is Smith's 1608 mention of Powhatan's sending her as one of two emissaries to Jamestown the next spring, knowing that Smith would immediately understand how precious she was to her father. A somewhat later bit of evidence is a Powhatan-language sentence that Smith included in his 1612 *Map of Virginia*: "Bid Pokahontas bring hither two little baskets, and I will give her white beads to make her a chain."[44] He was conferring special notice on the child, busy man as he was around Jamestown Fort. Her father's position had much to do with it, of course, but if she had not had a sparkling personality, it is doubtful that he would have said anything about her at all in that word list. His friends, who wrote the "Proceedings of the English Colony" that makes up the bulk of what is usually called the *Map of Virginia*, went further when they wrote that Smith could have married her if he had wanted to.[45] More about that later, but for now suffice it to say that such a strong statement says more about Pocahontas's interest in John Smith than about his interest in her. In the last days of December 1607, the sixteen-year age difference, the language barrier, and the flocking of the other townspeople around him would have kept the two from communicating very much.

Powhatan had succeeded, in his own estimation, in making Chawnzmit and the country he came from into allies of his own. Sealing the alliance may or may not have been done in some colorful way. Smith's 1624 account says that two days after his "rescue"—and thus the day he left Werowocomoco—he was taken to "a great house in the woods," presumably a temple, led inside, and set down next to the fire in the anteroom. This would have been a signal honor, if true, and one that indicated his new status as a weroance. Powhatan then emerged from behind a mat curtain along with "some two hundred" men and informed him that they were allies; in fact, Chawnzmit would be like a son to him.[46] The immense size of the entourage does not ring true, but the rest is culturally feasible, though not corroborated elsewhere.

Powhatan bade his new ally goodbye on January 1 and sent men with him to guide him back to the Strangers' fort. The trip could easily have been made in one day: Smith wrote later that the trip normally took six to seven hours.[47] Smith expected to be home soon, but he found that the men in his escort were dawdling. In fact they went so slowly that the party had to spend the night at "certain old hunting houses of Paspahegh." Smith therefore arrived at Jamestown on January 2, a few hours before ships arrived (captained by Christopher Newport, bringing the First Supply from England). Philip Barbour has suggested that Powhatan had gotten news from his Eastern Shore subjects about English ships entering the Capes, and he wanted his men to have a logical reason to be at or near Jamestown at the appropriate time to find out if that was the ships' destination.[48] That kind of intelligence work is precisely the sort of thing Powhatan would have ordered. But given how long it had taken poor Newport to sail up the winding James River the previous May, the mamanatowick would not have had to send to the Eastern Shore for reconnaissance. Eager observers would have lined the riverside (including picnicking families from Chiskiack), watching the watercraft with their "wings" spread and speculating about what the ships had brought this time.

7

The Alliance's Creaky Beginning

CHAWNZMIT'S BEHAVIOR in the next few months would disillusion Powhatan. The new "ally" would be willing to play upon his status when it benefited himself and the other residents at Jamestown, but he would be singularly insensitive to his "overlord's" proprietary feelings about his own hard-won dominions and the foreigners' movements within them. The disillusionment may have been harsher because Powhatan's relationship with Chawnzmit was phrased in a father-son way[1]—at least when both men were in Werowocomoco.

The mamanatowick had deliberately released his former prisoner with strings attached, both to satisfy his and his brothers' curiosity and for the protection of the people they governed. Nobody had yet come to Powhatan's capital bearing any of those interesting trade goods, much less any of those fascinating weapons. So he sent the foreigner home after agreeing on an exchange: bountiful provisions, carried along by the men who escorted him, to be repaid by two or three "great" ordnances. The deal quickly fell through, though, because the Tassantassas were unwilling to part with such valuable things. Instead they showed the men some large guns (demiculverins, or cannon), each of which weighed about two tons, after which they shot one off. Negotiation by noise! The escort hastily expressed satisfaction with lesser goods to take home.[2]

The foreign ships arrived later that day, and it is likely that the men who had escorted Chawnzmit got to see everything and report back to their paramount chief. However, in a few more days news arrived in Werowocomoco of a bad fire in the foreigners' fort,[3] so that hunger was stalking them once more. Here was Powhatan's golden chance to acquire the foreigners' goods, especially weapons, while generously coming to the rescue of his allies.

Powhatan, Opechancanough, and all the men they commanded remained intensely curious about the capabilities of muskets and pistols. Heretofore they had had few ways of learning those capabilities, since aside from the language barrier, the men could not exactly stroll up to one of those touchy foreigners and say, "Hey there! That was real sloppy shootin' at that deer last week. Was it y'all or the guns?"[4] Instead, the main way to determine the power of the aliens' armaments was by getting shot at. Not satisfactory! Now that the squatters were hard up, and in midwinter to boot, there seemed to be a fair chance to lay hands on those exotic weapons, the *poccasacks* (guns) that went off with such a bang and the *monacocks* (swords) and *tomahawks* (hatchets)[5] made of that unfamiliar hard metal. Then they could try them out for themselves. Ideal! It was true that last year's harvest had been poor, so that letting go of much corn to learn about such arms would be an expensive proposition. But the chance to demystify the metal cutting tools in particular was well worth it.

Accordingly, Powhatan began sending presents of food every couple of days, in the form of bread and game animals, to the Tassantassas and especially to Chawnzmit, who as the mamanatowick's "son" got half to do with as he pleased. Needless to say, lesser luminaries from the York River towns accompanied the presents, taking advantage of a chance to acquire trade goods for the first time. Only Smith's 1624 account mentions Pocahontas: in that version, which omits mention of any trading around the edges, she was solely responsible for the food that saved the Tassantassas.[6] Well, she may have visited the fort during that time, but as an eleven-year-old girl, she would have been a minor player.

Powhatan also wanted to meet the man his captive guest had described to Opechancanough and himself as his "father." Chawnzmit had continually presented this luminary (Christopher Newport) as the most powerful man among the Strangers. Powhatan also assumed that a visit would be an occasion for the Tassantassas' move to Capahowasick, so he issued an invitation for them to come to Werowocomoco.[7]

The visit, when it occurred, was a mixed success. Powhatan soon found out that the squatters did not intend to move themselves from the unhealthy island they were inhabiting to a place where he could control them better. He also would be deflected from trading for any weapons other than cheap iron hatchets. Only a fraction of the foreigners came to visit him, in a small sailing ship (a pinnace) towing a rowing boat (a barge) used for ferrying, yet they brought him a commodity that he would not be able to pass up. It was still the season popanow (near the end of February 1608), and the weather was bitter cold.

An Awkward Arrival

The visit got off to an uncomfortable start for the foreigners when a blunder occurred in handling the initial landing party.[8] In meeting a powerful chief who was unfamiliar with the local geography, protocol demanded that Powhatan send guides out to him when he arrived at the bay off York River. The guides on this occasion were Namontack, who would later travel to England, and the weroance of Chiskiack, who was known to be xenophobic. It was the guides who made the piloting error, bringing on a "test" of their victim's quick wits. That indicates that either Powhatan instigated the ensuing diverting spectacle, or else the guides did, knowing he would approve. John Smith hinted in his 1608 letter that he suspected as much, and he was probably correct.

Twenty Tassantassas, booted and "armed in jacks" (quilted jackets, perhaps plated with iron) and accompanied by a dog (a present for Powhatan), crossed the bay in the barge and were directed to the wrong neck of land (the one between Purtan and Leigh Creek). There they were politely met by Powhatan's son Naukaquawis (or Nantaquoud) and several other councillors who may or may not have been in on the joke. It was they who formally conducted the Strangers to the bank of Leigh Creek, where they came to a grinding halt. Well, now! They'll have to cross our bridge to get to the right neck (the one between Leigh and Bland Creek). But look at what they've got on their feet, and look how top-heavy they are—and look at those puny rails we're accustomed to walking on. Let's see what they do about it! By now spectators were probably gathering on the bluff across the creek, enjoying the fun.

(All of this may sound disrespectful toward the doughty English, but any cultural anthropologist doing fieldwork in someone else's country can testify that it is precisely this kind of embarrassing situation that we get put into occasionally by the people we work with, when they think they can get away with it. I myself have been the butt of several such pranks over the years. It

Aerial view of the site of Werowocomoco (1992). The landing place, indented into the twenty-foot-high neck of land, is out of sight, up the creek on the right. The creek on the left is the one John Smith had to try to cross on foot, to get to the town. (Photo by the author)

is a way that native people can put potentially threatening outsiders off-balance and remain in control. To Powhatan and his people, the English were not heroic settlers in Virginia; they were intruders into Tsenacomoco. Somebody needed to show them who was still in charge, to keep them from getting too big for those silly breeches they wore. Thus the bridge incident was exactly what Powhatan could be expected to set up when facing a first meeting with a powerful "chief" who was backed up by a ship carrying big guns.)

Chawnzmit tried to save face, but he failed. He intermingled his men with Naukaquawis, the Chiskiack weroance, and their companions and started them all across the bridge, which naturally began to sag dangerously under the weight. In Smith's later, more self-serving works, he and his men managed to get across. In his earlier letter they couldn't make it. A canoe put out from the opposite shore to rescue them. Chawnzmit and several others were hoisted down into it and taken ashore, after which they "stood guard" while the rest of their party was fetched. They could then proceed to Powhatan's house, leading the dog and marching "two in a rank" to retrieve their dignity.

In one respect, though, this "test" of the Strangers fell flat: Chawnzmit's "father" was not among those who came to the first meeting. Cannily, he had remained on board the aliens' ship, saving his grand entrance for the next day. Score one for each side.

Powhatan gave Chawnzmit the same formal welcome he had given him two months before.[9] Sitting in his reception room with his court around him, he greeted his guest "with such a majesty as I cannot express nor yet have often seen either in pagan or Christian" and then issued an invitation to sit down beside him. After being presented with "a suit of red cloth, a white greyhound, and a hat," he gave an acceptance speech and then had the good-looking wife of one of his subject chiefs (Appamattuck) bring the guest water for washing and meat and bread to refresh him.

A conversation then took place, unfortunately with no interpreter available. When Smith wrote about it a few months afterward,[10] he inserted dialogue to make a lively account. I cannot do that here, but some elements of the "conversation" are predictable. Powhatan asked him where his "father" was and was told that he was aboard and would come ashore the next day. Smiling to conceal his chagrin, the mamanatowick then asked for the big guns Chawnzmit had promised him when they last talked. We tried to give them to your men, was the reply. Then give us guns that are less heavy, was the riposte, uttered with a guffaw and the appropriate signs. Where were all the men who had come ashore with him? was the next inquiry. Chawnzmit indicated that they were outside the house waiting around. Powhatan then hospitably ordered them brought inside—which they agreed to warily, with some always remaining on guard outside—and had them given "four or five pound of bread" each. (That represented an extravagant gift to mere underlings after a poor crop year.)

Chawnzmit then asked for the corn and territory (Capahowasick) that had been promised to him as the mamanatowick's "son." You will have it, Powhatan countered, when your men all lay down their arms. He may also have pointed to the men of his court and bodyguard, who were presumably unarmed just then. But that is the demand of an enemy, not a friend, was the rejoinder. Instead his "father" (Newport) would give Powhatan one of "his children" the next day as a sign of friendship and would also help him fight the Monacans and Pocoughtraonacks. (The latter offer was actually phrased as "We will deliver them into your hands," but that subtlety was hard to convey by "body English" alone.) Powhatan waxed enthusiastic at this offer, and he gave Chawnzmit the impression (perhaps correct) that in return for the promise, he had made him "a weroance of Powhatan, and that all his subjects should so esteem us, and no man account us strangers nor Paspaheghans, but Powhatans, and that the corn, women and country should be to us as to his own people." Assuming that John Smith put the right construction upon this speech, the mamanatowick was offering to set up his new allies as a chiefdom directly under his own command and on an equal footing with his other subject chiefdoms. Ostensibly pleased with what he had been offered, the guest and his retinue took their leave. Powhatan sent another great pile of corn cakes along with them.

Leaving was one thing, but getting back to the pinnace was another, for Chawnzmit got to the water's edge and found that the tide was out. (Poor Smith had a positive knack for trying to stage dignified arrivals or departures and promptly running aground.) During his long visit with the paramount chief, as the afternoon became rainier, he had tried to find out what the tide was doing, but he had been misled. Now he had to accept Powhatan's hospitality for the night and go deeper into his debt while being unable to brief his "father" on the ship. The mamanatowick had the party lodged in a large building that served as an armory, where fires were lit, and the town's best orators entertained them with speeches assuring them of their safety. That evening Powhatan summoned Chawnzmit back to his presence, gave him "meat for twenty men"—which he was expected to share with his men back at the armory—and then chatted with him for another "two or three hours."

The next morning the two men met informally outdoors, and Powhatan took his visitor to the landing place, pointing to the canoes there and indicating that these were sent far and wide over his dominions to collect tribute. No sooner had he finished his discourse than he caught sight of a boat bearing several Tassantassas to the town. This would be Chawnzmit's "father" approaching, so Powhatan strode back to his house to assume his chiefly accoutrements while his visitor greeted his compatriots.

Sharp Trading

Chawnzmit and his "father" marched up the ramp from the landing and then up the rise to Powhatan's house "with a trumpet" announcing their coming—

another new sound in Tsenacomoco. Powhatan received his new guest indoors in his standard manner, and the day was passed, like the one before, in formal conversation and lavish hospitality for the powerful foreign chief.[11]

Powhatan was given a Tassantassa boy (Thomas Savage), which pleased him immensely. Now he could get somewhere! The boy's youth would enable him to learn the native people's language fairly fast, and then he could begin explaining things about the Strangers to the mamanatowick, who would treat him as a son and keep him close at hand for the foreseeable future. Powhatan's initial plan seems to have been to make it a one-way street, accepting that foreign boy. Although John Smith's later accounts say the exchange of boys happened that same day, Smith's 1608 letter, written when his memory was much fresher, says plainly that Powhatan did not reciprocate the "gift" of an interpreter-in-training until over a week later.

Over the next three days the two sides got down to business, which consisted of trying to take advantage of each other.[12] As usual, the 1608 letter gives far more details, including speeches that may or may not actually have been uttered by Powhatan. The only "interpreter" present as yet was Chawnzmit, armed with a word list from another foreigner's (Thomas Hariot's) stay among the Carolina Algonquian speakers, supplemented by what he had been able to learn during his captivity. Nonetheless, a vivid picture emerges of two experts haggling with each other, while an overgenerous, eager-to-please ship's captain officially did the bargaining for the Strangers. The later writings by Smith and his friends show a greedy Powhatan trying to hold them up for impossibly small amounts of corn, until he saw something among the outlanders' trade goods that he could not resist. The account written closer to the events depicts a more complicated situation.

First, after his guests came to his house again on the third morning, Powhatan fed them breakfast. Then a wrangle ensued over why the foreigners were acting so defensive. The mamanatowick's request that they disarm was refused, and when Chawnzmit's idea of sending his men away proved to be a relay of guards passing back and forth between landing and house, Powhatan found that move offensive, too. The paramount chief probably had good, if manipulative, intentions toward these hardheaded aliens. After all, ambushing them, as they seemed to fear, would have been detrimental to his plans for them that early in their relationship. But they simply would not cooperate with him.

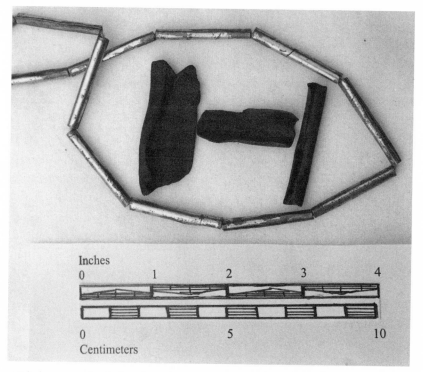

Tubular copper beads found at Werowocomoco. Darkened by four centuries in the ground, they are surrounded by shiny modern reproduction beads from Jamestown Settlement. (Photo by the author)

The trading session went no better. Powhatan was accustomed, as a great chief, to setting his own prices for goods and for women in the marriage market. He considered the Tassantassas to be his subjects, as Chawnzmit had supposedly agreed two months before. Therefore he expected to set the price of his own corn in the present negotiations. Accordingly, he asked the ship's captain, through Chawnzmit, to spread out all the "hatchets and copper" they had brought, so that he could take his pick. Chawnzmit refused, which was an insult. Then the ship's captain interrupted to offer twelve large copper cooking pots for whatever the mamanatowick would give in corn—and found that that the mamanatowick wouldn't give much. That made Chawnzmit seek some other trade goods that would tip the scales in his side's favor. He quickly found them: sky blue glass beads.[13] He had only a few bunches of them with him, and he assumed that it was the small number of the beads that piqued Powhatan's interest. He was wrong.

In Powhatan's world ornaments were made out of naturally occurring substances that had colors different from the gray, ivory, beige, and brown that characterized people's houses, tools, and clothing. Those substances, the luxury goods that chiefs were known to hoard, were native copper (reddish gold and shiny), freshwater pearls (opalescent), puccoon (a deep red dye), and shell beads (shiny). Those beads were usually white, being made from hard clams and whelks.[14] However, beads made from the lip of the hard clam were dark purple (also called blue and black in the literature), adding yet another color to necklaces, earrings, etc. Beads of that deep color were much more rare, due to the limited area of purple in the shells, and therefore more valuable than white beads. Powhatan had no idea—and lacking an interpreter and a reliable informant, he could not find out—that glass beads did not cost much to make and making them blue did not make them more expensive than beads of any other color. Powhatan had only his own cultural experience to draw upon. More to the point, he knew that his subjects would be more impressed by beads of blue than any other color. He simply had to have them!

Chawnzmit immediately took advantage of the intensity he saw in Powhatan's eyes, which of course is what Powhatan would have done if their roles were reversed. He bargained the mamanatowick up to a higher price and promised to fetch more beads from the ship the next day. On that note the interview ended, because the tide was getting low. Powhatan wanted the party to stay for supper, "which was a-providing," but they declined and left. Not to be balked of his intended hospitality and also proper protocol, the paramount chief sent the dinner of venison and bread out to their ship.

Before the fourth morning's trading began, Powhatan sent his son out to the Tassantassas' pinnace to ask them to leave their arms behind them when they came ashore. Chawnzmit disregarded that request, getting "twenty or twenty-five shot ashore." Upon meeting him and seeing him armed as usual with "sword, pistol and target," the mamanatowick asked him to stow them in the barge before coming up to the house. Chawnzmit refused, claiming that he and the "brother" whom the Monacans had supposedly killed (the story he'd made up during his captivity) had been lulled by just such a demand. That day's trading therefore went on uneasily, punctuated by requests to disarm and refusals to do so. Powhatan put up with the Strangers' intransigence because he wanted blue beads so badly. He paid for them with nearly a boat-load (barge, not pinnace) of corn.

It was his success in trading, though, that caused Chawnzmit to undergo another undignified experience. The laden craft plainly did not have enough room for him, his right-hand man, and their companions to fit in. So the hospitable townsmen of Werowocomoco offered them a canoe to help with the ferrying out to the ship, and the offer was accepted. Chawnzmit got into the canoe with six others and started out. That was when he discovered that he had stayed trading too late: the tide had gotten low, and the canoe ran aground when they were "a stone's cast" from shore. (If they launched from Wero-wocomoco's landing place and got that far out, they probably also misjudged where Bland Creek's channel ran and overshot it.) The right-hand man saw their difficulty from shore and decided to try Leigh Creek on the other side of the neck, so "with seven or eight more [men, he] passed [most of] the dreadful bridge" across a wide marsh to the creek—and found that channel to be no deeper. It was easier to finish the trek to the other neck, across a narrow marsh, so that is where some of the foreigners wound up.

Word reached the mamanatowick that two sets of guests were stranded out in the cold. He had provisions sent over to the other neck so that contingent could spend the night in some comfort. Chawnzmit's situation plus his pride made him more difficult to assist. Some of the townsmen seeing him off knew that the canoe would be aground until the tide rose again after dark, "ere midnight." Guests could not be allowed simply to sit out there in the cold. So the men "threw off their skins" (probably their mantles, leaving on their loincloths) and waded out into the mud and low water with the idea of carrying the foreigners bodily back to shore. Be carried like a child?! Chawnzmit was not eager enough to reach land dryshod that he would allow such a thing, so he asked instead for firewood and "mats to cover me." The men waded back to shore, undoubtedly calling to some of the many spectators to run and get those items, and then they slogged with the gear back out to the stranded canoe, "which pains a horse would scarce have endured." Their reward was "a couple of bells," which "richly contented them." Toward evening Powhatan fed the canoe-bound aliens, just as he did the others ashore. He sent the food via his son Naukaquawis, who like the others waded out into the creek and "seemed to take pride in showing how little he regarded that miserable cold and dirty passage, though a dog would scarce have endured it." (Well, dogs lack a culture that places a high value both on hospitality and on shows of manliness in front of foreigners.)

The next morning, when the Strangers came ashore, the tenor of the negotiations changed for a time from trade to military matters. Powhatan sent away all onlookers except his councillors and made a proposition to the Tassantassas: he and they were both enemies of the Monacans. Assuming that Smith understood correctly what Powhatan was saying, the mamanatowick would send spies out to discover their precise fighting strength, after which Chawnzmit, his right-hand man, 100 to 150 armed foreigners, a couple of his own sons (not named), Opechancanough, and 100 of his own men would pretend to go hunting. That would be a ruse to attack and overpower the Monacans. The enemy women and children were to be brought to himself as captives for farming and other labor. No reward was specified for the Strangers, who indicated that they would think the matter over.

The rest of that fifth day of the visit was spent in "trading, dancing and much mirth."[15] It was during the less formal festivities on days other than the first two that Pocahontas, as well as other lesser lights of Powhatan's family and capital, would have had a chance to say hello to Chawnzmit. It was most likely at such times during this February–March 1608 visit that her father's "son" and ally would have learned the words about giving her white beads for a chain that he later recorded in his *Map of Virginia*. They had no tête-à-tête, however. Not only was she still a girl of less than twelve years and Smith preoccupied with trading for food and avoiding an ambush that never came, but they would hardly ever meet without a crowd of people around them, scrutinizing one or both of them. That would be true at Werowocomoco, at Jamestown, and in London a decade later.

Opechancanough Got into the Act

Opechancanough, if not also his brothers Opitchapam and Kekataugh, had been at home upriver while Powhatan conducted his negotiations with the Tassantassas and acquired valuable trade goods. Now the Youghtanund chief could contain himself no longer. He wanted exotic goods, and he wanted badly to meet Chawnzmit's "father," that powerful chief. So on the fifth day that the Strangers were in his brother's capital, he sent a messenger there to invite them upriver. The mamanatowick, however, was unwilling to have his guests leave just yet, for although the people of Werowocomoco may have been ready for a break from producing feasts, there was the prospect of more trade goods. The foreigners had just sent overland to Jamestown for more metal hatchets to buy more corn. A verbal tussle with the brother's emissary broke out, and Powhatan won: the invitation was turned down for now.

The next day Opechancanough tried again, this time sending his daughter (unnamed) to say that he had hurt his leg, which forced him to stay home. But he very much wanted to see his brother's visitors, so would they please come upriver? Again, under pressure from Powhatan, the answer was no.[16]

The following day, however, the Tassantassas decided that Opechancanough's "importunities" were an excuse to move operations, so they took their leave of Powhatan. The mamanatowick may have been chagrined to see them go, but it is doubtful that was true of the people of his town, who were now relieved of having to provide enormous amounts of food for the seventh day in a row.

The wind must have been very "favourable" to the ship that day, for they made very good time going upriver. Around midday, at the town of Cinquoteck near modern West Point,[17] Chawnzmit went ashore and was met by the other chiefly brothers, Opitchapam and Kekataugh. Opechancanough and his family soon joined them. It was a genuinely joyous reunion as far as Chawnzmit could tell, so his "father" came ashore and a meal was laid on immediately. Entertainment probably was presented for a while afterward. This leg of the expedition, at either Cinquoteck or Menapacute, is the only one where the mock battle between "Powhatans" and "Monacans" that Smith later reported could have been staged "at Mattaponi" (i.e., by Mattaponis).[18]

The pinnace then moved up to Menapacute, as Opechancanough, whose leg had somehow healed, and Chawnzmit strolled the four-mile distance via a trail. A tremendous feast was held that evening inside a house specially built for the occasion. Its construction would have taken several days, though, especially in the freezing cold, so the brothers must have felt confident for some time that the Strangers would leave Powhatan and come to see them. Chawnzmit and his "father" wanted to start trading that day, but that was too precipitate to satisfy native hospitality. "The next day till noon we traded, the king [Opechancanough or Kekataugh?] feasted all the company, and the afternoon was spent in playing, dancing and delight."[19] Once more the visitors would have been surrounded by a welter of curious, friendly people, to whom European trade goods were exotic and well worth the expenditure of some of the winter's corn. Both sides were highly contented with the bargain.

The Tassantassas wanted to leave again that evening, but Opechancanough insisted on their staying for a plentiful breakfast the next morning. This meant another delay while his men went deer hunting, for he had "spent his first and second provision"—the first while waiting for the visitors to come upriver and the second in feeding them when they arrived. Once the meal was ended, however, he saw them off. Newport and the pinnace returned to Werowocomoco, but some foreigners in the barge stopped near Cinquoteck, where they were seen to dig in the ground looking for something ("a rock where we supposed a mine," as Smith put it). That group then headed off downriver, rejoining the pinnace "ere midnight."[20]

On the tenth day of their expedition, Powhatan received the Strangers once more in his capital to make their formal farewells. On this occasion, in exchange for the foreign boy, Powhatan "gave" them Namontack, a youth whom he treasured as a son, after which he saw them on their way. The wind seems to have been adverse to the pinnace, for it was not until the next day that the outlanders managed to reach Chiskiack, only ten miles (16 km) downriver, where they apparently stopped in hopes of acquiring still more corn. The inhabitants of that town, however, must have heard about all the trading upriver, for they decided to hold onto their winter stores. They met the aliens "scornfully," which got rid of them—that time.[21]

John Smith wrote darkly later on that he suspected Namontack of being placed among them as a spy, for he was Powhatan's "trusty servant, and one of a shrewd, subtle capacity." Of course he was a spy! And that was what Thomas Savage was expected to become when he had learned the Real People's language well enough. Both sides needed interpreters, and each side wanted more information about the other. In the rhetoric of formal gift exchange, both boys were presented as the sons of important people, but that was not really true. Thomas Savage was not related to Christopher Newport at all. Namontack at first was taken literally to be a son of Powhatan, and when he got to England, he was encouraged by the Virginia Company to claim a high status in native society, even refusing to doff his cap to the king of England. As he became fluent in English, though, his real status as a commoner became apparent, and word of his standing filtered slowly back to Jamestown.[22] His case is interesting: he was the predecessor of Pocahontas in being used in London as favorable propaganda by the entrepreneurs of the Virginia Company.

The subsequent fates of both boys can be summarized briefly. Namontack went to England with Christopher Newport in April 1608 and was returned to Powhatan after Newport brought the Second Supply in the following September. He apparently went back again when Newport sailed once more for England, for it was on his voyage home with the Third Supply, during its recovery from shipwreck in Bermuda in 1609–10, that he was killed by Machumps, a brother-in-law of Powhatan who was also returning from England.[23] No one had either the heart or the courage to tell Powhatan what had happened between the two youths; Powhatan would still be asking the boy's whereabouts as late as 1614. Significantly, Machumps remained among the English for quite some time after reaching Virginia. As for Thomas Savage, he returned to his own people in late 1609, after which he acted as an interpreter. He became especially close friends with the Accomac weroance on the Eastern Shore, and taking up the large tract of land the chief gave him (now called Savage's Neck), he settled there permanently in the 1620s, dying by 1635.[24]

Both boys were expected to report to their superiors, but it is far more likely that reports by Savage about the Powhatans were more accurate than the reports by Namontack about the Londoners. The ship that young man sailed on went directly to and from that big city. Seeing little of the country-side, he concluded that the English "had small store of corn or trees, . . . imagining that [their people] came into [his] country for supply of these defects."[25] This misconception probably remained among Powhatan's people until Uttamatomakkin returned from England in 1617, after having landing in Plymouth and traveled cross-country to London.

8

Allies Who Did Not Behave like Allies

POWHATAN'S SO-CALLED allies (he may have begun to have his doubts) had come and gone, taking away a substantial share of his stored corn and leaving behind some lovely blue beads with which he could deck himself and his favorites—and hire warriors if he felt the need. However, he and his brothers knew no more about the Tassantassas' weapons—how accurate they were at what distances—than they did before the intruders ever entered the country. That situation could not go on. For their part, the Strangers now had enough of the native people's corn that they did not need to be very concili-atory when they did not get their way. It was a prescription for trouble.

The powerful ship's captain (Newport) was still in Powhatan's country, and the paramount chief intended to draw him into further trade. So he sent five or six men laden with wild turkeys, with a specific request for Tassantassa swords in exchange. Smith's 1608 letter does not mention what the captain did about the "debt" he was in now; the later accounts say that a sword was sent to Powhatan for each turkey received, which encouraged him to send more turkeys, this time to his "son" Chawnzmit.[1] But Chawnzmit would not play the game. The mamanatowick then felt compelled to extract payment against the Strangers' will. He did it through the many people who flocked to the fort at Jamestown. These people were going there both to trade and to observe the entertaining Overdressed Ones, for they were the best show in town. By no coincidence whatever, thefts of tools began to occur.

What would Powhatan have done with those swords already sent to him? He could have done several practical things. Steel swords were obviously useful as weapons, so he may have held onto them until his warriors needed them. But steel swords were also useful as machetes, the standard field-clearing tool even today for people practicing the same kind of shifting cultivation that the Powhatans did. Steel machetes would be even better than cheap iron hatchets, which lost their edge sooner, for chopping down the saplings needed to build the native people's house frames. When more men and women had a chance to try out these superior tools, the demand for them must have risen steeply.

The obliging ship's captain left for England (on April 10, 1608), taking Namontack with him. On the way downriver, accompanied by Chawnzmit and others who were staying behind, he called in at Nansemond.[2] That "proud, warlike nation," whom Chawnzmit logically suspected of making the attack at Cape Henry the year before, gave the foreigners a prickly reception until the shooting of muskets scattered them. They then came back cautiously and made peace. The upshot was that Powhatan would soon have heard that one of his subject chiefdoms had been roughed up by the foreigners.

Another of the mamanatowick's subjects, Wowinchopunck, agreed to guide a stranger to "Panawicke beyond Roanoke" to search for any of his compatriots ("Lost Colonists") who might be living. However, when they got to Warraskoyack, he refused to go any farther.[3] He may have felt that his sovereign would be displeased by his involvement in what remained an awkward situation between the native people and the foreigners.

During that season of cattapeuk (spring 1608) when everyone was doing early planting and taking advantage of fish runs, the mamanatowick sent "some of his people, that they may teach us how to sow the grain of this country and to make certain tools [i.e., weirs] with which they . . . fish." That friendly gesture, to allies he still wanted to trust, meant that both women and men went to live temporarily among the Tassantassas. The Spanish later heard a garbled account and concluded that Powhatan's people were intermarrying with the aliens. Nothing like that happened, though enough liaisons occurred that William Strachey later wrote that the native people were "very voluptuous" and the women willing, with their husbands' permission, to "embrace the acquaintance of any stranger for nothing, and it is accounted no offense."[4]

With such warm cooperation prevailing between the two sides, Pocahontas may well have begun (or continued) visiting the outlanders' fort. No contemporary writer, however, mentioned her being there yet.

Uneasy Times

Powhatan's people continued "liberating" the Tassantassas' tools at an ever-increasing rate, extracting payment with interest for the turkeys sent to Chawnzmit. They did not get any swords, apparently, but they got a great many other things. The men seem to have made it into a game, rather like a substitute for their warfare, in which individual fighters took risks—which they had been brought up to enjoy—in order to prove their bravery. It was not enough to look a foreigner squarely in the eye while seizing his dropped tool with your toes and then, if he noticed it, daring him to take "your" new property from you.[5] It showed more courage to intimidate him first, an easy thing to do outside the fort where he felt vulnerable, and then snatch the item out of his hands. The honor was even greater if you went back the next day and did it again. And all this fun benefited the paramount chief[6] and therefore, eventually, your own family.

Those on the receiving end of this treatment, especially Chawnzmit, were less than enthralled. Before long, the flow of tools decreased because, Powhatan heard, his "son" and supposed ally was retaliating. Meanwhile, the paramount chief received word that another tall ship had reached the Strangers' fort (the *Phoenix*, on April 20), bringing them food from home (the remaining part of the First Supply). Now they would not really need to trade with the native people for a while longer.[7]

In spite of Chawnzmit's retaliation, Powhatan's subjects were still taking the foreigners' tools. Not surprisingly, the next news Powhatan got was that a number of Paspahegh men had been taken prisoner by the Tassantassas for "stealing"—certainly not the correct term in the native view. To even the score, the Paspaheghs managed to capture two foreigners, whom they planned to exchange for the "sixteen or eighteen" of their own being held in the fort. But Chawnzmit and his compatriots came out one night and burned one of their towns, after which they set the foreign prisoners free. The destruction of that town, a precursor to an even more destructive raid in 1610, seems not to have harmed anyone; "spoiling" property was the aim. The reason was the season: it was early in cohattayough, and most of the townspeople had planted some more crops and gone out foraging again.

With the help of a visiting Thomas Savage, the Strangers interrogated their prisoners and found that the information given by both Savage and

Amocis, an Indian who had been living at the fort, was correct. Powhatan considered himself an injured party, and he was planning to make a serious, lesson-teaching move against the foreigners once Namontack was brought back safely from England.[8] In the meantime he issued a protest against the way his "subordinates" (i.e., Chawnzmit and his compatriots) were behaving, and it was the protest that had brought Savage to Jamestown.

The mamanatowick sent the boy-interpreter to Jamestown with a gift of turkeys and a message: he understood that the Tassantassas intended to "come into his countries to destroy them." The evidence, he said, was the shooting off of firearms, which he claimed to be able to hear all the way to Werowocomoco (15½ miles [nearly 10 km] away, as the crow flies). Chawnzmit sent Savage back with word that the Strangers had a different intention: to go to the town of Powhatan to "seek stones to make hatchets." However, a Paspahegh man (probably Amocis) had told the outlanders that the paramount chief's men would shoot at them, and if this happened, they wanted him to know that they would destroy their attackers. This answer, which exposed Amocis's loose tongue, seemed also to assume that Powhatan was a fool and would believe that people with a fresh supply of metal hatchets would want stone to make more (the native people knew nothing of smelting ore). And on top of it, a rider added onto the message was truly insulting: Chawnzmit demanded that Powhatan order a high-ranking subordinate, the weroance of the Weyanocks, to be their guide up the river! At this, the old man took such umbrage that he sent the boy-interpreter home with all his belongings, asking that another boy be sent to replace him.

The Strangers sent messages and presents back to Werowocomoco to smooth things over, but they held off sending a boy to live there. That meant that now the one and only trained interpreter in Tsenacomoco (Namontack being in England) was living not with Powhatan but at Jamestown. Young Savage promptly reported to his compatriots that the paramount chief may have had another motive for sending him away besides feeling insulted by Chawnzmit. He was frequently in conference with the Chickahominies, which boded ill for the outlanders because the tribe was both populous and independent of his domain, and he did not want a foreigner around who understood the talk circulating in town about it.

Pretending to acquiesce to Chawnzmit's demand, however, the mamanatowick sent Kaquothocum, the Weyanock weroance, as the requested guide, though that canny man soon evaporated out of the fort, followed not long afterward by Amocis. The latter was a Paspahegh councillor who had been living part-time in the fort and playing both ends against the middle: spying for Powhatan but also letting on to the Strangers that Powhatan was receiving all the tools that found their way into the hands of the native people. Possibly for this slip of the tongue, and also for selling corn and staying "two or three days" without Powhatan's permission, the paramount chief had Amocis's brains beaten out when he arrived home.[9]

Enter Pocahontas

Several Paspahegh men still remained in the Strangers' fort, unable to go home because the native people no longer held anyone to exchange for them. Higher-level negotiations, covered briefly in the later accounts by Smith or his friends,[10] had to be initiated to get them released. They consisted of Powhatan sending "his messengers and his dearest daughter Pocahontas" to ask that any injuries be forgotten, after which Smith released the prisoners to "Pocahontas, for whose sake only he fained to save their lives and grant them liberty." This is a simplified version of what actually happened, which Smith wrote about in detail a few weeks later. It also makes Pocahontas a two-dimensional figure in this, her first appearance by name in Smith's two earlier accounts of his doings in Virginia. In real life the "messengers" were at least as important as she was, and another VIP was involved besides.[11]

Perhaps at Powhatan's urging, Opechancanough sent Chawnzmit his shooting glove and bracer as a personal token of esteem, asking that two captives who were particular friends of his be released. He got no reply from Jamestown, apparently. Then Powhatan sent a present of venison and bread with several men and his favorite daughter, Pocahontas; a welter of other people came, too. They arrived in the morning, indicating that they had broken the six- to seven-hour trip from her father's capital with an overnight stay somewhere. The leader of the party was Rawhunt, "his most trusty messenger, . . . exceeding in deformity of person, but of a subtle wit and crafty understanding." Rawhunt did the talking, which was proper protocol in a matter that concerned adult males. The mamanatowick, he said, esteemed the Tassantassas so much that he was trusting his dearest child to go among them. He wanted to see the boy-interpreter again, for he loved him "exceedingly."

Pocahontas played her role next. She had been looking on, as though nothing else was happening and no prisoners' fates were being decided. Then "suddenly" seeing and recognizing the captives' "fathers and friends" nearby, she began "in good terms [i.e., flowery language] to entreat their liberty." Everyone else began to do the same, at which Chawnzmit became angry and threatened them until they departed, leaving Pocahontas's contingent behind. That afternoon, after hauling the captives to Evening Prayer in the church (which cannot have meant much to people who spoke no English), he "gave them to Pocahontas . . . in regard of her father's kindness in sending her." After supper, the prisoners received their personal effects, Pocahontas was given "such trifles as contented her," and they made their farewells. Because of the lateness in the day, Pocahontas, Rawhunt, and the other messengers would have had to stay overnight either at a Paspahegh town or in the "hunting town" inland on their trip back to Werowocomoco. If Chawnzmit had granted their request earlier in the day, they could have been home by dark.

(Smith's *True Relation* ends here, except for a couple more paragraphs about being led on by Paspaheghs about a mine and beating them for their falsehood. He sent his letter to England soon afterward, when the *Phoenix* returned to her home port. Not until Ralph Hamor wrote in 1615 about his recent visit with Powhatan would there be another account of meeting the paramount chief written as close to the event and with as much vivid detail.)

Pocahontas probably had been visiting the Strangers' fort since soon after Chawnzmit's captivity ended. It is safe to say, however, that she did not go alone on those occasions. It was not so much that she needed bodyguards, for her hostage value was not very high yet. Nor need she fear being sexually assaulted by a lawless foreigner, since William Strachey's remark indicates that adult women made themselves available on occasion (no female aliens would arrive from England until the fall of that year). She was not a "princess" who required an entourage to uphold her status. A girl in her world who was about to turn twelve could perfectly well have found her way to Jamestown alone, once she got across the York River via dugout canoe. But it would not have occurred to her to try. The fact is that Powhatan females simply did not go around alone; neither, much of the time, did males.

Neither the Powhatans nor the English of that time put much value on privacy or on having "private time." Visual privacy was possible in the Powhatan towns, but aural privacy was virtually nonexistent. Both kinds of privacy were possible in the larger houses in England, but usually only the highest-ranking people in the household had access to those rooms. Consequently, for most people in both worlds, everything other than excreting was done in the company of others, partly to lighten the workload and partly for sociability.[12] That is why Pocahontas was almost never alone. A trip from Werowocomoco to Jamestown and back would take almost two days just for the traveling, or perhaps one long day at midsummer, and it would have seemed a senselessly lonely trip to make by herself.

When she got to the Tassantassas' fort, Pocahontas would not have seen much of John Smith in a group, much less would she have seen him alone. He was already a rising star among his people when Opechancanough captured him (in December 1607), for he had genuine organizational and military ability. After his return he was made the "cape merchant," with the job of supervising the buying and/or distributing of supplies for the denizens of the fort. During the summer of 1608, he was made the president of the colony, which gave him even more responsibilities. Further, in that summer he undertook major explorations of the Chesapeake region that kept him away from Jamestown most of the time. When he was in residence, he was thoroughly preoccupied. He would have paid the child some attention and given her presents, of course, because of who her father was, and perhaps also because she had a lively, friendly spirit. But none of his writings indicate any personal interest in her as a girl, much less as a blossoming young woman. (She would not have been very far along in that blossoming; it would be two more years before she began her monthly periods, if William Strachey can be trusted.) Smith's friends probably were accurate when they said only that "her especially he ever much respected."[13]

So how often did Pocahontas visit the fort, and what did she do there? Those Englishmen who were present and who could read and write did not mention anything about her at all. We have to rely on people who wrote long after the fact. Smith's friends wrote in 1612 that she came "very often," but given the kinds of work she would have done at home in Werowocomoco during cattapeuk and cohattayough and the travel time involved, that would not have meant going even as often as every few days once her people's winter food supplies ran out and people began foraging again. William Strachey is probably more reliable. He never saw her in person, for by the time he arrived in Virginia, she was living far away. But he was told by older hands that she "sometimes" had come to the fort and once there she would "get the boys forth with her into the marketplace" and make them turn cartwheels with her, "naked as she was," all over the fort.[14] In other words, she was still a girl—and unclad and bristle-headed accordingly—and she played active children's games with foreigners close to her own age. Many years later John Smith would say something a bit similar: she came "with her wild train" to a fort that "she as freely frequented as her father's habitation."[15] That latter phrase means she felt safe, not that she went to the fort all the time. The "wild train" probably refers to other children who came with her, which has the ring of authenticity. Given the exotic nature of the Tassantassas and the desirability of the trade goods they had, Powhatan people of all ages probably wanted to go and see the Pale (albeit Smelly) Ones whenever relations were friendly enough between the mamanatowick and Chawnzmit, his difficult ally.

Unauthorized "Discoveries"

If Powhatan used formal occasions to introduce new allies such as Chawnzmit to chiefs who were already in his organization and also to friendly neighbors outside his dominions, the protocol was never recorded. But it is safe to say that he organized such events and expected to preside over them. His Tassantassa allies, however, seemed blithely unaware of such politeness. Instead they went out and brazenly introduced themselves all over the Chesapeake Bay. They poked their noses into absolutely everything as they went; John Smith's friends would write later that they searched "every inlet and bay fit for habitation."[16] That kind of prying and asking of questions was transparent to everyone before long: these were not merely visitors.

Their offenses did not end there. When they met some of Powhatan's subject peoples, their first step was "to demand their bows and arrows, swords, mantles, and furs, with some child" as a hostage, so that they "could quickly perceive when [the local people] intended some villainy."[17] That, too, especially the grabbing of children, marked them as not being ordinary visitors. Further, they strong-armed their way into the capitals of Powhatan's newer and less firmly attached chiefdoms along the Eastern Shore and the Rappahannock and Potomac Rivers. This was a direct threat, for "pacifying" the people there could, in the mamanatowick's estimation, be the opening wedge in detaching them from his organization. Making friends with Eastern Shore

John Smith's map of the
Chesapeake region,
originally engraved by
William Hole and
published in 1612 in
London with Smith's
Map of Virginia

VIRGINIA

Mallaw. *Massawomecks*

Signification of these marks.
To the crosses hath bin discovered what beyond is by relation ✠
Kings houses 2
Ordinary houses 2

The Sasquesahanougs are a Gyant like people thus attyred.

Discovered and Discribed by Captayn John Smith
Graven by William Hole

Scale of Leagues

Leagues
and halfe

peoples also threatened to interrupt his supply of shell beads, one of the status symbols that validated his exalted position in the region. Worst of all, the Strangers were led by Powhatan's "son" and personal ally, Chawnzmit. It is no surprise, then, that before the Strangers had made many stops, they encountered people like the Onawmanients (Nominis) on Potomac River who had been ordered by Powhatan to attack them on sight.[18]

The foreigners made two six-week expeditions (June 1–July 21 and July 24–September 7, 1608).[19] On the first trip they started by going to Accomac, where the people were hospitable—and very likely reported the visit to Powhatan. Thomas Savage was not along, so that Chawnzmit acted as his own interpreter, but he may well have succeeded in communicating his planned itinerary to the chief. That news—which really was "news" to the native people—would have gone straight to Werowocomoco, too.

After leaving the Accomacs, Chawnzmit got initially hostile receptions among the (Maryland) Wiccocomicos and Nanticokes to the north. Calling in along the south bank of the Potomac River, he got similar responses from everyone in the lower part of the river: Sekakawons, Onawmanients, Patawomecks. The upriver Moyaones (Piscataways) and Anacostians, on the other hand, were friendly from the outset, perhaps because the moccasin telegraph had told them that the outlanders were doing something displeasing to Powhatan, who was a distant rival of theirs. The Tauxenents (Doegs) were also friendly, although they were within the far fringe of Powhatan's paramount chiefdom. If the downriver people heard of this and relayed it to the mamanatowick, it would be one more offense chalked up against the Strangers.

At the Potomac River's mouth, Chawnzmit's party had taken on a half-blood guide named Mosco (who was probably the son of a Spaniard of the 1580s). Mosco persuaded the Patawomeck chief to show them a mine that produced antimony (not the hoped-for silver). If the chief reported to Powhatan about that excursion, it would have confirmed the mamanatowick's suspicions that his allies were poking deep into the native people's business on the fringe of his domain: the Patawomecks traded the glittery antimony ore far and wide for use in face and body paint.[20] Stopping at Kecoughtan near the end of the first voyage, the mariners appeared frazzled enough that the local people—who knew all about their trip up the bay—assumed they had been fighting the dreaded Massawomecks. Smith wrote later that when his denials were disbelieved, he gave in and said yes, we fought them.[21] Pochins would then have sent word about it to his overlord, who may have believed it—and had some very mixed feelings indeed.

The second expedition began with a run right up to the head of the bay, and there the foreigners really did meet Massawomecks. In reality, the two parties treated each other like a pair of strange curs before making a truce and engaging in trade.[22] But the goods that the Tassantassas were able to acquire on that occasion later convinced many of Powhatan's subjects that they had beaten these ferocious enemies in a skirmish. The next people the Strangers met were the Tockwoghs, who, once they overcame their wariness, hospitably arranged a meeting with some Susquehannocks. Returning to the Northern Neck, Chawnzmit's party picked up Mosco again and probed far up the Rappahannock River, where they had a successful run-in with Mannahoacs, the Siouan-speaking enemies of Powhatan's subjects lower on that river. Powhatan may or may not have heard that they interviewed a captured Mannahoac, learning from him that his people had already heard about the aliens who had "come from under the world to take their world from them."[23] Heading back downstream, Chawnzmit meddled in the business of some more subject chiefdoms when he pressured the Rappahannocks and the Moraughtacunds to end their chiefs' quarrel over some women. After that, the Tassantassas made themselves allies of the Piankatanks, who promised to raise corn for them the next year. That may have been too much for Powhatan, for within a few months he had wiped the Piankatanks off the map and replaced them with loyalists of his own.[24]

While some of the Strangers were prying around in other parts of the Chesapeake region, their compatriots at Jamestown were doing things other than raising the corn they would need next winter. That must have seemed peculiar to native observers, but in the end it may not have mattered much, for 1608 was another drought year. Dendrochronology shows it was a drier year than the previous one.[25]

However, as time went on and nepinough did not come, the Strangers did not visit the towns of Powhatan's people, trying to trade for corn—at which the local chiefdoms probably heaved a sigh of relief. Some tall ships (the Second Supply) brought them food and personnel. So instead, the crazy foreigners ran around doing other things (on the orders of the Virginia Company and over Smith's protests): they sent out more expeditions, and they made another attempt to get news from the Carolina Sounds region about compatriots of theirs. Some of them went out on the island with some newcomers they couldn't converse with (company-hired Poles and Germans), and they went to work making extralarge quantities of weird things (commodities to export: pitch, tar, glass, soap ashes), none of them edible! Not only that, but the ships bringing women from their homeland brought only two of them![26] Not nearly enough to farm for all those men! Who could understand such demented creatures?

A Phony Coronation

Powhatan heard almost immediately that tall ships had returned to Jamestown (on September 29, 1608). He also heard soon afterward that the ship's captain he had met earlier in the year had returned with them and wanted to see him.

Chawnzmit was the messenger, along with several others; he took Namontack with him, both to deliver him home and to have him serve as an interpreter. First, though, Chawnzmit's party arrived at Werowocomoco and found that the mamanatowick was "some 30 miles off." The people left in town felt that the visitors should be honored with a dance and a feast, while a runner was sent out. The dance was a mock war dance, executed by thirty young women, and at first the Tassantassas were afraid it was an ambush. Smith added in 1624 that the women's leader was Pocahontas and that she offered to let him kill her if any harm was intended him.[27] She may or may not really have been the leader, but her dramatic offer would have been unnecessary once the visitors realized that the "attackers" were female.

Powhatan returned to Werowocomoco the next day (he must have rushed home by canoe, to cover thirty miles, nearly 50 km, in one day), and Chawnzmit delivered the message. The ship's captain wanted to give him presents sent by his king in London. More specifically, the captain invited the mamanatowick to come to the foreigners' fort to receive the presents.

What?! Here he was, a self-made man, the overlord of Tsenacomoco, and these squatters in his territory, who could not even feed themselves, wanted him to skulk to them like a dog and receive a pat on the head? The very nerve of it! Well, the answer was no. Definitely no. But with proper Native American manners, he waited until his guest had entirely finished speaking. Chawnzmit went on: the captain wanted Powhatan to "conclude their revenge [finish planning the campaign] against the Monacans." Another insult, as if he hadn't been successfully keeping those people at bay for most of his life! Controlling his anger, Powhatan made the following forceful speech (which is probably accurate, thanks to Namontack's presence, but still a paraphrase of what he said, because Smith's friends wrote it down four years later): "If your king have sent me presents, I also am a king and this is my land. Eight days I will stay [here] to receive them. Your father [Newport] is to come to me, not I to him nor yet to your fort, neither will I bite at such a bait. As for the Monacans, I can revenge my own injuries, and as for Atquanachuk, where you say your brother was slain . . . and any salt water beyond the mountains, [your geography is still wrong]." And with that, he began drawing a map with a stick on the ground. After more conversation between the two men, Chawnzmit took his leave.[28]

The presents from King James of England consisted of a "basin, ewer [pitcher], bed [feather mattress], bedstead [disarticulated frame], clothes, and such costly novelties," including a metal crown with fake jewels in it. Later on, the crown and "the beads" among those gifts would be stored in the temple treasury near Powhatan's new capital of Orapax.[29] The mattress and bedstead were bulky enough that they were sent to Werowocomoco in three large rowboats, while the ship's captain, Chawnzmit, and fifty more soldiers walked across the peninsula and then had the barges meet them to ferry them over the York River. According to standard protocol, the party was entertained and put up for the night, before everyone got down to serious business the next day.[30]

The exotic goods were given to Powhatan with a flourish, "his basin and ewer, bed and furniture set up, his scarlet cloak and apparel with much ado being put on him." Namontack had to assure the mamanatowick that the weird material (woven cloth) sewn into tailored clothing would not hurt him.

The actual "coronation" went badly, primarily because the mamanatowick subscribed to the same rules of thumb that many powerful rulers do. He who keeps his head higher than others ranks higher, hence Powhatan's custom of sitting on a platform while his councillors sat on the ground during a formal reception. And he who puts other people in a vulnerable position, without altering his own stance, ranks higher. Kneeling violated both of those rules. And now the Tassantassas expected the ruler of Tsenacomoco to kneel "to receive his crown." Fools! Other people knelt to him, not vice versa. The Strangers, thinking they had to explain European manners to him (Smith's friends said flatly that he did not know "the majesty nor meaning of a crown"), worked at persuading him until they were blue in the face. But he flatly refused to kneel. It took the combined efforts of several people "leaning on his shoulders," at which "he a little stooped," to get enough of a gesture of submission out of him that the crown could be put on his head. The English could claim afterward that he had submitted to King James, but it is extremely doubtful that Powhatan thought he had done anything of the sort.

The next moment there was a pop and then a terrible explosion, and Powhatan and his court nearly jumped out their skins. The Tassantassas had done something else that was part of their etiquette: as soon as the crown was tipped onto the paramount chief's head, Chawnzmit had a man at the door shoot off his pistol. Hearing it, the men back at the barges, at the landing place a third of a mile away, let loose a volley of shot to celebrate the "crowning" that had just taken place. It took a few moments, while the Strangers just stood there beaming at him, for Powhatan to realize that no ambush was afoot. Once he had collected his wits, he made a speech "to congratulate their kindness" and "gave his old shoes and his mantle to Captain Newport."

(Was that the "Powhatan's Mantle" that the Ashmolean Museum in Oxford owns today? It could have been, but no paper trail exists on that garment at all before 1638. Not only that, but long leather capes with similar circles embroidered in shells were specifically described among the Maryland Algonquian speakers in the 1630s.)[31]

More business followed. The Tassantassas wanted a large body of men and several guides from Powhatan to attack the Monacans. Chawnzmit held onto his lie: no arguments by Powhatan could persuade them that those Siouan speakers, whom he did not like, were nevertheless innocent of killing any Europeans. The paramount chief was not eager, either, to attempt a campaign with allies as untrustworthy as these Strangers were. If they had made friends with the Anacostians, who were known to be friends of the Massawomecks,[32] then they might cozy up to the Monacans and turn on their native companions. The mamanatowick therefore refused to send any men or, for that matter, any guide but Namontack. And there the matter seemed to end. Powhatan gave his guests' leader "a heap of wheat [corn] ears that might contain some 7 or 8 bushels," and after buying as much more shelled corn in the town, the visitors left.

If Namontack did not go with them that day, he joined them later, in time to sail back to England with the ship. Accompanying him on that voyage was Machumps, the brother of Powhatan's then-favorite wife, Winganuske. Both young men probably were intended by their chief for a career as spies and interpreters. Both of the youths, as well as Pocahontas, represented another Native view of the invaders: that of people who were too young and too far away from the seat of power to feel threatened by the behavior of the foreigners. All three of them lived in a place (Werowocomoco) where the aliens had not yet come bullying their way in, demanding food at gunpoint; and being young, until they saw such behavior for themselves, they probably did not believe it had happened elsewhere. Instead Namontack, Machumps, and Pocahontas saw exotic, rich newcomers who had fascinating gadgets and who represented a wider world that they were eager to sample. In their concentration on the glamour of the outlanders, they did not notice the arrogance.

The next thing Powhatan heard was that the bullheaded Tassantassas had gone into Monacan country on their own, in spite of him. No mention was made of Namontack as a guide, but he may have gone along. The captain's ship took a large force—120 Strangers—to the falls of the James, rudely passing by Powhatan's subject chiefdoms including Powhatan town without a word. Such wonderful allies! Chawnzmit was absent and personally opposed to the maneuver, though Powhatan may not have known that. The force penetrated deep into Monacan territory—some forty miles (ca. 65 km), reaching two towns—before it returned. It is impossible to know how much Powhatan found out about the results of the expedition, which in fact was more or less of a failure. (The people were indifferent to the foreigners, though probably silently hostile after one of their chief men was taken hostage and forced to lead the intruders around.) But the paramount chief did know that his allies had committed another serious breach of trust by sallying forth to meet those enemies after he had told them not to do it. The word of his disillusionment must have spread through his domain. His son Parahunt met the Strangers as they came back downstream past the falls. To hurry them out of his district, he told them that several ships had arrived in Chesapeake Bay, intending to kill everyone at Jamestown. Parahunt's people also refused to sell any corn, and when the foreigners tried to take it by force, they found that the people had hidden it in the woods, expecting just such a violent response.[33] Powhatan's other subjects along the James River were now getting braced for reenactments of the same kind of scene.

9

The Breakdown of the Alliance

IN THAT YEAR'S season of nepinough (harvesttime 1608), Tsenaco-moco's people saw that corn was going to be in short supply again, for the drought had not let up. Remembering the alternative of foraging in midwinter, they concluded that the Strangers' trinkets were not very desirable anymore. The Tassantassas at Jamestown idiotically had not tried to raise anything themselves, and it soon appeared that the ship had not brought them enough food. So the local people began to see a steady stream of foreigners coming to them in ones and twos, bringing tools they had filched from the fort, and when they could not get corn, they would purchase "furs, baskets, [gray squirrel pelts], young beasts [for pets], or suchlike commodities." Notice that with the exception of the baskets, those were all things that native men (not women) would procure for trade (though the women would tan the hides before sale). The women were holding back corn, not wanting to have to spend days in the freezing marshes digging tuckahoe.[1] The foreigners' purchases then found their way aboard the foreign ship, where the mariners were selling food (from the ship's supplies for the return voyage for their personal profit).[2] When the ship left for England, that last source of food would be gone at Jamestown.

Powhatan's people declined to bargain with the Strangers for foodstuffs unless they were forced to. So the foreigners began going in larger (official) parties from one tribe to another, pressuring people to sell food and encountering resistance at every stop.[3] At Chickahominy the people traded only after Chawnzmit and his companions landed and took up an offensive posture with their guns. "Their corn being that year but bad, they complained extremely of their own wants," but in the "four or five days" the traders stayed there, they gave in and sold them a hundred bushels. The people of Werowocomoco were visited by a pinnace and barge, whose hopeful captain (Matthew Scrivener) found them "more ready to fight than trade." Only through the persuasion of Namontack were the people induced to part with any of their winter supplies. After those two near fiascoes, which "affrighted us all with famine," Chawnzmit went to the Nansemonds. Those dutiful subjects told him that Powhatan had ordered them not to trade. The foreigners then prepared to shoot, at which time the townsmen decided to sell some corn rather than lose it all.[4]

When Chawnzmit moved back up the James, he found "neither corn nor savage" at the Quiyoughcohannock and Weyanock towns. Everyone had moved what corn they had deep into the forest. The Appamattucks, though, had not taken that precaution, so they had to give up half their supplies, as the Nansemonds had done. They got "copper and such things" for their corn, but they would have preferred to keep the food. Still other native people met Tassantassa trading parties with flat refusals, which made the foreigners become desperate.

Powhatan already knew about their desperation. Aside from getting reports from the Nansemonds and Appamattucks, he would have heard from Wowinchopunck of Paspahegh and Chopoke of Quiyoughcohannock everything their men had observed as traders in and around the fort. After conferring with his councillors as usual, he hit upon a plan. So those worthless "allies" of ours are hungry, are they? Let's rub it in. The paramount chief sent a messenger (probably Thomas Savage) to Jamestown, inviting Chawnzmit to visit him in Werowocomoco and asking him to bring several of his compatriots to build him an English-style house there. He also offered an exchange: if Chawnzmit brought "a grindstone, fifty swords, some pieces [guns], a cock and a hen, with much copper and beads, he would load his ship with corn." The affirmative answer was brought by five foreigners (three of them Germans) who went to work cutting lumber for the house. The mamanatowick must have expected one or more of them to be a spy, which was in fact the case: it was one of the Germans. But he and his countrymen, seeing the contrast between Powhatan's prosperity and Jamestown Fort's poverty, also quickly noticed preparations for an ambush. Being hirelings of the Virginia Company, they had no particular loyalty to Powhatan's foreign "allies," so they turned their coats, threw in their lot with Powhatan, and confirmed how hungry the Tassantassas really were. They also revealed Chawnzmit's plans for an ambush of his own.[5] That was no surprise, but it was nice to get corroboration. The paramount chief then had only to wait for Chawnzmit and his cohort to show up. They had broken the alliance, after all, and he owed them nothing.

Ambushing a Traitor

The Strangers set out in a small ship (a pinnace) towing a rowboat (a barge) and stopped at three of Powhatan's subject chiefdoms on their way to Werowocomoco. The Warraskoyack weroance, Tackonekintaco, put them up overnight, sold them some corn, and warned them against visiting Powhatan. He also accepted a young man to learn the language, as well as providing guides for another inquiry, this time among the Chowanocks, about Tassantassas ("Lost Colonists") still living in their region. Chawnzmit phrased his request for guides as an intention to send presents to the Chowanock chief, to "bind him his friend [ally]."[6] If Tackonekintaco later relayed his actions to Powhatan—and the records indicate that he remained firmly in Powhatan's camp for many more years—then the paramount chief must have been thoroughly displeased with everyone involved.

(From this trip to the Chowanocks, a follow-up on what Opechancanough had told a newly captured John Smith about Ocanahonan, came "little hope and less certainty." A subsequent meeting with the Mangoags [probably Nottoways], aided by Quiyoughcohannock guides, produced a report that all such survivors were dead.)[7]

The Strangers were then delayed by over a week of bad weather (probably a northeaster that they could not sail against without being beached). They had to stay "six or seven days" at Kecoughtan, only fifteen miles (24 km) by water from Warraskoyack, where Pochins made them welcome but divulged no advice on handling his father. Then the aliens managed to get as far as Chiskiack before adverse winds stalled them again for "three or four days." Their reception at that town was hostile, but they forced themselves upon the people until the weather abated.[8] More reports would have flowed toward Powhatan, because windy weather did not hinder men running overland and then paddling across the York River. Finally (on January 12, 1609) Chawnzmit and his compatriots managed to reach Werowocomoco. The weather was bitter cold, and the bay in front of the town had frozen over.

Once more the tide played Chawnzmit false and ruined his entrance. In a show of eagerness to get ashore, he had the barge's rowers break through the ice, and it took so long that well before he reached shore, the tide left the barge stranded. This time, before another ignominious rescue could take place, he and the crew jumped overboard and pushed their muddy, icy way to shore. Less entertaining for the spectators! A few Strangers were left in the lightened barge, now afloat again, with orders to take it back to the pinnace. Powhatan soon received word up at his house that his visitors had been taken straight to the nearest buildings to dry out and warm up, so he sent over "plenty of bread, turkeys and venison." There the guests stayed the night.[9]

Pocahontas may have been among the spectators watching the Tassantassas' arrival ashore that day. It is unlikely, though, that she was an onlooker at any of the negotiations the next day. Danger was in the air, and it was not the place of a twelve-year-old girl—or any other valuable female person[10]— to meddle in matters where they could come to harm.

Powhatan laid on a generous breakfast feast, as protocol required. On their way to partake of it, however, the foreigners had to pass a gruesome sight, staged by the mamanatowick to teach them their place in his world. He had had the Piankatank people punished for their overfriendliness to the aliens not long before. The dead men's scalps, with long hair still attached, were now on display, "hanged on a line between two trees; and of these Powhatan made ostentation as of a great triumph." He showed "them to such [of] the English as came unto him at his appointment to trade with him for corn, thinking to have terrified them with this spectacle, and in the middest of their amazement to have seized them."[11] That timing is a bit beforehand. Why kill the detested foreigners while the town's women were cooking a huge meal to feed to them? And before the start of a final trading session??

Once the lavish repast was over, the paramount chief set about to put his visitors off-balance again. Why had they come, when he had not invited them? Was it corn they wanted? Well, there was little to be had (which was true), but for these favored guests he would make a very special concession: forty swords for forty baskets of corn. Chawnzmit pointed out the men, present in the room, who had delivered the invitation and asked how he could be so forgetful. Powhatan laughed, as if to say, So you caught onto the joke, after which he added, All right, show me what you've brought to trade with. Hmmm. No, I don't want any copper, for we can't eat that. Did you bring any swords or guns to exchange? Chawnzmit got tougher, telling the mamanatowick that he could not spare any weapons. Not only that, but if Powhatan thought that he could starve out the powerful Strangers by ordering his people not to trade and then delaying any bartering himself, he had better think again. The Tassantassas could take what they wanted, said Chawnzmit, though they would not do that to an ally unless he behaved badly. Powhatan managed to listen politely to this insolent speech, and then, feigning acquiescence, he promised to have whatever corn his people could spare brought to Werowocomoco within two days.

The paramount chief then said he had heard news that made him reluctant to feed his allies yet another winter, and he became blunt: "Many do inform me your coming hither is not for trade but to invade my people and possess my country." Not waiting for a rejoinder—for he was merely informing Chawnzmit of what strong suspicions he had by that time—Powhatan went on to try a bit of blackmail. His people, he said, had been afraid to bring any corn in time for the Tassantassas' arrival the previous day because they knew that the foreigners always came so heavily armed. So to expedite the transfer of corn they seemed to want so badly, the Strangers really ought to leave their arms in their barge, "we being all friends and forever Powhatans." That demand got no further with Chawnzmit than others like it had gotten on previous visits, and the rest of the day was spent in verbal sparring, after which the visitors were lodged that night "in the king's houses."[12]

The next day saw the final breaking of the alliance, when each side tried to ambush the other.[13] Not, however, before more diplomatic niceties had taken place. They held a formal review of the English-style house that was a-building for Powhatan (it cannot have gotten very far along) and did a bit of sharp trading before the mamanatowick and Chawnzmit resumed verbal jousting.

Powhatan began by letting his adversary know that he had had long experience of both peace and war: "Having seen the death of all my people thrice . . . I know the difference of peace and war better than any in my country." But he was old, he said, and he wanted himself and his successors to be at peace with the Strangers. He had heard from the Nansemonds that Chawnzmit's countrymen intended to "destroy my country." (The Nansemonds, as then-allies and neighbors of the Chesapeakes, had heard in detail about the Roanoke Colonies and probably had met some of those foreigners personally in the 1580s. That, coupled with English actions in the previous eighteen months would be enough to make them send a strong warning to Powhatan.) Why did the foreigners take things by force when they could have them for the asking from their friends, whose labor they depended on in any case, in order to eat? Why "destroy them that provide you food?" Did Chawnzmit think that he, Powhatan, was so simpleminded that he would not prefer to "eat good meat, lie well, and sleep quietly with my women and children, laugh and be merry with you, have copper, hatchets, or what I want, being your friend," than to be an enemy and forced to flee from everything? Besides, if the Tassantassas chose to be enemies, their "rash unadvisedness" would bring them, too, to a miserable "end, for want of that [food] you never know where to find." Far better to remain on friendly terms—and not go visiting armed to the teeth, "as [if] to invade your foes."

That was good advice, but his adversary would not admit it. Chawnzmit's reply was that the Strangers had kept the alliance, and Powhatan's subjects had not. Only his compatriots' high personal regard for the mamanatowick had curbed their "thirsting desire for revenge" on his miscreant subjects. Surely Powhatan had seen, by their "adventures" (explorations the previous summer and fall) and their advantage in weapons, that they could already have conquered him and his people if they had wanted to do it. (Doubtful, thought the paramount chief.) Warriors were admitted to the fort at Jamestown with their arms, because the Strangers understood that they, too, considered weapons to be part of their normal apparel. As for any dangers from enemies, "in such wars consist our chiefest pleasure" (not true of most people in England!). And they would not starve, either, even if the native people hid their food in the woods, for the outlanders had sources of supply that were "beyond your knowledge." Powhatan recognized this as the bluff it was.

Another attempt at trading led to a protest from Powhatan: he had shown this "son" of his more favor than any of his other weroances, who willingly laid themselves down at his feet, but Chawnzmit was the least submissive or cooperative. He let Powhatan have only what he himself did not want, but he demanded that Powhatan give him whatever he desired. Captain Newport had been generous and had made his men lay aside their arms. Chawnzmit, he complained, called both Newport and himself "father," and yet he went on doing whatever he felt like doing, and "we [Newport and Powhatan] must seek to content you." Rotten behavior from a "son" and "ally"! He was speaking this strongly to him, he said, because of the "love I bear you."

Neither man believed this statement. It was only a delaying tactic while the soldiers on both sides prepared for a fight. Chawnzmit sent his companions to begin moving the purchased corn to the landing place. Powhatan probably guessed that he was also having them finish breaking a path to shore through the ice, as well as signal the pinnace to send more men ashore immediately in the barge. Meanwhile, the captain temporized with another speech to the effect that he refused to live as the mamanatowick's subject but would live as his friend. In fact, he said expansively, the paramount chief was welcome to bring all his people to Jamestown as a bodyguard, and their faithful allies would not object. This claim was followed by a truly far-fetched offer: tomorrow he would meet with Powhatan without any arms at all. "I call you father indeed, and as a father you shall see I will love you. But the small care you have of such a child caused my men to persuade me to look [out for] myself."

At that point Powhatan excused himself "temporarily" from the conference. While Smith sat waiting for his return, the mamanatowick was in fact hurrying into the woods, along with "his luggage, women, and children"— which would have included Pocahontas. Two of his wives remained behind, sitting with Chawnzmit and entertaining him and the soldier with him, while a large number of warriors quietly surrounded the house. But Chawnzmit caught onto the plot, and making good use of their pistols and shields, he and the soldier broke out of the ambush and rejoined their compatriots down at the landing place. A second barge put out from the ship in the river to come ashore and enlarge the Strangers' forces. The ambush had been foiled.

The townsmen remaining in Werowocomoco quickly began trying to smooth things over, as if it had all been a misunderstanding. They were seconded by a talented orator sent by Powhatan with presents for Chawnzmit. Powhatan had fled the town, the speaker said, because he was afraid of the Tassantassas' guns and, moreover, because when the rest of the ice was broken, the barge would return and a greater force of potential enemies would be ashore in his town. The men around the house were not an ambush, he declared; instead they were merely guarding the boss's corn so no one would pilfer it. The ice was open now, the barge was at the landing, and the visitors could take their corn out to the ship. If Chawnzmit wished to see Powhatan and continue their conference, the speaker went on, then please have his men lay down their arms, which were scaring away the people who were still coming in, bringing yet more corn for the Strangers. The townspeople would be more than glad to furnish baskets in which the guests could carry the corn and to provide men to guard their stacked-up weapons from theft while they worked! Chawnzmit's response to this palaver—for everyone involved knew it was precisely that—was to have his compatriots cock their guns. Under threat of being shot, Powhatan's people then had to put the corn in the baskets themselves, carry it to the landing place, and put it in the barge. When Powhatan heard about that, he must have been livid.

Once again, the tide was low by the time the Tassantassas tried to shove off. It did not help that the barge was overloaded, what with corn and passengers and weaponry. Once more Chawnzmit could not make his exit until "the next high water" (the *Generall Historie* adds that it was the midnight tide), so once again he and his company had to bed down in a house near the landing. And Powhatan's people were stuck for a while longer with the stinking foreigners.

Smith's *Generall Historie* gives most of the details of that evening's events. Some things are plausible, but many are less so. The outlanders, now unwillingly restored to the status of guests, "spent that half-night with such mirth as though we never had suspected or intended anything." That sounds probable, being bravado. So does Smith's suspicion, implied in that sentence, that Powhatan would make another attempt on his life. A warning to that effect from Pocahontas was completely unnecessary, but since it appears in two different accounts,[14] it could well have happened. The girl sneaked away from wherever her father was (supposedly still out in the woods rather than back at his own lodgings in town). She crept into the house where the Strangers lay, even though it must have been closely watched by Powhatan's men. Once inside, she informed them that her father would send them food presently (which protocol demanded anyway), but beware! He was preparing another ambush before the night was out, and the foreigners should leave as soon as possible (she may have been unaware that they had already tried their best to get away). Her life was at stake for telling him that (true), so she could not accept a thank-you gift from Chawnzmit before she left. All well and good, but the 1624 version begins the story with something truly preposterous, which a great many people have chosen to believe since then: it was only Pocahontas's warning that saved the party from death that night! As if nobody could have guessed Powhatan's intentions, given the afternoon's scare!

Sure enough, the mamanatowick sent his unwanted guests food that night, as was only right in a leader of his standing. The outlanders made the bearers taste all the dishes, fearing poison (not a bad idea, for Powhatan's people knew a good deal about it). Other townsmen came to call during the evening, checking on the visitors in relays (and, yes, hoping for a chance to do them dirt) until the tide rose enough to enable their departure. Meanwhile, everyone was horribly polite to everyone else.

More Things Going Awry

When the Tassantassas left Werowocomoco's vicinity the next morning, they were observed to head upstream, toward Pamunkey, rather than downstream as though returning to their fort. That meant trouble for Opechancanough and his brothers and their subjects, who had not participated in the goings-on at the capital. Powhatan sent word, by one or more runners, for his brothers to organize a reception the Greedy Ones would not forget. He also encouraged two of the three Germans, who had been glad to be left behind to work on his house, to go to Jamestown Fort and requisition more weapons and tools, supposedly at Chawnzmit's order. This they did, bringing several more malcontents into the scheme. Powhatan was now richer by 300 hatchets, 50 swords, 8 guns, and 8 pikes,[15] with the promise (which was kept) of a steady siphoning-off of more. Now, those were results! Thomas Savage and the other (English) housebuilder saw all this and tried unsuccessfully to run away. A close watch was kept on them thereafter.

The messengers upriver need not have run, for the wind was "unfavourable" again: it took the Strangers' ship "two or three" days to sail up to Pamunkey territory (presumably Menapacute, nearly twenty-five miles [40 km] away by water). There Opechancanough feigned friendship and entertained them for another two or three days. Then (about January 21, 1609) he began the trading, as though he were unaware of the unpleasantness that had occurred at his brother's town. He was vividly aware of it, though, and the indications are that he had planned an ambush all along. His own limited forces were joined by men from miles around, who were outraged at the treatment of their mamanatowick and eager to take revenge. Fifteen armed out-landers were invited to his house, "near a quarter of a mile from the river," and found it and the surrounding houses abandoned. Then Opechancanough arrived with an escort of armed men and some other people with a few piti-ful baskets of corn. Balked of the plentiful trade he had expected, Chawnzmit reminded his host of the profitable bargains they had made last year and stated that he was determined to have part of the people's supplies this year. The chief appeared to give in, selling the corn for a low price and promising that his subjects would bring more to sell the next day. He led them into his house for more conversation, after which "six or seven hundred" of "his" men (only 300 or so being Pamunkeys) "environed the house and beset the fields" nearby. But one of the foreigners left at the riverside saw these movements from a distance and rushed up to the house to warn Chawnzmit, who heard his cries. No interpreter was present, Thomas Savage having been detained by the paramount chief, so Opechancanough could only guess that the alarum had been given and that the speech Chawnzmit immediately began to make concerned strategy. (John Smith later claimed to have challenged Opechan-canough to single combat at this point, which was highly improbable given the differences in their ages [twenty-nine and about sixty].)[16] The ambush had to be put on hold for a while.

The mamanatowick's brother tried to assuage his guests' fears, and he promised Chawnzmit "a great present" if he would go outside the house to receive it. But this was too obviously an attempt to turn Chawnzmit into a pincushion, especially because the doors on the native people's houses were so low that one had to duck to get through them (Henry Spelman wrote of "a little hole to come in at").[17] Chawnzmit did not fall for it. Instead he had a couple of his companions precede him and the weroance through the door, and then he seized Opechancanough by his leather forearm protector and held a pistol to his chest. (The 1624 version is more degrading and less likely: he was seized by the hair and the pistol held to his head.) In that manner Chawnzmit then "led the trembling king (near dead with fear) amongst all this people.[18] This humiliation would have been horrifying for an ordinary Powhatan man; it was excruciating for a man who was also a weroance. The onlookers would have been appalled: the unthinkable had happened. And it is very likely that Opechancanough never forgave Chawnzmit—or the Tas-santassas—for doing such a thing.

"C. Smith taketh the King of Pamavnkee prisoner, 1608." Engraved by Robert
Vaughan for John Smith's *Generall Historie* (London, 1624).

In the face of such a calamity, everyone disarmed. If Chawnzmit made the long, crowing speech his friends later recorded for him, no one understood a word of it, though its gist would have been plain enough. In 1624 Smith added that while he uttered it, he held onto Opechancanough "by the hair." The Pamunkeys (and their neighbors) got the message and began bringing out their winter supply of corn. Chawnzmit then let go of his captive and retired, exhausted, back into a house to rest, where he fell asleep. His companions outside proved a distracted guard, though, and that was too good an opportunity to miss. A mass of armed men pushed their way into the house, intent on releasing their chief and eliminating the miscreant who had offered to kill him. But the framework of a Powhatan house—especially one with some age on it—was just shaky enough that it made noise as people pressed through it. Chawnzmit woke up and grabbed his sword and shield, while his companions did the same. The warriors backed out of the house again. Now Opechancanough and his councillors had to try to reassure their captors once more.[19]

Sometime during that day another foreigner from the Jamestown fort reached Pamunkey on foot and conferred with Chawnzmit. He had gone first to Werowocomoco, thinking the boats were there, and Powhatan had lodged him for the night while pretending (unsuccessfully) that no hostile actions were afoot. (Smith added in 1624 that Pocahontas had to hide this unwanted guest, to keep him safe. It is unlikely that she had the power to do such a thing, even if she wanted to.) Now he made his report, the import of which Opechancanough could listen to but not understand in the absence of an interpreter. But the report did accomplish something: it encouraged the Arrogant Ones to leave for the night, at least. Chawnzmit released Opechancanough, and amid pretenses of friendship the foreigners went back to their boats.[20]

Early next morning Opechancanough had his people gather at the riverfront, laden with baskets of corn, to entice the detested foreigners ashore once more. Chawnzmit had to go himself when the local people refused to trade without his being present. They also declined to cooperate unless the Tassantassas left their arms on the boats, a concession that Chawnzmit agreed to, though he brought the boats close inshore, within musket range for the soldiers left in them. Chawnzmit's landing was a defensive one, too, standing not far from the riverbank that could give him cover, and he refused to go farther, much less as far as the chief's house. Opechancanough therefore came to him, along with the women bringing baskets of corn. He also had a large force of men, "in the form of two half-moons," ready to close in on his quarry. However, when all these people got close enough to the boats, Smith jumped back down the bank, into cover, and the soldiers in the boats brought up their muskets as if to fire. The Pamunkeys scattered before anyone could be hurt. There would be no trade that day, nor any more feigning of friendship.

That night Opechancanough's people heard the sound of oars in rowlocks: the foreigners' barge was leaving the pinnace and heading downriver (to Queens Creek and the overland route to Jamestown). They assumed that Chawnzmit was sending for reinforcements, which would make an even greater threat to themselves, their houses, and their winter food supplies. The great weroance decided to call a truce, which he did with a chain of pearls for Chawnzmit as a personal gift. His subjects would bring corn to trade, he said. And his word was good: "Five or six days after from all parts of the country within ten or twelve miles [i.e., 15–20 km] in the extreme frost and snow they brought [the Strangers] provision on their naked backs." They also expressed their resentment when they offered cooked food, which the Arrogant Ones ate and found to be poisoned. The poison was not strong enough, however, for "it made them sick, but expelled itself." A son of Opitchapam, Wecutanow, seems to have been the major player in that attempt, for as the Pamunkeys saw the aliens off, they tried to excuse him. He himself with some companions went upriver to another town, Potauncack, and when the Tassantassas' ship came within range, he tried unsuccessfully to ambush them there, as though preempting their taking revenge on him.

Once again the native people were dismayed to see the aliens push upriver instead of going back to their fort. This time they were heading up the meandering Pamunkey River, the breadbasket of Powhatan's domains, stopping at towns and demanding that people trade with them (extortion is a more accurate word). Not only that, but they did the same along the Mattaponi River. They noticed the tearful heartburning with which the women and children gave up their food supplies, but they went on "trading" anyway.[21] It probably did not occur to them that they were condemning those women and children to many extra days of guddling out tuckahoe roots from the freezing marshes. Faced with thugs who pointed muskets at them at any sign of resistance, the men of the towns had to acquiesce in the looting of their wives' stores. But they and their weroances, especially Opechancanough, must have been fuming. And reports of all these outrages must have been taken to Powhatan, though that, too, did not occur to the foreigners.

Eventually the Tassantassas presented themselves back at Werowocomoco, as though everything had gone peacefully upriver. John Smith's friends wrote in 1612 that the plan was to "surprise" the mamanatowick—as if mere "savages" could not recognize enmity masked by false affability—and take the remainder of his corn. But Powhatan had seen something of the sort coming and had outsmarted the aliens. Probably while the Thieving Ones were well up the Mattaponi River, he and most of the population of his capital had moved out, very likely by canoe up the Pamunkey River, taking all their belongings with them. Only house frames would have been left behind, for house coverings took long enough to make that they would have been packed along with the deerskin blankets and the baskets of corn. Whatever timbers had been cut for the promised English house would lie neglected.[22] When the foreign harassers appeared at Werowocomoco's landing place, the few men remaining in the town greeted them with such hostility that they left again in a hurry.

Pocahontas's visits to the aliens' fort, which may have dwindled the previous fall as relations worsened, were over. Her father would not dream of letting her go where she might fall into enemy hands now that she would definitely be considered a valuable hostage. Not only that, but visits to Jamestown Island were no longer easy for anyone living with Powhatan to make, for he moved his capital a long and difficult distance away.

Powhatan's Subsequent Capitals

After his flight from Werowocomoco (in late January or early February 1609), Powhatan established his new capital at a place called Orapax, "in the deserts at the top of the river Chickahominy between Youghtanund and Powhatan [town]."[23] That was the general area in which John Smith had been captured a year before, after he borrowed a canoe to get that far upriver, and it was a measure of how anxious the mamanatowick was just then to get away from any place that the English could reach him by the form of transportation they preferred, namely, their boats. Circumstantial evidence, however, shows that the paramount chief did not intend to remain there indefinitely, aside from the fact that by 1614 the English found him living elsewhere. Powhatan probably did not spend more than a couple of years "keeping state" at Orapax.

The giveaway is the location of the town, in the Chickahominy's swampy headwaters. William Strachey wrote that "at Orapaks Powahatan himself co-maundes with 50 [bowmen]," meaning a population of as many as two hundred souls.[24] An Indian town of that size would be an anomaly in the area, given the Virginia Algonquians' preferences for village locations. Usually the native people located their larger, more permanent towns in places that offered a substantial amount of good, flat farmland. The head of the Chickahominy River lies in rolling uplands. The people also chose sites bordering rivers, not swamps, because the moving of people and foraged materials by canoe on a daily basis was a major consideration. Unless Powhatan could somehow keep more than the usual amount of annual tribute corn coming in, he would have to cut back on hospitality when his subject chiefs or foreign emissaries visited, and this was a reduction he could not afford for long now that he badly needed his subjects and allies to oppose the Tassantassas.

Two other major inconveniences to Orapax's location make it likely that the town was merely temporary: it was at the fringe of Powhatan's dominions, making communication with many of his districts difficult, and it was very near to Monacan territory, making living there dangerous.

Powhatan had already moved from Powhatan town, on the western side of his original dominions, to Werowocomoco, in the center of his expanded dominions. Continual communications were needed to keep that big a polity together. And before the English began seriously wooing away his fringe chiefdoms, Powhatan's "empire" was still a very large one for native North America at that time. Orapax was definitely on the periphery of things. Further, it was a long way by water from any subject chiefdoms whatever, for the Chickahominies downstream were still independent of Powhatan. Emissaries to and from Powhatan at his new capital would have to travel—and carry tribute to him—either by canoe through Chickahominy territory or else over hilly country for a considerable distance on foot. The nearest important chiefs' towns were Opechancanough's seat at Youghtanund on the Pamunkey River and Parahunt's seat of Powhatan on the James. Neither was close or easy to reach.[25] Even for a people who prided themselves on endurance, the way to Orapax would have been unpleasant when they were heavily laden with tribute goods.

As for the danger of Orapax's location, the Monacan towns were all located along the James River beyond the falls, but Monacan people claimed—

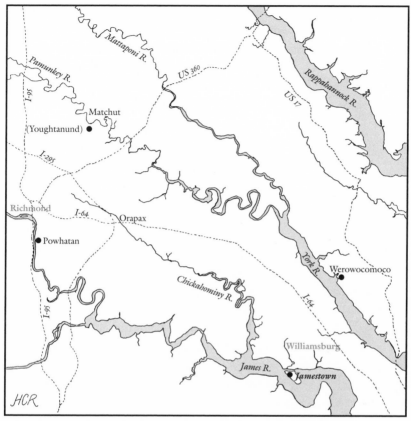

Powhatan's known capital towns: Powhatan (town of origin); Werowocomoco
(1580[?] to 1609); Orapax (1609 to before 1614); Matchut (1614–18)

and actually used—a foraging territory that extended down to the fall line
and beyond. That probably included the area in which Orapax was built. The
two peoples had been enemies at least since 1570. However, the English intrusion into the Monacans' country in the fall of 1608 must have left a sour
taste in their mouths, one that may have made them see Powhatan in a less
hostile light. Now Powhatan was at their borders, and he had been driven
there by English outrages. It is impossible to say which side made the first
overtures, though it clearly would have been in Powhatan's own immediate
interests to have done so. By the time William Strachey lived in Virginia

(1610–11), the two peoples had become allies against the English, and the danger to the residents of Orapax would have abated.[26]

Orapax's precise location is hard to ascertain. Archaeological survey of the Chickahominy River's headwaters has been very limited, except where highways have pushed through. The best candidate at present for Orapax is site 44NK100, now destroyed by the building of Interstate 64 at Bottom's Bridge.[27] A subdivision, formerly a farm, named Orapax is about two miles (ca. 3 km) to the north, though the farm may simply have been named by someone who read Captain John Smith. The archaeological site was at the eastern (New Kent County) side of the swamp at Bottom's Bridge, under and just north of the interstate highway. A survey located a large Late Woodland site there, exactly the kind of anomalous phenomenon that Orapax would have been. It is a pity that no actual excavation was done before the highway went through, for more extensive investigation might have shown whether or not the site was palisaded. It might also have brought up European trade goods to confirm an Early Contact period date.

Powhatan and his household took everything of value from Werowocomoco with them to Orapax. That included the fake-jeweled crown and other gifts he had received from the Tassantassas' monarch back in the fall of 1608, for Henry Spelman, who lived with him at Orapax in late 1609 and early 1610, saw them stored in the temple that was built about a mile away.[28] The town remained occupied at least through mid-1611, when William Strachey returned to England. Strachey's informant, Machumps, told him Powhatan still lived there.

Powhatan's next, and apparently his final, capital was the town of Matchut on the Pamunkey River. He was definitely in residence by 1614, when the final negotiations about Pocahontas's captivity were conducted outside the town, but no colonist bothered to mention when he was first known to be settled there. The location of the town is not that of the "Matchut" on John Smith's much-published map, down at the mouth of the Pamunkey River, but far upstream. Ralph Hamor went to visit Powhatan in May 1614, and he wrote specifically that "Matchcot" was "at the head almost of Pamunkey River," and that it was on the north or King William side, "the main river [being] between him and us lest at any time we should march by land unto him undiscovered."[29] Hamor added that the distance from Jamestown was "threescore," or sixty, miles (97 km), and he indicated that he and his party traveled overland. These data can be combined to arrive at a location a little upriver from the U.S. 360 bridge, somewhere between Mehixen and Millpond Creeks.[30] Smith's map, originally sketched in 1608 after he had been in that vicinity as a captive, shows a town there named Wahasatiack.

Close by—almost opposite, on Edward Haile's reconstructed map[31]—was Opechancanough's capital of Youghtanund. Opechancanough was an extremely important person in Powhatan's organization by that time, and it made sense for the old mamanatowick to settle near his strongest and ablest brother. The actual overland distance between Jamestown and this likely location of Matchut is about fifty miles (ca. 80 km). The spot was still far from central in Powhatan's dominions, but it was accessible for his subjects by canoe. Powhatan could still receive tribute and govern his domain.

10

Contain Them, Then Let Them Starve

P O W H A T A N A N D his people played a major role in the "starving time" that the denizens of Jamestown endured in the winter of 1609–10. True, the dispersal of the ships of the Third Supply by an Atlantic hurricane the previous summer helped immensely. But most of the causes of that terrible famine stemmed from the actions of both sides in Virginia—during another dry year.[1]

Letting Them Run Out of Food Again

Powhatan and his people would have known that the Tassantassas expected more ships to come to Tsenacomoco, loaded with supplies. It is doubtful that they, any more than the aliens in the fort, knew of the hurricane out to sea that wrecked the fleet, which in any case had started out very late (in June 1609). It is likely, however, that the Eastern Shore subjects of the mamanatowick continued to keep watch on anything that came through the Capes and that he would have his people in Kecoughtan and Nansemond (now spread out into Chesapeake) thwart its arrival if they could. There is a bit of evidence that they had a chance to do precisely that. A longboat was sent out from the shipwrecked fleet in Bermuda with the aim of reaching Jamestown with news of what happened. That longboat was never heard from again, and William Strachey suspected that it reached Powhatan's country only to be assaulted and destroyed on its way up the James River.[2]

Before the fish-runs season of cattapeuk was over, the foreigners ran out of the food they had extorted from the native people a few months before.

They could hardly expect those people to welcome them when they came around again wanting to buy food. Few people would let them have anything at all, not that there was much to sell. One chiefdom and only one remained really friendly to the Tassantassas, and that one was probably serving as a conduit for information sent to Powhatan about conditions at Jamestown. Chopoke, the chief of the Quiyoughcohannocks across the river, often sent "presents" to Chawnzmit, asking him "to pray to his god for rain, or his corn would perish, for his gods were angry."[3]

Some of the local people, especially the Chickahominies, were willing to sell food (probably meat) to the Strangers, though, because tools and weapons and ammunition kept disappearing from the fort and finding their way into the local people's hands. Much of the drain was accomplished by the intrigues of the Germans still living with Powhatan and their accomplices in the fort. The result was that by the time the planting season of cohattayough was underway (late spring 1609), Powhatan's warriors had learned the capabilities of the foreigners' weapons and were practicing with them, while the few aliens who were willing to work at feeding themselves—most were not, preferring to wait for the ships—soon had little with which to clear and till the ground.[4]

Powhatan's, not to mention Opechancanough's, thirst for personal revenge on Chawnzmit remained unslaked. Suspecting that the Tassantassas' leaders had guessed the Germans' betrayal by now, he had Wowinchopunck, the Paspahegh weroance, prepare an ambush. Sending a German as a decoy to the aliens' glasshouse (the appointed rendezvous for the pilferers), a force of several dozen warriors lay in wait for Chawnzmit to come over from the fort to arrest the turncoat. Chawnzmit took the bait, sallying out with a couple of dozen armed companions. His escort was drawn into the woods before catching the German, but when he himself turned to go back to the fort alone, Wowinchopunck intercepted him and took aim at him. The captain promptly foiled that attempt by grappling with him, and in the ensuing struggle both of them fell into the river. The weroance tried to break and run when he saw two foreigners (Poles) approaching, but Chawnzmit held onto him until the three of them could wrestle him ashore. The ambush had backfired. Wowinchopunck was held as a hostage pending Powhatan's turning the other two Germans over to Chawnzmit, and the siphoning-off of arms came to an end for the time being.[5]

In spite of Wowinchopunck's repeated requests for the exchange, Powhatan made no move at first to return the Germans. The weroance's wives and children visited him frequently at Jamestown, and before long he escaped while his men ambushed the foreigners who chased him into the forest. Chawnzmit then retaliated by capturing two other Paspaheghs, named Kemps and Tassore. Paying them copper to betray their chief and serve as guides, he sent them with a force of soldiers one night to raid the Paspahegh capital and recapture Wowinchopunck. However, the leader of the soldiers (Peter Winne) made such poor time that daybreak revealed his arrival. In the skirmish that followed, a few people were hurt, and the chief's house was burned, but the chief himself remained at large.

Chawnzmit then made a raid of his own there, burning more houses, killing several people, and pulling up some fishing weirs. As he moved up the Chickahominy River (for reasons unknown) past another town,[6] the men there initially offered to fight him but then desisted, claiming that Wowinchopunck's quarrel was not with him personally but with the captain (Winne) who had attacked them earlier. There was more oratory, excusing the weroance's actions, but no interpreter was present to make sure that the Strangers understood what they were hearing (the oratory recorded by Smith's friends is probably a literary device). Chawnzmit agreed to make peace in exchange for their bringing him food, presumably when the summer's corn became ripe enough (if it ever did). The summer was already proving to be another dry one, so Wowinchopunck made no more attempts on the foreigners' safety for the time being. Powhatan may have heard what soon befell two Chickahominy men who were caught filching tools from the fort, but that would not concern him except insofar as that tribe might become more willing to align itself with him.[7]

By well into cohattayough, when the native people were accustomed to foraging for wild foods, the Tassantassas were seriously hungry. (The last of their extorted corn was lost to rats—a European import.) Kemps and Tassore, now freed to go home and feed themselves, remained among the aliens a while longer, probably because they had turned against their chief and could expect retribution for it. Their efforts at helping the foreigners get gardens under way paid no more dividends that year than the efforts of the women elsewhere in Tsenacomoco paid their families. The sturgeon were still migrating up the James to spawn, and that was the outlanders' main food. Some of Powhatan's people (probably Quiyoughcohannocks) brought tuckahoe and wild game to the fort and (probably) carried away information as well as trade goods.

Soon Powhatan received word from his sons, created weroances, that parties of Strangers tried to set up camps, one at the falls of the James beyond Parahunt's town of Powhatan, and the other at Point Comfort, near Pochins's town of Kecoughtan. These squatters hoped to feed themselves in those places, but without luck. At the latter place it was the bumbling foreigners' own fault: "In six weeks they would not agree once to cast out the net." The hogs brought in the Second Supply had been taken to Hog Island, across the James and downriver. They and the chickens had to be eaten sparingly, which must have puzzled the local observers. (William Strachey wrote that the native people "devoured" any animals that came within their grasp.)[8]

Some of the outlanders, however, found the diet at the fort too meager and went to live in the native towns. Some years later both John Smith and the "ancient planters" surviving from this time would remember its being a dispersal rather than a problem with runaways; both may have happened. Smith inadvertently admitted there were runaways when he recounted that when some miscreants decamped to Paspahegh, searching for Kemps and Tassore, Kemps accused them of being lazy and returned them to Jamestown for punishment, thereby discouraging others from deserting the fort.[9]

Meanwhile, Powhatan was still harboring the Germans, Thomas Savage, and another countryman of Savage's. When the Tassantassas sent someone (a "Switzer") to retrieve them, the messenger, too, turned his coat and encouraged Powhatan to have his people wipe out both the Strangers in the fort and those living in the native towns. Still others in the fort were drawn into the plot, except that two of them relented and informed Chawnzmit, who quickly sent two soldiers all the way to Orapax to assassinate the plotters. Powhatan saw their purpose and promptly stood back from it all. His message to Chawnzmit indicated that he would remain neutral: he would neither detain the Germans nor prevent their murder.[10] After all, unloading them would mean fewer mouths for his household to feed.

Some of the "billeting" came to an end not long after, when a ship arrived at Jamestown (in July 1609). Those still resident at the fort were able to buy part of its supplies (captained by Samuel Argall, it had been on a fishing expedition). They lost ground, so to speak, when the first ship of the Third

Supply straggled up the river to Jamestown (in August 1609). It too was short of provisions, and along with the news of the "loss" of the rest of the fleet (this ship was separated from it in the hurricane), it brought a welter of new-comers who had to be fed. Gabriel Archer arrived back in Virginia on it, and he noted that "many were dispersed in the savages' towns, living upon their alms for an ounce of copper a day. . . . Neither were the people of the country able to relieve them if they would."[11]

The first crop of corn had not come in yet; nepinough was late in coming again. Harboring foreigners, whether runaways or guests, put a strain on the native people's labor, not to mention their patience, that must have been considerable, for in this fourth drought year in a row, their foraging was not producing as much sustenance as usual even for themselves.

Repelling Attempts to Spread Out

In that unhappily extended foraging season of cohattayough (after August 1609), the outlanders decided to move part of their forces out of their fort and into the Real People's territory.[12] This time they did it in a highly organized and decidedly forceful way that was guaranteed to spark opposition. The land's owners began to think that the Tassantassas were like *tahkemi* (lice):[13] pests that spread unless picked off and crushed.

The first attempt was at Nansemond, and the intruders did ask for permission first. But the place they wanted for a fort was the site of the people's temple. It did not seem to cross the Strangers' minds that anybody would object, one piece of non-Christian ground being much like any other. Needless to say, the Nansemonds did not take kindly to anyone proposing to settle on sacred soil. But how could they explain it to infidels, especially in the absence of an interpreter? When the answer came slowly, the impatient Tassantassas occupied the site anyway, which led to open conflict. The intruders were driven out, but only after some of them destroyed "the temple, took down the corpses of their dead kings from off their tombs, and carried away their pearls, copper, and bracelets wherewith they do decore their kings' funerals." Nansemond retaliation for this sacrilege was swift. Some of the invaders broke away and went to Kecoughtan, where Pochins's people disposed of them, but the others were gleefully picked off by the locals, to be found later "with their mouths stopped full of bread, being done as it seemeth in contempt and scorn."[14] The Nansemond weroance, Wehohomo, could report to Powhatan that the Abrasive Ones had even less respect for sacred things than he had suspected, but they had been defeated this time.

Almost simultaneously, another party of foreigners went up the James and sat themselves down on the riverbank just below the palisaded town of Powhatan. They informed the residents there that they were going to build a fort, and they began cutting trees. Well, that was too bad. The town's residents were not thrilled by the presence of 140 enemies perching on their flank, in a place where other enemies (Monacans) had been making annual raids on them. Sniping operations commenced. Before long, Chawnzmit arrived from Jamestown, and officious man that he could be, he made things worse for everybody. His compatriots were not glad to see him or eager to do what he wanted. And what he wanted was to buy the town of Powhatan, up on the terrace away from the river's floods, and move them into it. Accordingly, apparently without consulting anyone else, he made an offer.

Parahunt—and Powhatan, when he heard about it—must have thought that Chawnzmit's "offer" stank of arrogance, because it was actually a demand not only for the mamanatowick's hometown but also for much more: "the fort [palisade] and houses and all that country [in exchange] for a proportion of copper; that all stealing offenders should be sent him [Chawnzmit], there to receive their punishment; that every house as a custom should pay him a bushel of corn for an inch square of copper, and a proportion of *pocones* [puccoon root] as a yearly tribute to King James for their protection [from enemies] as a duty; what else they could spare to barter at their best discretions."[15] Finally, the puffed-up little creature bragged that his forces would defend the townsmen against the Monacans. All this from a set of aliens who were known to be on the verge of starvation! And whose copper was so devalued after two and a half years of trading that a big kettle would hardly fetch a bushel of corn anymore. What an idiot!

Now everybody was mad at Chawnzmit. Parahunt seems to have made some sort of temporizing answer, for William Strachey later claimed that Powhatan himself had sold the town.[16] But the intruders, who were still engaging in skirmishes with the local people, refused to cooperate with a lame-duck leader (which Smith was, pending the new governor's arrival with the Third Supply). After nine days Chawnzmit gave up and pushed off downriver in a snit—and promptly ran aground on a shoal. According to Smith's friends in 1612, that was a lucky occurrence, for the local people had made a concerted attack on the remaining Tassantassas as soon as Smith left shore. Now his compatriots were willing to listen to him, for the moment. So he went back, ran out the town's inhabitants (let us hope they took that devalued copper with them), and moved his gang into the "savage fort . . . built and prettily fortified with poles and barks of trees, sufficient to have defended them from all the savages in Virginia." Thus the "sale" went through—for now.[17]

Seeing that "all were friends," as he thought hopefully, Chawnzmit returned to Jamestown. Of course, as soon as he was out of sight, his compatriots moved back into their flood-prone fort on the riverbank, and the town's former residents moved back home. Not long after that, the hostility of Powhatan town's people (we don't want you over there, we want you out!) caused so much loss of life and property that the foreigners were forced to give up altogether and leave.[18] The second attempt at making a satellite settlement had failed.

The third attempt was made shortly thereafter. A fort, called Fort Algernon, was established on a sandy island at (Old) Point Comfort, about a mile from the hostile Kecoughtans. This time the satellite was a success, probably due in part to its nature as a base for fishing and keeping watch through the Capes.[19] There would be no conflict over sacred soil or farmland there.

Something else was "sold" during the imbroglio at Powhatan's hometown: another boy (Henry Spelman) was to be an interpreter-in-training. The boy thought that he was being handed over to Parahunt in exchange for Powhatan town; perhaps that is what Chawnzmit told him, to ensure his cooperation. He would, of course, wind up living with the paramount chief. Now the mamanatowick would have two interpreters, while the Tassantassas would have only one. That one, the Paspahegh man Kemps, would remain at Jamestown until he died of scurvy—something he would never have contracted among his own people—in 1610.[20]

Spelman arrived at Powhatan's capital of Orapax in a roundabout way that indicated his "sale" was not a straightforward one. He stayed about a week with Parahunt before returning to the ship, still at anchor before Powhatan town, and he returned with it to Jamestown. Not long afterward, Thomas Savage came from Orapax bringing a present of venison and a message to Chawnzmit's successor (George Percy, with whom Powhatan was trying to establish a personal relationship). Before he returned with an answer, Savage asked for company, and Spelman went with him rather than stay in the fort and go hungry.[21]

The Departure of John Smith

Half a moon before Powhatan heard about the building of Fort Algernon (in October 1609),[22] he would have heard about the calamity that happened to Chawnzmit, news that probably made him rejoice. On the way downriver to Jamestown, his former "son" and "ally," now seemingly a taunting enemy, was badly hurt in a powder explosion. He was being taken back to his home country, but he would probably not survive the voyage.[23] As though the mamanatowick cared by now!

One person who did care was Pocahontas, though her exact emotions about the departure—or about Smith himself, except for respecting him[24]— were never recorded. Smith, for his part, never speculated about her feelings, for being a man of his century and a military man at that, he was not interested in such things. The lady herself did not have her opinion of him written down by her second husband, who was literate. However, she reacted strongly when she saw Smith years later, and one of the emotions she expressed plainly was anger at him for the way he had double-crossed her father.

Legend has it that the poor, starstruck girl came to the fort looking for him, as usual, and one day she was callously told that he was dead. After he left, according to Smith himself,[25] she ceased her visits to the fort. Well, she was told he was dead, and she did stop visiting, but not in that order; once again, Smith was making a good story.

Since early February 1609, Pocahontas had been living at her father's new capital at Orapax. Even if the distance were not so great, her father would not have let her near the Tassantassas' fort, for he was rarely sending even messages there. The Strangers' attempts to found satellite forts would have intensified his enmity toward Chawnzmit, who was now the official leader of those intruders. Correspondingly, Pocahontas's potential value as a hostage kept on rising. As the Strangers showed themselves ever more willing to use force to get what they wanted, so the mamanatowick would have kept his favorite daughter ever closer by him. Pocahontas would have heard the news, after it reached her father in Orapax, that Chawnzmit had been injured, perhaps mortally. She seems to have heard that news from her father, for her words to John Smith later on were, "They did tell us always you were dead." She was talking about her father and herself at the time,[26] and the "always" indicates that Powhatan asked more than once in succeeding months or years whether Smith had survived. He may not have liked the man anymore, but he continued to respect him. Pocahontas seems, later at least, to have shared that opinion.

Legend—and even worse, the Disney cartoon—speaks of a love affair between Pocahontas and John Smith; many Americans today actually believe that he was her second, English husband. There is no historical evidence at all for such a thing. Instead the legend seems to be based on a misinterpretation of something Smith's friends wrote in 1612, when they indicated that some of their contemporaries had speculated about whether Smith could have used Pocahontas to expand his power base in Virginia through a "royal" marriage of convenience. They helped along the fantasy they were contradicting by adding a couple of years to her age:

> Some prophetical spirit calculated he had the savages in such subjection he would have made himself a king by marrying Pocahontas, Powhatan's daughter. . . . She was the very nonpareil of his kingdom, and at most not past 13 or 14 years of age. . . . her especially he ever much respected. And she so well requited it. . . . But her marriage could no way have entitled him by any right to the kingdom [correct: it was inherited matrilineally], nor was it ever suspected he had ever such a thought, or more regarded her, or any of them, than in honest reason and discretion he might.

Of course, they added obsequiously, if Smith had wanted to marry her, or do anything else he felt like doing, nobody could have stopped him.[27]

Pocahontas went right on with her life after Chawnzmit's departure. In fact, she got married. It happened sometime in 1610, the year she turned fourteen. She would have begun her menstrual periods, the sign in her society that a girl was marriageable, and by that age she and most other girls had learned most of what they needed to know to participate fully in the adult women's world. (The Powhatan world had no artificially prolonged childhood or adolescence.)

Pocahontas appears to have had her own choice of husband, unlike one of her younger sisters, for the man was not a chief picked out for her by her father. All that was ever recorded about him is half a sentence written by

William Strachey in 1612: Pocahontas was "now married to a private captain called Kocoum some 2 years since."[28] The words "private" and "captain" meant the same thing in Strachey's time as they mean now: Kocoum commanded (or was at least an informal leader of) some men, but he did not hold public office (he was neither a weroance nor a councillor). His middling status in Powhatan society indicates that Pocahontas was not—at that time— particularly ambitious to raise her status by "marrying well," so that other considerations about the man may have outweighed his nonchiefly position. How romantic those considerations were is open to question. Kocoum may have been a Tsenacomoco girl's dream, but where he wanted to live may have mattered as well. Pocahontas had much to gain by remaining her father's favorite daughter. Daughterly affection was probably involved as well, but in the Powhatan world, as in ours, comfort mattered, and her father was a rich man. She did keep her favored position after marrying,[29] which points to the couple's staying in Powhatan's vicinity. As with many potentates, to be his favorite she had to be accessible, even on call. Marrying a weroance, even one she loved, would have meant moving to the district he governed (not to mention becoming one of a bevy of co-wives). Kocoum was somebody who did not require her to leave her father. He may have been a nice boy from one of the Youghtanund towns, which would give Powhatan an additional motive for moving to Matchut, in that district, a couple or three years later. Alternatively he may have come from farther away but have been a member of the mamanatowick's bodyguard, based right there in Orapax. We will never know why Pocahontas chose as she did. The historical record is also completely silent about whether or not the couple had children.

The Native People Almost Won

Powhatan must have viewed Chawnzmit's departure as a stroke of good fortune, for he was the most able leader the Tassantassas had had up to this time. The others were either incompetent or quarrelsome or both, which left the Strangers even more vulnerable to famine than before. The paramount chief encouraged his people to harass the foreigners[30] and then set about playing upon their hunger in order to eliminate another leader. Henry Spelman, now living at Orapax, was an eyewitness to the preliminaries.[31]

The mamanatowick followed the same procedure he had used almost a year earlier: he invited the aliens to come and trade with him for corn, at which time he ambushed them. This time the stratagem worked. The scene of the ambush was one of the Pamunkey River towns, for Orapax was much too far into the Chickahominy's headwaters to be reached by a ship. Spelman is clear that a ship went to the town. George Percy added, at second hand, that Powhatan allowed his "son and daughter" to visit on board, to lull any suspicions that the ship's occupants might have had. If that is true, then the daughter in question was probably Pocahontas, who would have been familiar to many of those present from her visits at Jamestown. To resume from Spelman's version, a longboat carrying over twenty Tassantassas ferried Powhatan's children ashore. The captain (John Sicklemore, a.k.a. Ratcliffe) met with Powhatan in the usual formal manner, exchanging gifts, and he and his companions were lodged for the night in a house about half a mile from the riverfront (and from the barge in which they could escape).

The next day the foreigners were escorted to the "storehouse" to barter for the corn there. A contretemps broke out, however, when Powhatan's people were found to be pushing up the bottoms of the baskets offered, to reduce the amount of corn being sold. At that point Powhatan made his exit, along with his wives, Spelman, and one of the Germans who still lived with him. A large force of warriors who "lay lurking in the woods and corn about" the town then began shooting at the outlanders, who were hurrying toward the barge with their purchases. All but two were killed, those two managing to get to Jamestown by land and report what had happened; the mariners on the ship had taken fright at what little they saw and retreated downriver without them. Spelman, who had served as the messenger to invite the captain to come from Jamestown, saw everything but the ambush itself. Knowing he was still loyal to his countrymen, the departing Powhatan sent him and the German upriver to Youghtanund, Opechancanough's capital, and told him to stay there (under his brother's watchful eye) till Powhatan came through on his way back to Orapax. That was when Spelman learned from Thomas Savage about the ambush; Powhatan trusted Savage enough to keep him close by while the killing went on.

Spelman lived with Powhatan for another six months or so, during which the mamanatowick treated him well but showed evidence of valuing both boys less than before. Neither boy was tempted to go back to Jamestown that winter, however, for there the Tassantassas were in dire straits. Eventually the brother of the Patawomeck weroance came to visit Powhatan. Iopassus's treatment of the young foreigners was so friendly that they and the remaining German decided to go with him when he left for home. But Thomas Savage changed his mind on the trail and turned back; he would go on living with Powhatan for another several months.[32] Savage tattled about the others' leaving. Powhatan sent men after them, asking them to return, which they refused to do. In the chase that ensued, the German was killed, and Spelman barely escaped into the forest, after which he "shifted for myself" and made his way to Iopassus's town of Passapatanzy.[33]

(The welcome Spelman got at Passapatanzy was testimony to the Patawomeck people's ability to differentiate among foreigners, for they had been maltreated by Spelman's compatriots a few months before. Shortly after Powhatan's successful ambush of Ratcliffe, the desperate leadership at Jamestown had sent a ship to the Patawomeck capital. There the captain bought a good deal of corn, but his contempt for "savages" [he was Lord De La Warre's brother, and therefore an aristocrat] had led him to take offense at something and kill two people and injure several others.)[34]

The Strangers Starved like Dogs

The Tassantassas could not afford to alienate even a distant chiefdom like the Patawomecks any longer, for by winter they were starving in good earnest. They were also under constant guerrilla attack by Powhatan's people, who killed hogs as well as anyone foolish enough to venture out of the fort to retrieve them. The men of Tsenacomoco now knew the limitations of the foreigners' firearms, and they showed little fear of them.[35] Powhatan forbade his people to trade, though that did not include the independent Chickahominies. Strachey even claimed that the paramount chief's men "drave all the deer into the farther part of the country."[36] The foreigners ate up the last of their supplies and livestock, sold away their tools until none were left and the native traders evaporated, and then they ate each other. By the beginning of the planting season of cohattayough (in 1610), Jamestown Fort was almost depopulated: "Of five hundred men, we had left only about sixty."[37] Others survived either by holing up in Fort Algernon and living on oysters (it was discovered later) or else by running away to the native people's towns, where they were "never heard of after."[38]

English coins made into ornaments, found in James Fort. It is a measure of the residents' desperation at being "abandoned" that they took silver coins, instantly tradable to Europeans, and bent them into stringable beads. The beads' being found still inside the fort means that the native people weren't buying, either.
(Courtesy, APVA Preservation Virginia)

Powhatan watched all of this through his observers and probably gloated. So much for their arrogance! So much for their strong-arm methods! The priests, who had become unremittingly hostile to the outlanders, would have believed that the prayers Our People were making to Okeus to send a plague upon those horrible pests were being answered. The common people were singing the latest hit song, which derided the Strangers for being such fools as to be killed in spite of their supposedly superior weapons. Guns! Swords! What good did they do for such incompetents? Just let the morons' leaders try to buy the Real People off with copper! Our Real Men can capture and kill foreigners whenever they want to![39]

Some modern readers may wonder why the mamanatowick did not make a massive strike and wipe out the Jamestown squatters completely during this time. The answer is that he didn't think he had to bother. He and his people had never seen very many of the foreigners at once, and they seem not to have believed Namontack's account of how many people he saw in London. (Hence Powhatan's 1616 order to the priest Uttamatomakkin to make a careful count while he was in England.) These Tassantassas had to be a nation no more populous than Tsenacomoco, thought Powhatan, so if more of them came to infest his country, their numbers would be about the same as before; ditto their inadequate supplies from home. As for the aliens at Jamestown, they were dying out all by themselves, and he need take no further action than to let his men have some target practice. His opinion seemed to be confirmed when another ship sailed up the James (after May 23). It stayed at Jamestown for half a moon, during which Powhatan's people came around only to watch the invaders and kill a few stragglers. Then (on June 7, 1610) the ship took aboard the walking skeletons who had survived the famine and sailed back down the river again, leaving the fort empty.[40] What a welcome sight!

11

Return with a Vengeance

WOWINCHOPUNCK'S welcome report from Paspahegh about the ship's departure probably reached Powhatan simultaneously with a more ominous one from Pochins at Kecoughtan: more Tassantassa ships had just entered the Capes. The Nansemonds, now using the old Chesapeake territory, actually met the ships, which had anchored in order to go fishing, and some ostensibly friendly trading took place,[1] after which another message would have gone to Powhatan. Not long afterward (after June 10, 1610) Wowinchopunck would have sent word that the ships had reached the empty fort, where they not only unloaded many people (and surprisingly few provisions) but also a new chief (Thomas West, Baron De La Warre). This was the first in a kaleidoscope of royal governors—none lasting longer than two and a half years, and most of them less, until the 1620s (see Appendix B)—that Powhatan and his successors would attempt to deal with personally.

It would soon become apparent that in many ways Powhatan had met his match. Both he and De La Warre had limited manpower in Virginia with which to make war, so they used what they had to great effect. Both men were aristocrats in their own world, and as such they had little tolerance for non-cooperation, much less outright disobedience, from people they considered their inferiors. The trouble was that each man thought the other one was his inferior. Powhatan was unaware that he was now being officially charged by the Virginia Company with the extermination of the "Lost Colonists."[2] It did not matter whether or not all of them had died violently (the Carolina tribes never said that) or whether he had ever even been in contact with them (the earlier records give no hint of it). He had been accused, and his adversary arrived already primed to see him as a criminal. Powhatan, for his part, had some hopes of parleying with the new chief, during which he could try to maneuver this set of foreigners into becoming his subjects. He had his men resume sniping at the intruders, and he persuaded the Chickahominies to do the same.[3] Relations between the two leaders immediately became strained, and then they snapped.

Escalating Hostilities

It was still cohattayough; nepinough was delayed, for the year was proving to be yet another drought year, the fifth in a row and the worst yet.[4] The Tassantassas approached the local people about trading—people who had nothing but hard-won wild foods to eat—and walked into ambushes instead. Powhatan later heard that the ships had left his country for a time and come back (from Bermuda) with more exotic animals (pigs and chickens) for the residents of Jamestown.[5]

Soon the aliens began attacking the towns of Powhatan's subjects—without reason, as far as he could see.[6] The country was his and his people's, to use as their ancestors had taught them, and it was everyone's duty to repel interlopers who tried to push into it. Obviously, the invaders disagreed.

The first victims were at Kecoughtan (on July 9, 1610), where several townsmen were killed in the attack.[7] Pochins was away at the time, which was just as well, for shortly he had no town to return to. The Strangers had taken it over, along with all its fields; they now controlled that strategic tip of the main Virginia peninsula. This attack seemed gratuitous to the native people. True, a foreigner had been captured and killed by some Southside people (either Nansemonds or Warraskoyacks) when he went after a stray longboat that had blown away from Fort Algernon.[8] But that was ordinary business nowadays to the native people, like smashing a bug. Perhaps the Tassantassas were angry at the Kecoughtans for killing those would-be settlers of the Nansemond temple site when they had washed ashore in their territory the previous year, or maybe they were just put out that the townsmen would not sell them food. Who knew?[9] But the loss of such a strategic town and the insult to the paramount chief and his kin must have hurt.

Two emissaries from Jamestown then arrived at Orapax with a message from the foreign leader. Thomas Savage may still have been in residence there, to serve as an interpreter. Machumps, returned from England with the Third Supply, may have been with the messengers, though he seems to have spent most of 1610–11 away from his people.[10] De La Warre sent a statement, that Powhatan's people had been harassing and killing his own, and an ultimatum: Powhatan, being a great chief, would order the hostilities to cease and also send the killers to Jamestown for punishment. Otherwise there would be retribution. Further, Powhatan was to "return such men as he detained of ours"—more runaways had taken off for the native towns—or De La Warre would recover them by force. They were, he reminded the mamanatowick, subjects of the same foreign king to whom Powhatan, "on his knees," had sworn "not only friendship but homage."

Powhatan, remembering how little dignity he actually had given up at his "coronation," was infuriated. The gall of these pipsqueaks! This new batch of them could obviously not keep from starving any better than the previous lot, yet they thought they had dragged him into subjection to some leader across the ocean. Well, they didn't rule his domain; he did. So he sent the messengers back with a scorching reply to the effect that if the squatters insisted on staying, which he didn't want, they had better confine themselves "to James Town only" if they didn't want to be annihilated. Furthermore, the leader in that fort need not bother sending another message to him unless it was accompanied by "a coach and three horses, for he had understood by the Indians that were in England how such was the state of great werowances and lords in England to ride and visit other great men."[11] Powhatan could not have gotten under the aristocratic De La Warre's skin any better if he had tried.

The paramount chief's men continued either to hang about Jamestown Fort, spying until they were run off, or to wait in the woods to ambush any aliens who came within range "to gather strawberries or to fetch fresh water" while the fort's well was being redug. Most of the watchers were Paspahegh men, now entrenched in their hatred for the invaders who had settled within their territory. Their feelings were intensified when the Strangers captured one of their number, cut his hand off, and sent him to Powhatan as a warning that if he did not return the foreign runaways and all the captured guns and swords turned over to him in the past few years, his people would find their towns and cornfields burned.[12] Powhatan did not give in.

The next victims of the Tassantassas were the Paspaheghs (on August 10).[13] Guided by an unwilling Kemps, seventy foreigners attacked the capital by night, killing people of both sexes and scattering the rest. Wowinchopunck escaped harm, but one of his wives and two of his children were captured and taken away. The bodies of the children were found in the river later; they had been thrown overboard and shot in the water. The fate of the wife may or may not have become known: she was taken into the woods near Jamestown and put to the sword. Killing children and women was simply not done in Powhatan warfare: aside from the fact that they were noncombatants, they were too valuable as food producers for their captors. So this atrocity, coupled with the destruction of that town and another one belonging to the Paspaheghs—along with the temple near it, which was a sacrilege—cemented the deadly hatred felt by the lower James River chiefdoms for the criminal outlanders.

No more messages went back and forth between Powhatan and his opposite number in Jamestown. Even though no large-scale, open-field actions were fought, both sides were now at war.

Losing Ground

Powhatan would be slow to realize it, but hunger was no longer his ally. The Tassantassas from now on would be better supplied from home than they had been heretofore. More ships came in than before, bringing not only food but also newcomers with tools and weapons. The more populous nation began to show the advantage it had that ultimately defeated Powhatan's people: replaceable personnel. When the paramount chief's warriors killed some, and the local diseases killed many more, the empty places filled and then overflowed. The process started slowly and would not really accelerate until the last year of Powhatan's life—aided, ironically, by the propaganda value of his daughter—but it must have seemed unsettling for him to watch even in the early stages. For Opechancanough, still two places away from the position of mamanatowick, it must have been horrible, but he held his peace for now. No one knows what Pocahontas thought about it. Politics were not supposed to be her sphere: being a new wife was, within the women's world.

Reports began coming in to Orapax from subject chiefdoms. The Warraskoyacks were roughly handled. Their weroance and his son were taken prisoner, the latter being kept as a hostage and taken to England on a returning ship. The father was made to promise peace and a share of his people's

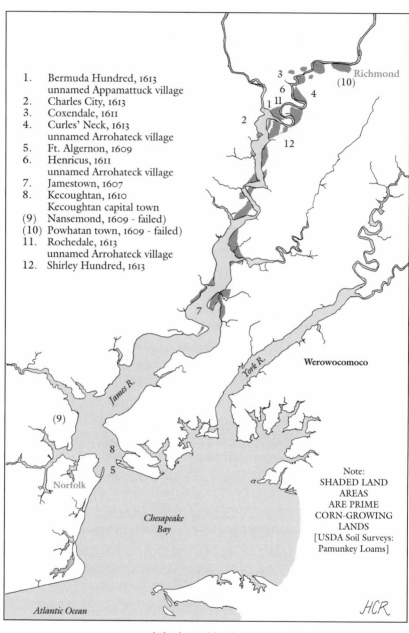

1. Bermuda Hundred, 1613
   unnamed Appamattuck village
2. Charles City, 1613
3. Coxendale, 1611
4. Curles' Neck, 1613
   unnamed Arrohateck village
5. Ft. Algernon, 1609
6. Henricus, 1611
   unnamed Arrohateck village
7. Jamestown, 1607
8. Kecoughtan, 1610
   Kecoughtan capital town
(9) Nansemond, 1609 - failed)
(10) Powhatan town, 1609 - failed)
11. Rochedale, 1613
    unnamed Arrohateck village
12. Shirley Hundred, 1613

Richmond

Werowocomoco

James R.

York R.

Norfolk

Chesapeake
Bay

Note:
SHADED LAND
AREAS
ARE PRIME
CORN-GROWING
LANDS
[USDA Soil Surveys:
Pamunkey Loams]

Atlantic Ocean

HCR

English-claimed lands to 1613

harvest before being released. A supposed nephew was still in the Strangers' hands as another hostage, but he escaped, after which the Warraskoyacks mocked the aliens every chance they got. Soon afterward a ship's captain (Samuel Argall) went to their town and destroyed it, but failed to kill any of the people.[14] They were probably out foraging, for in that driest year of the seven-year drought, the crops may have failed altogether, so that there was no nepinough at all.

The Appamattucks saw a Tassantassa boat going upriver and enticed the occupants ashore, promising them a feast. The credulous foreigners were then attacked, only the "taborer" (drummer) escaping by holding the boat's rudder as a shield and sculling the boat out of arrowshot range. That score would be evened a year later, when the satellite town at their river's mouth was burned, and Opossunoquonuske, its weroansqua, was wounded.[15] Another boat carrying the governor himself managed to reach the falls of the James River (in the autumn of 1610), where the foreigners built and occupied a fort for a while in spite of the local people's ferocious response, which killed many intruders. The intruders returned the favor, destroying many houses in Powhatan town.[16]

During the cold months of popanow (of 1610–11), Powhatan would have received word that the Patawomecks had been visited by the Tassantassas. That chiefdom, at the fringe of his sphere of influence, had given haven to the runaway Henry Spelman earlier. Spelman occasionally had had a thin time of it while living there, thinking himself a guest but sometimes being treated as a servant. Once he even got into fisticuffs with two of Iopassus's wives after he refused to obey the orders of one of them.[17] If Powhatan and his brother heard about that incident, they may have found it amusing. Less amusing was the fact that now the Patawomecks were approached by a ship's captain (Samuel Argall again) who had been sent to trade for corn. He had heard from a downriver group that a foreign boy was among them, and he decided to retrieve him. Iopassus gave up the boy readily enough. His brother and overlord (name never recorded) sold corn so willingly that the Strangers would thereafter make a practice of trading there.[18]

Powhatan could not know it, but in the long run the Strangers dealt him a worse blow by making friends with the Patawomecks than by what came next. In the depth of the winter (on February 9, 1611), he lost one of his greatest weroances, Wowinchopunck. That doughty warrior had taken a party of men and gone to lie in ambush at the foreigners' blockhouse, which guarded the isthmus entry to Jamestown Island. A skirmish took place in which Wowin-chopunck was thrust twice through the body with a sword, mortally wound-ing him. His men managed to retrieve the body and retire into the woods with it, and while they did that, an outlander, bolder than the rest, managed to kill a Paspahegh councillor as well. It was almost six months to the day since the chief's wife and children had been murdered. A few days later the Paspahegh men settled the score when they managed to kill several of the invaders.[19] But their losses had been too great, and they had been unable to dislodge their hated neighbors. By May the Paspaheghs had abandoned their towns[20] and gone to live with relatives in other chiefdoms. The aliens took over their lands.

It was in the next planting season of cohattayough (May 1611) that the Nansemonds received a visit from the foreigners in their boats. This en-counter went no better than previous ones had. As the boats went upriver, the priests came to the waterside and conjured up a rainstorm to put out the matches on the intruders' guns. Unfortunately, as conjurers their aim was not very good: the rain fell in the wrong place, and the boats kept on going up-river. The Nansemonds became even more embittered.[21] Machumps was in the boat with the intruders that day, serving as their interpreter; Powhatan's brother-in-law seems to have gone over entirely to the enemy.

The war had not gone on long before some people began to entertain se-rious fears about their future. Before he left Virginia in mid-1611, William Strachey learned through Machumps that the paramount chief's priests had made two prophecies. In the earlier one a great power would come from the Chesapeake Bay and overrun his land. Thus Powhatan's crushing of the hold-out Chesapeakes. But another version said that the native people would push back such invaders twice but fail in their third attempt and become a con-quered people.[22] That sounded more ominous. (It later came true.)

In that year and successive ones, wherever the Tassantassas were success-ful in holding onto the native people's land, they built forts, the precursors of farming communities. At first they made their choices simply to acquire al-ready cleared ground, but later they knew they were also getting the best farmland available to Powhatan women.[23] When the Strangers took over a native town, they looted it before burning it. The prizes they carried off in-cluded not only whatever corn they could find but also household goods. William Strachey wrote of "a delicate-wrought, fine kind of mat . . . with which, as they can be trucked for or snatched up [during raids], our people do dress their chambers and inward rooms."[24] Replacing all those lost goods would have fallen upon the women more than the men. The invaders' expansion thus was costly for women in work time and for men in prestige.

Although the Accomacs, the Quiyoughcohannocks, and even the Chiskiacks had a truce with the Strangers during that time (mid-1611–early 1613),[25] other chiefdoms were less amenable, for the moving-in of the hated trespassers continued. Another party of them tried to settle fairly near the falls of the James, this time managing to stay permanently within Arrohateck territory. No efforts of the local people succeeded in dislodging them.[26] Then they appeared at the falls, very near Powhatan town, with the same intention. The paramount chief had heard about the plan and specifically warned the governor (Thomas Dale by now) against doing this, saying he would make the would-be settlers "drunk." When his threat was ignored, the mamanatowick had some priests put a hex on the Tassantassas one evening in their camp outside the town. The soldiers began hooting and falling all over themselves, a condition that lasted seven or eight minutes. The experience frightened the invaders but did not make them leave. Instead their resolve hardened, and they took more land.[27] All this pushiness caused the Monacans to feel threatened enough that they were willing to lay aside their traditional hostility to the Algonquian speakers. Powhatan at Orapax was not the only one who needed the alliance that resulted.[28]

A Forced Truce

The intruders now consolidated their hold on lands that had belonged to Powhatan's originally inherited chiefdoms of Powhatan, Arrohateck, and Appamattuck, while the people of those towns, not needing orders from their paramount chief, continually fought back. The obvious questions here are: Why didn't Powhatan organize a multitribal assault, like the later one in 1622, during this period? Wouldn't that have nipped in the bud the foreigners' attempts to conquer Tsenacomoco? The second question is easy to answer: in the long run, no multitribal assault then or later would have made any difference. England's population was too big, and ultimately nothing could have stopped a swarm of aliens from migrating across the Atlantic. The first question is harder to answer, and the attempt is part of my later discussion of Opechancanough because he was deeply involved. Here it is enough say that Powhatan seems not to have taken the new settlements as enough of a personal threat to make a large-scale assault worth the bother.

Then a real calamity then fell upon the mamanatowick and his people, and the war slowly ground to a halt (in early April 1613).[29] The Tassantassas succeeded in taking his favorite daughter hostage.

Eyewitness accounts of Pocahontas's capture and subsequent captivity are few and extremely brief. It is a shame that the writers of the time focused so little on individuals and their feelings and station in life—unless they were nobility back home. John Smith, with his somewhat greater attention to Powhatan's daughter and, through her, himself in 1624, was the exception, not the rule. For instance, there are several detailed accounts written close to the event that explain the mechanics of her capture, but the "ancient planters" who like Smith wrote in 1624 did not even mention her as a factor in the truce.[30]

Pocahontas was visiting "friends" among the Patawomecks. Given the early seventeenth-century meaning of the word, that could mean visiting people who were anything from casual acquaintances to blood relatives. Interestingly enough, she was not at the capital, on Potomac Creek. Instead she was at the town of the tanx weroance Iopassus, on Passapatanzy Creek downriver, where Henry Spelman (whom she knew) had lived. The contemporary records do not mention her husband Kocoum, either because he was not along or because he did not matter (to the Tassantassas he was "Mr. Pocahontas").

People for miles around knew that the great Powhatan's daughter was visiting; according to one account, albeit one written two years later, she had been among the Patawomecks for three months, exchanging "some of her father's commodities for theirs." Native people in other towns along the river now mentioned her presence to a ship's captain (Samuel Argall yet again), who had returned to buy more corn. Aware of her value as leverage to recover some captured compatriots and their arms that her father was holding, he hastened to meet with Iopassus and intimidate him into betraying her. Iopassus was initially unwilling, knowing that Powhatan would retaliate against his people for their perfidy. He turned the matter over to his brother, the district weroance, who very properly called a council to discuss the matter. The upshot was that of the two powers, the Patawomecks preferred to cooperate with the Tassantassas—especially if they could convince Powhatan that they had been coerced, which indeed they had been.

When Pocahontas understood that a ship from Jamestown was in the area, she was "desirous to renew her familiarity with the English." That friendliness is an exaggeration by the writer of the account, as her subsequent behavior shows. Argall took advantage of her willingness and pressured Iopassus to help take her hostage, after which Iopassus recruited "his wife" (or one of them) as a fellow plotter. She persuaded Pocahontas to join them in walking down to the waterside. There she pretended to have a great longing to tour the ship, which she claimed—falsely—never to have had a chance to do before. No other women were conveniently around, and Iopassus refused to let her go aboard unaccompanied. She resorted to tears, at which point Iopassus agreed to let her go if Pocahontas went with her. Pocahontas was unwilling, for she sensed a trap, but the importunities of the wife finally won her cooperation. The party went aboard, where they all sat down to supper, and then Pocahontas was shown to the gunner's room to spend the night.

The next morning she was the first person up, anxious to go ashore in case some treachery was afoot. Needless to say, when the party disembarked, Pocahontas was held back. A supposedly surprised Iopassus asked why. The captain said it was because eight of his countrymen were held prisoner by Powhatan, along with a great stock of stolen weapons. Pocahontas "began to be exceeding pensive and discontented,"[31] not suspecting that her Patawomeck host had had any part in the affair. She was sufficiently upset that it took "much ado . . . to persuade her to be patient, which with extraordinary courteous usage, by little and little, was wrought in her." Iopassus and his wife had gone ashore, richer by a small copper kettle and some other rewards. Argall remained on board with his prize, who put the best face on it that she could.

12

Hostage Situation, with an Unusual Denouement

POWHATAN WAS now faced with a horrible dilemma: lose his country or lose his favorite child. If he gave back the foreign weapons he had, thereby partially disarming his men, his country would be overrun for certain. If he gave up his daughter, aside from not having her company anymore, he would lose a close family member to the squatters he detested. And worst of all, in a culture in which shame was something to be avoided at all costs, he would lose face no matter what he did. His brothers, his councillors, and his priests could not help him much. He initially opted for ransoming his daughter, but the way the Tassantassas went about it put him off.

The foreign ship remained anchored in the Potomac River, and its captain sent a local man to the capital (probably now at Matchut) of the mamanatowick with the bad news. Powhatan replied immediately, to the effect that the captain was to treat Pocahontas well and was to come "into his river" (the Pamunkey) to make the exchange. The captain set sail (on April 13, 1613) but went instead to Jamestown, to confer with his superiors and turn Pocahontas over to the governor (Sir Thomas Gates by this time). That delay seems to have scotched any chance of a quick and complete exchange. Not seeing any ship coming up the river—for three months, according to Ralph Hamor[1]—Powhatan finally sent part of what he was holding to Jamestown: seven of the eight aliens, "three pieces [guns], one broadaxe, and a long whipsaw, and a canoe of corn."[2] With them went a message offering to complete the exchange whenever the foreigners were ready. Powhatan received a return message that he would have to send the rest of the goods before he saw his daughter, who was being well treated. Meanwhile, the ship's captain, his mission over, went exploring along the Eastern Shore, where Powhatan's subjects the Accomacs welcomed him after hearing good reports of him from the Patawomecks.[3] Another fringe of Powhatan's domain was beginning to come loose.

There things rested for the time being. It did not help that some of the returned "prisoners" became runaways back to Powhatan again.[4] (It is significant that this set of runaways had sampled the native people's world already and had found it to their liking.) The Tassantassas made no move to come to Matchut with their captive, and the paramount chief and his council could not decide what to do next with enemies who took such a hard line. In the meanwhile, Pocahontas was becoming Anglicized, which would eventually mean that the Strangers would have it both ways.

Pocahontas in Jamestown

The residents of the Jamestown fort, at least those who were literate, seem not to have taken much interest in the "savage" prisoner. Their writings say next to nothing about her. A Spaniard held captive there at the time never mentioned her in his letters either,[5] indicating that to yet another European she was not worthy of much notice. It was mainly the political leaders in the fort, who oversaw her captivity and were responsible for her well-being, who said anything, and then it was about her religious conversion. Sir Thomas Dale, who became governor in April 1614, wrote in June that he had had her "instructed in Christian religion, who after she had made some good progress therein renounced publicly her country idolatry, openly confessed her Christian faith, [and] was[,] as she desired[,] baptized." Rev. Alexander Whitaker, a minister who served at both Henricus and Jamestown, wrote in the same month that "she had openly renounced her country idolatry, confessed the faith of Jesus Christ, and was baptized—which thing Sir Thomas Dale had labored a long time to ground in her."[6] And that is all the information we are given by eyewitnesses during the first few months of her stay in Jamestown.

The rest must be reconstructed, based upon what is known about the two cultures involved: the one from which she came and the one into which she was being drawn. It goes without saying that she had to adjust to her kidnappers' houses and food. At least she had sampled them before, on visits to the fort when she was a child, although by 1613 the native mats she would see adorning some of the houses' interior walls would have been bought or stolen from her people. But having to live full-time among the aliens and conform to their ways was another matter.

The very first thing that her captors would have done to Pocahontas, probably as soon as the ship set sail, was to put more clothes on her. The Strangers' notions of modesty were far more extensive than the Powhatan ones. Pocahontas was used to working in only an apron; when going visiting, she wore an over-one-shoulder garment that may have shown a good deal more than a low-cut bodiced dress would. The foreigners' clothes were distinctly uncomfortable until one got used to them; we would not like them today. For one thing, they constricted a woman's movements, especially the dress-up clothes: tight bodices, long skirts, and multiple layers. For another thing, the aliens wore those multiple layers even in the scorching summertime, without bathing themselves or laundering the garments very often. So the prisoner had to get used to feeling dirty. It must have been immediately plain to her that clad as they were, Tassantassa women could not possibly do all the kinds of work—gardening, gathering firewood, digging tuckahoe—that Real Women did at home.

That brought up another matter. While she was a captive, Pocahontas was probably not allowed to go outside the fort and perhaps, for some time, not outside the house where she was being kept. This kind of confinement would have been very hard to bear, judging by the reactions of other traditional Native Americans over the centuries when they were captured and jailed. In their cultures men and women both had work that took them in and out of the camp or town on most days; only the sick and the very old were stay-at-homes. Pocahontas had grown up moving about within her mother's district, wherever it was, according to what season it was and what jobs needed doing. Now she was stuck in one small place. Not only that, but she would gradually realize that the women in the fort were restricted in their movements, too, even in peacetime. In her captors' culture women worked close to home, in a special "domestic" sphere, made possible by the intensive farming and animal husbandry that made foraging in the woods unnecessary. It was a slightly less strenuous life, but the scenery never changed. What a different world!

Pocahontas would have been treated as a person of high status at

Jamestown, to keep her father happy, and that would have meant having servants to do the physical work. Depending upon her character, she either would have welcomed the chance to "live easy," or she would have champed at the bit to be out and about and getting things done. Her upbringing had emphasized the latter. But now she was given "work" to do of a different kind: learning a new language, probably learning to read and write in it (the historical record is silent about whether she ever became literate), and trying to absorb all the social rules and religious tenets that her captors threw at her.

The food she was given to eat differed radically from what she had grown up knowing, because it featured more starchy dishes and fewer fruits and vegetables. One of her fellow countrymen named Kemps had lived too long in the fort ("almost one whole year"), eating that diet, and in 1611, a fairly prosperous year at Jamestown, he had died of scurvy.[7] Pocahontas may have feared, with good reason, that she might suffer a similar fate. But what must daily have struck Pocahontas as weird about the Tassantassas' eating was the rigidity of their schedule. Instead of dipping into the stewpot whenever they were hungry and their work allowed a meal break, the Strangers ate at set times of day whether they were hungry or not. Certain people cooked and served, and others came together in a clump to eat the product. Not only that, but one had to sit upon a bench (or perhaps a chair for a VIP), because the food was on a table. At least one could use one's fingers as usual (forks being not yet common among her captors), and the aliens knew enough to give proper thanks before the meal, as the Powhatans did.[8]

Another rigid schedule among the Tassantassas was the religious one. The outlanders knew enough about proper religious observance that they had prayers in the morning and evening, as the Real People did, although theirs were held indoors instead of out. But community rituals were held every seven days, whether any current events justified it or not. Whatever for? Why not do it the Powhatan way and have the people gather for thanksgivings when things went well or ask for help when real danger threatened, with just the ordinary daily prayers in between? Not only that, but the major festivals were a bit haywire. One took place in midwinter (Christmas), as was proper after the harvest and the communal hunt. But why have a big to-do in the spring (Easter), when food was scarce and people needed to be dispersed? And another in the late spring (Whitsunday) before the corn became ripe, and then nothing much when the corn did ripen enough to eat? She was told that the foreigners' big celebrations were a commemoration of events in the life of a Savior who had lived in a distant land over a millennium and a half before.[9] That had none of the immediacy of the deities that the priests in Pocahontas's culture actually saw and talked to,[10] so for some time she must have wondered if she was living among lunatics. Lunatics who were absolutely positive that their ways were "right" and her people's ways were "wrong." And meanwhile, her father would not lift a finger to ransom her!

Pocahontas eventually came around to the Tassantassas' way of thinking about many things. For one thing, a strict, even harsh, captivity can bring about an alignment of captive with captors (nowadays called the Stockholm syndrome), especially if the siege goes on for any length of time. Pocahontas was not treated roughly in a physical sense, but the confinement, the rigidity of the scheduling, and the insistence that her people were "wrong" would have been psychologically harsh on her. For another thing, she was young: sixteen turning seventeen. That is an age at which new languages can still be learned fast and new cultural practices can be fairly readily adapted to, for they may be seen more as an adventure than as a trial. Pocahontas had had friendly, interesting experiences among the denizens of Jamestown in 1608, so the groundwork had been laid for her to have a positive attitude in 1613–14. She seems, as a personality, to have been lively and adventurous anyhow, and her ability to make friends and entertain people would have served her well in captivity.

Another major factor was that Pocahontas would have perceived the contrast between her future position among the Tassantassas and her future position among her own people. Her future at home had not been exactly stellar, because as time went on she would have been farther removed from the paramount chief. Among the Strangers, on the other hand, she was treated as the daughter of a VIP and therefore something of a VIP herself—and one who, in their patrilineal system, would continue indefinitely to be so. As a potential convert to Christianity, who could gratify the foreigners' feelings of being "right," she was the center of attention, at least among the individuals who were trying to convert her. Judging by the behavior that made her into her father's favorite, she liked being the center of attention, and she would have wanted to stay there. Staying among these outlanders held more promise of celebrity than returning to her own people did. And because being an important person in the aliens' world meant being the opposite of lively and insolent, she also became "very formal and civil after our English manner."[11]

The last and probably deciding factor in Pocahontas's "conversion" in culture and religion was that one of her teachers was a warm-hearted, earnest widower, the twenty-eight-year-old John Rolfe. All the accounts agree that she and Rolfe fell in love with each other.[12] Rolfe, at least, also fell in lust with her, which caused that proper gentleman no end of guilt.[13] It is doubtful that Pocahontas, coming from a culture that was far less straitlaced in those matters,[14] shared the guilt.

Taken all in all, by the time the governor decided to force Powhatan's hand and make him choose between his daughter and his "prisoners" and "stolen" weapons, his daughter was hoping that he would not ransom her after all.[15]

Forced to Decide

At length Powhatan had to make up his mind when the Tassantassas forced the issue. The two eyewitness accounts do not fully agree with each other.[16] One writer was Sir Thomas Dale, Pocahontas's mentor and the commander of the foreign party. A ship, a frigate, and other boats carrying Pocahontas, Dale, and 150 soldiers, started up the Pamunkey River, "where Powhatan hath his residence, and can in two or three days draw a thousand men together." Some of those men met them almost immediately, demanding to know what they were doing there. When told that Pocahontas was aboard, ready to be exchanged, and that the Strangers were prepared to burn everything along the river if Powhatan did not keep the rest of his promise, they said they had to send word to him upriver.[17] Pairs of hostages were exchanged while this was done.

At midday the next day an answer arrived: Powhatan was three days' journey away (probably at Matchut), but Opechancanough, who could deputize for him, was nearby. Dale already had an impression that the younger brother was "his [Powhatan's] and their [his subjects'] chief captain, and one that can as soon (if not sooner) as Powhatan command the men." Power had begun to shift in the paramount chiefdom. Dale might have been willing to deal with Opechancanough, but the two Pamunkey hostages insisted that only Powhatan would do. The pairs of hostages were sent back to their own people, and the native side offered to give up a runaway named Simons. Dale liked that idea, for Simons had run away three times, and "his lies and villainy much hindered our trade for corn." However, the proposal was only a delaying tactic, and when the aliens came ashore, they walked into an ambush. The

Pamunkey side lost the encounter, however, seeing several killed and a number of houses burned. To ram home their victory, the Strangers camped ashore for the night. Opechancanough would have been told that he now had a truly threatening situation on his doorstep.

The boats pushed upriver the next day. As they passed another town or two, the residents came out and demanded to know why the aliens had come, as though they did not already know the answer.[18] They got the same reply as the people downriver. This time the people promised to bring "all" that was demanded the following day. Dale and some companions went ashore upon that promise, and when a large number of local men came and mingled among them, they merely "stood to [their] arms." A similar scene was played out when the outlanders finally reached Matchut.

Pocahontas then came ashore. She ignored her countrymen, except a few of "the best sort," probably her uncle's councillors. She angrily told these men that because her father seemed to value "old swords, pieces, and axes" more than he valued her, then she would stay among the Tassantassas, "who loved her." The second writer, Ralph Hamor, adds details here: Powhatan had refused to see the two foreign emissaries who were sent to him (one being John Rolfe), but Opechancanough, "one who hath already the command of all the people," met them and promised to help bring about a resolution. Meanwhile, two of Powhatan's sons came forward to see for themselves that that their half sister had been well treated. Seeing her in excellent health, they promised to try to persuade their father to redeem her. Only Powhatan was the holdout now.

Soon a message came from Powhatan himself. He could not return two of the captive foreigners, for one had run away from his capital, going to Nand-taughtacund on the Rappahannock River (this was later found to be true) and the other (William Parker) had died (this was false). The mamanatowick promised to send all the weapons to Jamestown in fifteen days, along with corn. Pocahontas was free to stay among the outlanders or not, he said. He repeated his promises of keeping peace and returning runaways, and he added a promise, demanded of him back in 1610, that he send any of his people who injured the Strangers to Jamestown for punishment.

This was a capitulation of major proportions, and Powhatan subsequently kept his word about sending things. Opechancanough may or may have not agreed with this course of action, but at the time, before Dale's boats returned downriver with Pocahontas, he too asked for an alliance. It was a personal al-

The abduction of Pocahontas. Engraving by Johann Theodor de Bry, plate 8 in
Amerigo Vespucci, *America*, pt. 10 (Oppenheim, 1619).

liance with Dale, however. He told Dale, through the interpreter, that "he
was a great captain and did always fight; that I was also a great captain, and
therefore he loved me, and that my friends should be his friends." And thereafter "every eight or ten days [Dale would] have messages and presents from
him." Hamor added that Dale had extended the deadline for sending the corn,
"giving them a respite till harvest to resolve what was best for them to do."
No drought came in 1614, and 1613 had been a decidedly wet year. Powhatan
probably had plenty of tribute corn that March, which he could have spared.[19]
The extension of the deadline therefore sprang from generosity in Dale, not
necessity for Powhatan.

A Way Out

Pocahontas sailed back downriver with Dale, pending her father's sending the
weapons and corn agreed upon. As far as Dale and Hamor tell us, she had not

set eyes on her father during the expedition. Technically, until her father kept his promise, she was still a hostage, and the Tassantassas had scored only a simple "win." Before long, though, the governor was given news that turned things around: the hostage wanted to marry one of her captors and stay among them. Dale seems to have been unaware of Pocahontas and John Rolfe's feelings for each other until very late. Ralph Hamor claimed he had been the one to break the news, during the parley with Pocahontas's brothers, and that it was at that time that he had handed the governor Rolfe's letter asking permission to marry the prisoner. Hamor is regrettably vague, though, about just when the news was carried to Powhatan. He merely says that the mamanatowick gave "his sudden consent thereunto" and "some ten days after sent an old uncle of hers, named Opachisco [probably Opitchapam], to give her as his deputy in the church, and two of his sons to see the marriage solemnized; which was accordingly done about the fift[h] of April [1614]."[20] Dale himself was more laconic: "Her father and friends gave approbation to it, and her uncle gave her to him in the church." The church was presumably the one at Jamestown. The minister who most likely performed the ceremony, Rev. Alexander Whitaker, was even more terse: "Pocahuntas, or Matoa[ka], the daughter of Powhatan, is married to an honest and discreet English gentleman, Master Rolfe."[21]

No chronicler of the time mentioned the delicate matter of Pocahontas's already being married. Kocoum may as well never have existed. His wife's extended stay with the Patawomecks may indicate that she was still childless, perhaps due to adolescent infertility. That would make divorce, Powhatan-style, easier. Opechancanough's own experience with Pepiscunimah was a precedent within her own family: losing a wife by abduction was the first step in dissolving the marriage to her. When Pocahontas was kidnapped at Passapatanzy, Kocoum would have known that much. When she later sent word to her father about wanting to marry Rolfe, that would have broken the tie to Kocoum in the eyes of Powhatan society at large. Kocoum may have had a variety of feelings about the situation, but he could do nothing except acquiesce. By the time she entered the church, whose parishioners did not consider her "savage" marriage a "real" one, Pocahontas was a free woman according to the rules of both cultures.

Pocahontas changed her name twice. At her marriage she received a surname for the first time: Rolfe. At her baptism, which preceded the marriage by an unknown length of time, she took on the name Rebecca (though we will continue to call her by her famous nickname). It was at that time that she revealed that she had had a second name, besides Amonute, since infancy: her private, very personal name was Matoaka. She had not let any of the Tassantassas, or even most of her own people, know what the name was because those very personal names could be used by malevolent people in spells to hex victims (a very common belief in traditional Native American societies). But now she was girded with a new, stronger name, and she could reveal the old one.[22]

Nothing is known for certain about the Rolfes' married life, not even where they lived. The records are silent on the matter. In later years John Rolfe patented land directly across the river from Jamestown, along what is now Powell's Creek in the vicinity of Smith's Fort. (The creek used to be called Rolfe's Creek.) Legend has the couple living at Varina, across the river from Henricus in the old Arrohateck territory, but the records do not indicate that Rolfe had any landholdings there. John Smith's *Generall Historie,* written a decade later, indicates that Mrs. Rolfe's training in English language and culture continued after the marriage, at the hands of John Rolfe and "his friends."[23] Within the next two years Pocahontas gave birth to a son, Thomas. However, his birthplace is unknown; it could have been on either side of the Atlantic, since his birth date is equally a mystery.

One thing is virtually certain, though: because it was now peacetime, the couple would have gone to visit Powhatan, for keeping up with relatives was highly valued in both cultures. Rolfe also met and became friends with Opechancanough during this period, for in a later letter he indicated that although relations between the two peoples were strained, Opechancanough still "loved" him. The in-law relationship was a good one—but, then, John Rolfe was as good at drawing people to him as Pocahontas was.

13

Interview with a Wily Old Man

HOSTILITIES BETWEEN the Powhatans and the Tassantassas had ceased for the time being. The records left by the latter indicate that they did not trust their new allies; the native people probably felt the same way, especially because the foreigners were not giving back any farmland. Not surprisingly, the arrogant Strangers took advantage of Powhatan's seemingly good humor, for Sir Thomas Dale proceeded to press his luck.

Although he had a perfectly good wife in England, he decided to offer marriage to a younger half sister of Pocahontas, to forge a still firmer bond between the two sides. If Powhatan knew of Lady Dale's existence, he would not have been shocked; great men in his world were polygynous. Dale may have intended to pass the girl to some bachelor in his council, which would also fit with native practice. But we shall never know what he would have done with the girl, for he did not get her. Instead his emissary, Ralph Hamor, got unsettling confirmation that Powhatan had lied about a few things during the peace negotiations. We are lucky enough to have Hamor's eyewitness account.[1]

Midnight Hospitality

Powhatan had not been notified to expect visitors at his capital, Matchut. The first he and his people knew of their coming was when the guides accompanying Hamor and interpreter Thomas Savage called across the river for a canoe to ferry two foreigners, come on official business, over to the town. It was nearly midnight (on May 16, 1614).

Powhatan met the visitors in person at the landing place, a signal honor. He first directed his attention to Thomas Savage, who had lived with him as a family member for nearly three years. His greeting to the young man was awkward, however, for he gently chided him about his desertion (in 1610): "My child, you are welcome; you have been a stranger to me these four years, at what time I gave you leave to go to Paspahegh [Jamestown] . . . to see your friends, and till now you never returned. You . . . are my child by the [gift] of Captain Newport in lieu of one of my subjects, Namontack, who I purposely sent to King James his land to see him and his country, and to return me the true report thereof. He as yet is not returned, though many ships have arrived here from thence since that time. How ye have dealt with him I know not." Unwilling to report that the boy had been killed by the paramount chief's own brother-in-law four years earlier, Savage gave no answer.

Having simultaneously greeted young Savage and put him off-balance, Powhatan then focused on Hamor. Wordlessly, he went up close and began feeling around the foreigner's neck with his hands. The astonished emissary managed to hold still—with difficulty, he admitted later—and when the mamanatowick did not find what he was looking for, he stepped back. Where was the chain of pearls, he asked through Thomas Savage? What chain? replied Hamor. The one "which I sent my brother Sir Thomas Dale," the one that Dale had told him he would have any of his countrymen wear around his neck when sent on official business, "otherwise I had order from him to bind him and send him home again." So where was the chain, if he was really there on business?

An uneasy pause ensued. (Hamor was thinking fast. Dale had delegated the handing over of the chain, and an explanation of why it was needed, to his page, who forgot the errand. Hamor had never heard of the chain-as-token.) Then came an elaborate explanation which seems to have amused the old politician more than anything else. It was like this, Hamor said: he knew about the chain, of course, but the governor had really meant it to be used only in an emergency, when he had to send an emissary without one of Powhatan's people as a guide to vouch for his coming on legitimate business. In the present case not only were there two guides, but one of them was one of the paramount chief's own councillors. No chain needed this time!

Smiling at that answer, the paramount chief led his guests to his house, which was "not full a stone's cast from the waterside," and into the reception

Eiakintomino in St. James's Park, 1615. Detail of a Virginia Company lottery broadside. This young man probably traveled to England in the wave of good relations following Pocahontas's marriage in 1614. (Courtesy, The Society of Antiquaries of London)

room. Formalities had to be observed. He sat down on the bedstead across the house's end, with a young, nubile wife on either side of him and the other wives ranged in front, and "a hundred bowmen with their quivers of arrows at their backs" on guard outside. A pipe of tobacco was lit, and after taking a smoke himself, he handed it to Hamor, who took his turn and handed it back. All was done in ceremonious silence, as was proper. Then, while behind the scenes the women of the town were rushing to pound corn into meal and cook the meal into cornbread, small talk could be made at a leisurely pace before getting down to business. Powhatan asked politely after Sir Thomas Dale; "after that of his daughter's welfare, her marriage, his unknown 'son' [John Rolfe, whom he had refused to meet back in March], and how they liked, lived, and loved together." The reply was that Dale was well, "and his daughter so well content that she would not change her life to return and live with him, whereat he laughed heartily, and said he was very glad of it."

Then the mamanatowick asked Hamor to deliver the message he had brought. Hamor demurred, saying that only Pepaschicher, the councillor-guide who had come with him, should be present. Powhatan then sent everyone else away, except for the councillor and the two wives beside him, who never left him on formal occasions. The visitor began talking, with Savage interpreting. The request for the daughter's hand was delivered in a flowery oration, which mentioned that not only did Dale want her but her sister Pocahontas was eager to see her. Powhatan began to fidget and then to interrupt—a major breach of etiquette in his world, indicating fury as well as impatience. Hamor asked him to allow him to finish but was interrupted several times more.

Finally, when the speech was over, Powhatan gritted his teeth, assumed a demeanor of "much gravity," and carefully worded his refusal for Thomas Savage to translate: "I gladly accept your king's salute of love and peace, which while I live I shall exactly, both myself and my subjects, maintain and conserve. His pledges thereof I receive with no less thanks, albeit they are not so ample—howbeit himself a greater weroance [chief]—as formerly Captain Newport, whom I very well love, was accustomed to gratify me with. But to the purpose: My daughter whom my brother desireth I sold within these few days to be wife to a great weroance for two bushels of *roanoke* [mussel-shell beads] . . . and it is true she is already gone with him three days' journey from me."

Don't you have the power to reverse that exchange? came the question, especially because the girl was "not full twelve years old and therefore not marriageable"? Wasn't his "brother" Dale's affection worth retrieving her and bringing her home? Especially when Dale was willing to pay three times that bridewealth in "beads, copper, hatchets, and many other things more useful for him."

> His answer hereunto was that he loved his daughter as dear as his own life, and though he had many children, he delighted in none so much as in her, whom if he should not often behold, he could not possibly live, which she living with us he knew he could not, having with himself resolved upon no terms whatsoever to put himself into our hands or come amongst us; and therefore entreated me to urge that suit no further, but return his brother this answer:
>
> "I desire no firmer assurance of his friendship than his promise which he hath already made unto me. From me he hath a pledge: one of my daughters, which so long as she lives shall be sufficient. When she dieth, he shall luring[2] have another child of mine. But she yet liveth. I hold it not a brotherly part of your king to desire to bereave me of two of my children at once.
>
> "Further [you must] give him to understand that if he had no pledge at all, he should not need to distrust any injury from me or any under my subjection. There have been too many of his men and my [mine] killed, and by my occasion there shall never be more. I, which have power to perform it, have said it: no, not though I should have just occasion offered, for I am now old and would gladly end my days in peace. So as if the English offer me injury, my country is large enough; I will remove myself farther from you. Thus much I hope will satisfy my brother. Now, because yourselves are weary and I sleepy, we will thus end the discourse of this business."

Powhatan then sent one of his men to fetch the bread the women had ready, while he explained that he could not put on a proper feast because he had not received advance notice of the party's arrival. Indeed, there would be only bread tonight, "as usually they do eat up all their other victuals." In a country with brazen scavengers like bears, raccoons, and opossums, and with no refrigeration, that custom made good sense in May. The bread was brought and proved to be boiled dumplings the size of tennis balls—"two great bowls the quantity of a bushel," requiring a large amount of corn in a season when all the common folk had run out of it. The visitors ate a few pieces and, observing etiquette as well as being generous, gave the rest to the mamanatowick's "hungry guard which attended about [them]." Powhatan himself then had someone bring one of his presents from a Tassantassa visit of six or so years before: a three-quart bottle of sack (dry white wine). The bottle was nearly full, only a pint or so having been doled out over the years to special guests.[3] Hamor and Savage (and possibly Pepaschicher and Powhatan) each received three spoonfuls' worth in a large oyster shell. With that courtesy, the evening ended. The visitors were lodged in one of the houses in town, where they found the fleas so persistent that they had to go outdoors, under an oak tree, to get any sleep.

Caught in an Untruth

Everyone was up with the sun the next morning. Powhatan came personally and conducted his guests back to his own house, where they were served the first of several enormous meals that they could not possibly eat by themselves (fortunately, they had help): "a great bowl of Indian peas and beans boiled together, and as much bread as might have sufficed a dozen hungry men; about an hour after boiled fresh fish, and not long after that roasted oysters, crevises [crayfish] and crabs, his men in this time being abroad a-hunting some venison, others turkeys and suchlike beasts and fowl as their woods afford; who returned before ten of the clock with three does and a buck (very good and fat venison), and two great cock turkeys, all which were dressed that day; and supper ended, scarce a bone to be seen."

An awkward incident occurred, though, during that second day of the visit (May 17). Into the town strolled a foreigner named William Parker, one of the two "prisoners" that Sir Thomas Dale had demanded from Powhatan the previous year. The paramount chief and his people had claimed he was dead, but now here he was, hale and hearty, "grown so like both in complexion and habit" to the native people that only when he greeted Hamor in his own language was his nationality revealed. He seemed glad to see some fellow countrymen. His apparent freedom of movement may indicate that he had been captive long enough to be adopted into a family, but his feelings for his homeland were still strong. Now he asked Hamor to get him released and take him to Jamestown.

Hamor immediately took him to Powhatan and confronted the mamanatowick about the lie and demanded that he be allowed to accompany the party when it returned. He added that if the prisoner was detained any longer, his "brother" (the governor) would come looking for him. Powhatan did not like being caught out; he also did not want to give up someone who could be useful as an interpreter and an explainer of the Tassantassas' ways.[4] So he snapped at Hamor: "You have one of my daughters with you, and I am therewith well content. But you can no sooner see or know of any Englishman's being with me but you must have him away or else break peace and friendship. If you must needs have him, he shall go with you. But I will send no guides along with you, so . . . if any ill befall you by the way, thank yourselves." Hamor retorted that he was willing to go without guides—he could find his way home by himself, thank you—and further, that if anything did happen to him, his countrymen would bring retribution down on the people's heads. Besides, he added in another thrust, his king across the ocean would take it as a serious mark of disrespect if no guides were provided him on the return journey. Powhatan stalked out of the house at that point, refusing to deal with such a visitor for the rest of the day.

That evening, apparently over his anger, the paramount chief invited his visitors to supper, which was passed with the usual pleasantries and small talk. It was not until about midnight, after the guests had retired, that he came to them with some more business to transact. Pepaschicher and another man would guide them to Jamestown, he said. And he wanted Hamor to have the governor send him the following things:

> ten pieces of copper, a shaving knife, an iron froe to cleave boards, a grinding stone not so big but four or five men may carry it, which would be big enough for his own use; two bone combs such as Captain Newport had given him (the wooden ones his own men can make); an hundred fishhooks or, if he could spare it, rather a fishing seine [net]; and a cat, and a dog—with which things, if his brother [Dale] would furnish him, he would requite his love with the return of [deer]skins, wherewith he was now altogether "unfurnished," as he told me, which yet I knew he was well stored with, but his disposition, mistrustful and jealous, loves to be on the surer hand.

That sizable list was important; Powhatan made Hamor repeat it, to be sure he remembered it all. Still not satisfied, he had someone bring him the finely made "table-book" (notebook) that had been one of his presents in previous years, and he made Hamor write the list in it. Hamor then pressed his luck and asked to keep the book, saying it was of no use to its current owner. The current owner took the book back, retorted that "it did him much good to show it to strangers which came unto him," made Hamor write the list in his own lower-quality notebook, and then left his guests to the fleas.

The next morning began early, with the visitors (and, it is safe to say, Powhatan) wanting to be away from each other. First, though, they had to eat another lavish meal: "a good boiled turkey, which ended, he gave us a whole turkey besides that, and three baskets of bread to carry us home." More presents had to be given to both foreigners: "an excellent buck's skin very well dressed and white as snow, and sent his son and daughter [the Rolfes] each of them one." Then in one last gesture toward the Tassantassas, Powhatan uttered a threat: "I hope this will give [your governor] good satisfaction. If it do not, I will go three days' journey farther from him, and never see Englishman more. If upon any other occasion he send to me again, I will gladly entertain his messengers and to my power accomplish his just requests." He may have put some emphasis on the word "just." With that, the mamanatowick personally conducted the pushy emissary, the former "son," and the ex-prisoner, with their guides, to the riverside and saw them off.

Within the next two years, Powhatan's star would fade within his domain, while Opechancanough's rose. When he said he was old and wanted peace, he was telling the truth. Unfortunately, his timing was poor: his people were being pushed off their land by invaders, and the hard-liners among his brothers and councillors were coming to the fore. By the spring of 1616, though he still held the paramount chief's position, Powhatan had all but withdrawn from public affairs. He was visiting (or perhaps living) at least that threatened three days' journey away from his capital—somewhere to the south, according to the rumor current in Jamestown. The location is uncertain; perhaps he was visiting the Chowanocks. "Some thought [he did it] for fear of Opechancanough . . . , a man very gracious, both with the people and the English, jealous lest he and the English should conspire against him, [and they thought] that he will not return; but others think he will return again."[5] Powhatan eventually returned, but not to power.

14

Pocahontas in England

HAVING WON the daughter of Powhatan to their religion and culture, the Tassantassas then decided to show her off in England. Little is actually known about this famous trip, except for a very few incidents, and only one of those—the reunion with John Smith—has come down to us in any detail. Pocahontas made a splash in London Society (with a capital "S"), but regrettably no one she met was given to the keeping of a journal, in which she might be mentioned. The only Londoner, in fact, to mention her in his everyday writings was John Chamberlain, a gentleman with Virginia Company connections who had little use for "savages." Rev. Samuel Purchas, who collected so many accounts by colonizing Englishmen, was less interested in her than in the priest who accompanied her. The lady was simply not a legend in her own time.

Pocahontas's visit to England was a propaganda venture subsidized by the Virginia Company of London. That may sound harsh, but it is true nevertheless. Our authorities are John Smith, who wrote in 1624 that "the Treasurer and Company took order both for the maintenance of her and [her son]," and John Chamberlain, who reported that "the poor Company of Virginia out of their poverty are fain to allow her [four] pounds a week for her maintenance."[1] John Rolfe went along with it, for he was not wealthy enough to provide his wife with the many changes of fine clothing she needed to go about in society at the level the company wanted for her.

She traveled with an entourage of ten or twelve, of both sexes and various ages. One of the was a priest, Uttamatomakkin, who was also a councillor of either Powhatan[2] or (more likely) "Opechancanough, their king and governor in Powhatan's absence." This luminary was expected to report back in detail on what he saw and heard, since those in power in Tsenacomoco trusted him, a grown man unlike Namontack, to "get it right this time." Uttamatomakkin was also one of Powhatan's many sons-in-law, for his wife Matachanna was the mamanatowick's daughter.[3] The limited historical records are silent about whether or not she accompanied her husband to England, though it is probable that she did.

Seven-Day Wonders

The party disembarked not in London but in Plymouth, in the West Country, and then (after June 3, 1616)[4] they proceeded overland to the capital. Thus Pocahontas and her retinue would see much more of the Tassantassas' country than Namontack or Machumps had done. They knew now that Namontack had been wrong: though much of the forest in England had been cut down, trees could still be seen. And in the south of England thousands of fields were producing crops and feeding animals. Impressive! Arrived in London, they moved into lodgings paid for by the Virginia Company, after which Pocahontas began to be taken around. The densely populated city with its huge public buildings must have seemed utterly strange to her, even after hearing about it from her husband and his friends. Because she would be moving in the upper social stratum, she probably would be insulated from the narrow, fetid streets where the poor subsisted. Her view of London would be London at its most glamorous.

Her introduction into society was effected by Sir Thomas Dale, the company's man who had brought her to England.[5] John Smith wrote later that he himself had taken "divers courtiers and others my acquaintances to see her," but he was not her mentor. He also said that she was well received by "divers persons of great rank and quality,"[6] but only two can be identified from the few records made about her at the time. The Reverend Mr. Purchas wrote, "I was present when my honorable and reverend patron, the lord bishop of London, Doctor King, entertained her with festival state and pomp, beyond what I have seen in his great hospitality offered to other ladies."[7] The other dignitary she saw was King James I. No details survive about his meeting with the Virginia natives nor any clear indication that they were formally presented to him. The only scraps of evidence for their having even seen him in person are a complaint by the priest about King James's lack of dignity and John Chamberlain's snippy comment that "the Virginian woman [not lady!] Pocahuntas, with her father counsellor, have been with the King [meaning: in the same room with him] and graciously used [by his court functionaries]; both were well placed at the [Twelfth Night] mask."[8]

The encounter, at whatever distance, of Pocahontas with the king has led to another legend about her, one that John Smith started. In 1624 he wrote, "I have heard [that] it pleased both the King and Queen's Majesty honourably to esteem her, accompanied with that honorable lady the Lady De la Warre and that honorable lord her husband."[9] Referring to the letter that Smith supposedly wrote directly to Her Majesty, Robert Beverley enlarged upon the matter in 1705:

> Pocahontas had many honors done her by the Queen upon account of Capt. Smith's story, and being introduced by the lady Delawarr, she was frequently admitted to wait upon Her Majesty, and was publicly treated as a prince's daughter; she was carried to many plays, balls, and other public entertainments, and very respectfully received by all the ladies about the court. Upon all which occasions she behaved herself with so much decency, and showed so much grandeur in her deportment, that . . . she gained the good opinion of everybody, so much that the poor gentleman her husband had like to have been called to an account for presuming to marry a princess royal without the King's consent, because it had been suggested that he had taken advantage of her being a prisoner, and forced her to marry him. His Majesty was pleased at last to declare himself satisfied.[10]

It is a lovely story, possibly based on oral tradition that had come down to Beverley from other planters in Virginia. And Pocahontas seems to have had more than enough poise to have brought off a coup with every host and hostess she met. But no contemporary historical evidence exists for those responses to her by Tassantassa royalty.

Uttamatomakkin the priest made a less good impression—and a more indelible one upon the one person other than John Smith who was willing to write details about the Virginia visitors. That person was Samuel Purchas, who as a priest himself was enthralled with the opportunity of interviewing his opposite number from another culture. Unfortunately, on each occasion the interview turned first into an interrogation and then into a diatribe. Maybe the trouble was that a competent interpreter was present ("Sir Thomas Dale's man," meaning Henry Spelman), so that Uttamatomakkin could understand the condescending nuances of the questions he was asked. He met English ministers several times at Dr. Goldstone's house, willingly talking about his beliefs and demonstrating some of the ceremonies he knew, and he listened politely to the words of his counterparts. However, after enough encounters with Tassantassa prejudice against his religion, he had had enough. Even then, though Purchas denominated him a "blasphemer of what he knew not," he was more liberal than the priests he was rejecting: he told them they could evangelize the younger people in his party if they wanted to, but he himself was "too old" to change.[11]

By the time Uttamatomakkin ran into John Smith, he was more than ready to vent his frustration. First of all, it had proved impossible to make a tally of the population of England, as he had been ordered to do. Namontack had been right in that respect: there were too beastly many of them! He had also been told to see the English God and bring a description back. Good luck! He had been told to find out if Chawnzmit was alive, so that mission was successful. But he had also been directed to see and describe the king, queen, and prince (later Charles I), and he was still waiting. Smith said he had heard that the priest had indeed seen the king. What?! That awkward man?! (James I's public behavior was notoriously unkingly.) Well, he didn't give me a present, which kings are supposed to do. "You," he said ruefully, "gave Powhatan a white dog, which Powhatan fed as himself. But your king gave me nothing, and I am better than your white dog."[12]

Departing London, Departing Life

Not long after the king's masque (of January 6), it was time to return to Virginia. However, the wind was in the wrong quarter for sailing downriver in the ships of that day, so a lengthy delay followed. John Chamberlain is our source for both the delay and Pocahontas's feelings about leaving London: he wrote on January 22, 1617, "She is upon her return (though sorely against her will) if the wind would come about to send them away."[13] She had enjoyed all the attention and luxurious settings immensely, and she did not want it to end. Workaday life in Jamestown or out on a farmstead across the river was a dull business by comparison! Sometime during the wait for the wind to change, the Rolfes moved up the Thames to Brentford,[14] now a western suburb of London but then a rural community.

One of the things that passed the time was that Pocahontas had her portrait done. It was not a painting, for that would require too much time (and money). Instead the engraver Simon van de Passe, who would later create a portrait of John Smith,[15] made a sketch of her and then produced engravings from it that were circulated to interested parties. One such party was John Chamberlain, who sent a copy of it to a friend (on February 22, 1617), noting sourly, "Here is a fine picture of no fair lady and yet with her tricking up and high style you might think her and her worshipful husband to be somebody [unless you know the Virginia Company is paying her upkeep]."[16] That engraving was the only portrait of her done from life, so it is unfortunate that van de Passe was no expert at depicting an Amerind face with epicanthic folds over the eyes. Artists in later centuries largely ignored that picture and painted their own, ever paler, more Europeanized "princess."

While the Rolfes were in Brentford, John Smith finally made time to visit them.[17] Pocahontas had found out he was alive as soon as she had landed in Plymouth. Still thinking there ought to be some sort of friendship between Chawnzmit and herself, she expected him to seek her out as soon as she arrived in London. But the weeks and then the months passed, and he did not come. He was in London, all right, but he was engrossed in promoting the colonization of New England. It was as he was preparing to sail there, he wrote in 1624, that he stopped by to see the Rolfes.

Smith was announced and walked into the room expecting a warm welcome from Pocahontas. Instead she took one look at him and "turned about, obscured her face, as not seeming well contented. And in that humor, her husband with divers others we all left her two or three hours." If it took her two or three hours to compose herself, she was a good deal more than "discontented" with the sight of him. The major cause proved to be more Smith's treatment of her father than his tardiness in calling.[18] When she began talking with him, she started off reminding him of "what courtesies she had done" him back in Virginia. The rest should be paraphrased, since the speech Smith remembered—perhaps accurately—is convoluted.

She said: You promised Powhatan that what was yours was his, and he promised you the same. You called him "father" when you were a stranger in

Engraved portrait of Pocahontas by Simon van de Passe. Made in early 1617, this was the only portrait of her done in her lifetime. (Courtesy, Virginia Historical Society)

his land, and now that I am a stranger in yours, I must call you "father." Smith replied with an attempt at flattery, saying he dared not allow her to use the word, because she was "a king's daughter." That set off Pocahontas's temper again. "With a well set countenance" she spat out at him: You weren't afraid to come into my father's country and threaten everybody—except me. So why do you hesitate now to let me call you "father"? Well, I will call you "father," and you will call me "child," for (I am not a Powhatan woman anymore, as you seem to think,) I am forever an Englishwoman. The people at Jamestown always told us you had died, which I learned was a lie only when I arrived in England at Plymouth. But my father suspected the truth and sent Uttamatomakkin to find you—"because your countrymen will lie" frequently. At that point Smith's *Generall Historie* cuts off the interview, switching to the subject of Uttamatomakkin, which may be an indication that the conversation with Pocahontas went downhill from there.

On March 10, 1617, the Virginia Company made a very generous grant of £100 to the Rolfes in order that they might set up a mission to native children in Virginia.[19] No details of a plan were given. The warrant merely says that besides being partly in honor of Pocahontas's conversion, the money was granted "partly upon promise made by the said Mr. Rolfe on behalf of himself and his said Lady his wife, that both by her godly and virtuous example in their particular persons and family, as also by all other good means of persuasions and enducements, they would employ their best endeavors to the winning of that People to the knowledge of God, and embracing of true religion." Given the company's concurrent exhortations that families at Jamestown take in native children to rear, it is likely that the Rolfes were expecting to do the same while mentoring other evangelizing families. John Rolfe had more than enough evangelistic zeal to get such a project underway. In 1616 he had written of his wife's country: "There are no great nor strong castles, nor men like the sons of Anak to hinder our quiet possession of that land. What need we then to fear but to go up at once as a peculiar [special] people marked and chosen by the finger of God to possess it? For undoubtedly He is with us."[20] Mrs. Rolfe's opinion of her husband's juggernaut plan was not recorded. She may have been as fervent as he was, or she may have been more cautious, knowing her own people well, while her optimistic husband disregarded her warnings. English custom and law did not encourage husbands to listen to wives' advice.

One other thing is significant about the March 10 warrant: the writer assumed that Pocahontas was in perfectly good health to go home and undertake a physically taxing project. Neither the warrant nor any other surviving contemporary record in England says anything about her being sick, much less wasting away from some pulmonary complaint, as so many writers have alleged. In any case, Pocahontas would not have suffered from the smoky air of London, when she had grown up in even smokier Powhatan houses. The move out to Brentford, with its lesser social life, was probably made for reasons of economy.

Finally the wind shifted and the Rolfes could go aboard their ship, the *George*,[21] and start for Virginia. But when the ship reached Gravesend, downriver from London, Pocahontas had to be taken ashore to die. All the contemporary accounts of her death are aggravatingly brief. John Chamberlain wrote merely (on March 29), "The Virginian woman (whose picture I sent you) died this last week at Gravesend, as she was returning homeward." Not very informative! Samuel Purchas added only that she made a good Christian end, which was what his readers really wanted to know in those days. Nobody wrote anything about her deathbed scene, as Frances Mossiker did in the twentieth century.[22] Nor did anybody think at the time to mention what the poor woman died of, at the age of twenty going on twenty-one. Many young women of that age died of various causes back then, in both England and Tsenacomoco. Childbirth often did the job, but just as often it was contagious diseases for which there was then no cure. And plenty of those were going around.

One of the most contagious killers in the seventeenth century, other than smallpox, was the "bloody flux," a hemorrhagic form of dysentery that mutated into something else in the next century and disappeared from the records. Circumstantial evidence indicates that a shipboard epidemic of this unpleasant malady was what carried off Pocahontas so suddenly—and her death does seem to have been unexpected, if we can believe the March 10 warrant.

The epidemic is easy to document. John Rolfe wrote on June 8, both grief-stricken and guilt-ridden, about having had to leave his and Pocahontas's son, Thomas, in Plymouth, England, while he had sailed on to Virginia. The reason for committing the boy to someone else's care was this: "In our short passage [along the south coast of England] to Plymouth in smooth water I found such fear and hazard of his health, being not fully recovered of his sickness, and lack of attendance—for they who looked to him had need of nurses themselves."[23]

The "sickness," which probably (but not certainly) attacked Pocahontas as well as all the others on board, is harder to pin down. But while the Tassantassas in Virginia were healthy as of June 1617,[24] a terrible outbreak of bloody flux occurred later in the summer. Survivors in Jamestown remembered the ships that arrived: the *George* (in May, with Rolfe aboard) and the *Neptune* and the *Treasurer* (in August, after being separated from the *George*). "With them [the last two, or all three?] was brought a most pestilent disease called the bloody flux, which infected almost the whole colony." It was summertime, the James River was undrinkable again, and if we can believe John Smith writing seven years later, the town's well had been "spoiled." The residents probably drank the water and beer that remained on the ships, which through careless sanitation and shared drinking vessels could easily have become contaminated, and then they got sick—a sequence of events specifically recorded as happening in 1623 and which probably took place in 1617 as well.[25] In addition, even nowadays, with much better sanitation, up to 40 percent of people in their late twenties (and lesser percentages in other age groups) are symptomless carriers of one cause of dysentery, *Endamoeba histolytica*. Carelessly handled feces from infected people, in a culture with only rudimentary notions of hygiene, can and often does spread the disease rapidly to other people.[26] Therefore the form of dysentery called the bloody flux, specifically mentioned as being brought to Virginia by some or all of the fleet of ships in which the Rolfes had traveled, may well have been the disease that killed Pocahontas.

The young woman was buried in Gravesend, under the chancel of St. George's Church, on March 21. Chancel burials were for high-status people, so she was honored in death by the nation she had joined, the nation she had been reluctant to leave. Her bones lay in that place until 1727, when the church burned and had to be rebuilt. English churchyards, like those in many other European countries, go back so far in time that getting filled up would be a problem were it not for the custom of reusing graves: periodically collecting old tombstones, and any remnants of bone found while making fresh graves, and putting them (and interring the bones) to one side of the cemetery, making space available for new burials. The practice is not considered disrespectful as long as the bones remain in hallowed ground. When St. George's

Church was rebuilt, all the burials under the floor were treated this way: they were reburied in a mass grave out in the churchyard. Because Pocahontas was not a celebrity in that century, no one tried to distinguish her bones from the rest, much less note where in the mass grave they were placed. In 1923 the grave was uncovered, and British archaeologists, including Sir Arthur Keith, examined the skulls (other bones are not useful), looking for Amerind features such as wide cheekbones and shovel-shaped incisors. Keith found no skull that he could identify as native North American and label "Pocahontas." Her bones must therefore be considered lost.[27]

Recurrent movements arise in the United States to "bring Pocahontas home." Ignoring her recorded preference for staying in England, bringing "her" (the bones) back to Virginia would mean either arbitrarily picking out bones for packaging or else bringing back the bones of everybody buried under that church floor along with her.

Pocahontas's reluctance to return to America was true of some of her retinue as well. Three of her "maidens" are known to have remained voluntarily in London into the 1620s—at the Virginia Company's expense, of course. One of them was sick with consumption (pulmonary tuberculosis) in 1620 and may have died not long after. She had been living happily in the household of a cloth merchant in Blackfriars, and on May 11 the company made an allowance for two months' worth of medicines for her. The other two women were healthy and willing to emigrate, but not to back to Virginia. Just as some foreigners liked life among the Powhatans, some Powhatans liked life among the Tassantassas. So instead, when the company proposed sending the women to the Summer Isles (Bermuda) to find husbands, they agreed. An English servant was to go with each of them, the servant's labor serving as a dowry, and the governor there was to arrange for "the careful bestowing of them" in marriage among the planters there.[28]

A Broken Family

John Rolfe returned to Jamestown in the same condition in which he had arrived in 1610: widowed (again) and without the child his second wife had borne (his child by his first wife also had died). In a letter he sent to England in June 1617, he justified leaving son Thomas in England, and he testified that he and everyone he knew grieved for the loss of Pocahontas. He did not say so precisely, but he must have gone (or sent a messenger) to see his father-in-law to tell him of their mutual loss. Thus it was very probably about Powhatan that he wrote in the same letter that his "child [was] much desired when it is of better strength to endure so hard a passage, whose life greatly extinguishes the sorrow [to Powhatan] of her loss, saying all must die, but 'tis enough that her child liveth." He went on with his own life, however, taking care to petition the governor for land for himself and his surviving child. Rolfe would remarry and have yet another child, a daughter, and then he would die himself in 1622,[29] though not at the hands of his second wife's people.

Thomas Rolfe grew up in England as an Englishman, though he retained a sympathy for his mother's folk. His passage to Virginia was paid in 1635, when he was nineteen or twenty, by his stepmother's father, and he took his place in Anglo-Virginian society as a landowner, his father's heir. Although he visited his uncle Opechancanough (and his aunt, "Cleopatra") in 1641, he retained the trust of the leadership at Jamestown in the next war. At the end of that war, he was made the commander of James Fort on the Chickahominy River, and he later patented adjacent land. Meanwhile, he was selling his father's lands south of the James. His later career is shadowy, and he was dead by 1681.[30] He, like his mother, was not a celebrity during his lifetime.

Nobody in Virginia, elsewhere in America, or in England seems to have taken much interest in either Pocahontas or her descendants until well after 1800, when the aristocratic Randolph family's oral tradition of descent from her (through the Bolling family) began to be publicized. Before that, none of her descendants' ancestry was any more the subject of record making than that of most other Virginians. In the eighteenth and early nineteenth century, people usually entered the public records only if they owned land, became public officials, or broke the law.[31] Recording family "vital statistics" was for the literate, and often those family bibles did not survive the Civil War. Marriage registers began to be kept spottily in the mid-eighteenth century; birth and death records were not required to be kept in Virginia until 1853.

Consequently, the tens of thousands of people proudly claiming descent from Pocahontas today—or asking genealogists to prove such descent for them—cannot actually trace a line of authentic, contemporary documents stretching back to Thomas Rolfe.[32] No one can. Elements of Pocahontas are out there in the gene pool, all right, but they probably dwell in a great many people with whom the "blue bloods" would rather not associate.

15

Unofficially in Control

THE TASSANTASSAS remembered the years from 1614 to 1618 as a "golden age," in which they could expand without hindrance and the "savages" paid them "tribute" and traded so freely as to go into debt. Though still outnumbered, the foreigners thought they were in charge, and that felt good.

Such expansion and prosperity among the Strangers meant that for the Powhatans, times were bad. They lost ground, and they ended up owing their wealth, in the form of their corn, to the aliens, which meant that families had to forage harder to get enough to eat. The two ordeals were related, for the ground lost was the prime farmland of the James River tribes. A mania for raising and exporting tobacco seized the Strangers during these years, so that they raised less food than ever for themselves and relied more heavily on the native people, whom they illogically treated as dependents. As tobacco farming took hold, and more newcomers raised it and wore out the soil and wanted to move to new plantations, the country's Real People would find it ever harder to hold onto their land. The foreigners also rubbed salt into their wounds by their pushy evangelizing, which often took the form of "offering" aggressively to take the local people's children to raise them in the "right" way. It did not matter to the native people that the evangelists meant well; the offers were a deadly insult.

All these things darkened the end of Powhatan's life, and yet he abided by the terms of the peace he had made with Sir Thomas Dale. He probably knew of his brother Opechancanough's activities aimed at turning the tide, but personally, he was old and tired now, so he held himself aloof.

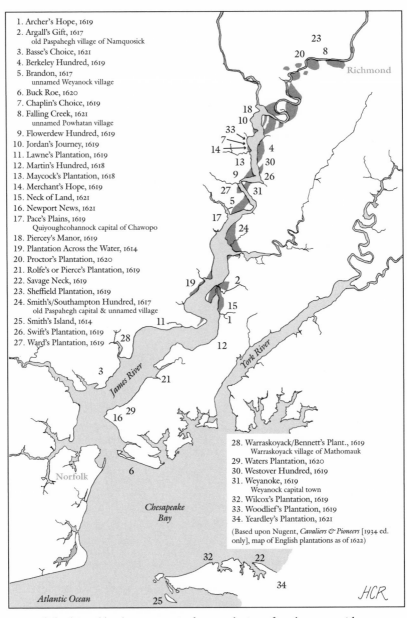

1. Archer's Hope, 1619
2. Argall's Gift, 1617
   old Paspahegh village of Namquosick
3. Basse's Choice, 1621
4. Berkeley Hundred, 1619
5. Brandon, 1617
   unnamed Weyanock village
6. Buck Roe, 1620
7. Chaplin's Choice, 1619
8. Falling Creek, 1621
   unnamed Powhatan village
9. Flowerdew Hundred, 1619
10. Jordan's Journey, 1619
11. Lawne's Plantation, 1619
12. Martin's Hundred, 1618
13. Maycock's Plantation, 1618
14. Merchant's Hope, 1619
15. Neck of Land, 1621
16. Newport News, 1621
17. Pace's Plains, 1619
    Quiyoughcohannock capital of Chawopo
18. Piercey's Manor, 1619
19. Plantation Across the Water, 1614
20. Proctor's Plantation, 1620
21. Rolfe's or Pierce's Plantation, 1619
22. Savage Neck, 1619
23. Sheffield Plantation, 1619
24. Smith's/Southampton Hundred, 1617
    old Paspahegh capital & unnamed village
25. Smith's Island, 1614
26. Swift's Plantation, 1619
27. Ward's Plantation, 1619

28. Warraskoyack/Bennett's Plant., 1619
    Warraskoyack village of Mathomauk
29. Waters Plantation, 1620
30. Westover Hundred, 1619
31. Weyanoke, 1619
    Weyanoke capital town
32. Wilcox's Plantation, 1619
33. Woodlief's Plantation, 1619
34. Yeardley's Plantation, 1621

(Based upon Nugent, *Cavaliers & Pioneers* [1934 ed. only], map of English plantations as of 1622)

Richmond

James River

York River

Norfolk

Chesapeake
Bay

Atlantic Ocean

HCR

English-claimed lands, 1614–21. Such an explosion of settlements, with more apparently in the offing, threatened the native farmers.

The Last Days of Powhatan

Powhatan spent his last months touring his territories and presenting an affable face to the invaders, whose governor wrote complacently that the mamanatowick was "taking his pleasure in good friendship with us." He and Opechancanough both had been notified of Pocahontas's death, and they expressed sorrow while being "glad her child is living . . . both want to see him but desire that he may be stronger before he returns" to Virginia.[1]

Wahunsenacawh, alias Powhatan, died in April 1618, according to a letter that John Rolfe wrote on June 15 of that year.[2] No information has come down to us about where he died, what he died of, who was with him at the time, or any other details. His body received the same treatment as those of other chiefs: it was disemboweled and placed on a scaffold to decompose. Three years later his bones were collected, wrapped into a bundle, and carried to their final resting place. "At the taking up of Powhatan's bones," a ceremony was performed, which a very large number of people were expected to attend. No further information about it was recorded, except that Opechancanough had tried to procure poison to distribute at the gathering, to which dignitaries from Jamestown were invited, so that the people could then fan out and kill a large number of Tassantassas.[3] Powhatan's bone bundle would have been deposited in a temple—probably the holiest temple, at Uttamussak—not in a burial mound, as some people are led to believe. No early eyewitness source mentions mounds in the Virginia coastal plain, and no verifiable burial mounds have been found there by archaeologists.

A parting glimpse of Powhatan, or perhaps an anticipatory glimpse of Opechancanough, comes from an anecdote written down in 1621, which seems rather late for Powhatan.[4] From what is known of the personalities of the two, it could have been true for either man. The mamanatowick was on his "annual progress" around his dominions and had come to rest at Patawomeck. Here he was greeted, feasted, orated at, and danced for, as was good and proper. Another entertainment was set up for him, in which the young men who had participated in the huskanaw ("such as were fit for war") got up, one at a time, and announced their exploits, thereby impressing their august visitor with their prowess as warriors and hunters. The trouble was that the visitor was so august and had such a formidable reputation, that exaggeration began to creep into the stories. A tall-tale contest soon developed, to the consternation of the host weroance and his councillors. What would happen when the mamanatowick caught on that he was being lied to? The paramount chief simply sat there, listening gravely, as Native American etiquette demanded; no one could tell what he was thinking. Fortunately the last youth in line had a quick wit. When it came his turn to speak, he faced his overlord stoutly, made the required obeisance, and began. "And I, my lord, went this morning into a great marsh, and there I valiantly killed six muskrats! For although that is no more than the boys in the town do daily, yet this, my liege, is true, and most of the other stories only fables." This turnabout made Powhatan burst out laughing—for he did indeed have a sense of humor, as Pocahontas had proved years before. Everyone present laughed along with him, in relief as well as appreciation of the joke. And the young man was rewarded with more presents than anyone else.

Second in Rank, First in Power

Less information was recorded about Opechancanough in his personal dealings with his own people and with the foreigners than about his predecessor. By the time he achieved a measure of official power, so that governors in Jamestown were forced to pay closer attention to him, the Tassantassas were beginning to smell success in their takeover project. Thus their writings from that time onward are almost entirely concerned with themselves. Anyone who, like Opechancanough, threatened to upset their plans was described in two-dimensional terms: a canny man to appease or a fierce enemy to destroy.

The times were definitely stressful for the native inhabitants of Virginia, so that the very few eyewitness accounts we do have of Opechancanough show him not as a generous though wily host but as an able leader who had been put on the defensive. This is a pity, for reading between the lines, among his own people Opechancanough was at least as able a politician and diplomat as his brother had been. Samuel Purchas talked to some who had met him and then wrote that he was "a man very gracious, both with the people and the English."[5] Sadly, with one exception, Ralph Hamor's 1614 account is the last one that portrays a mamanatowick's doings in enough detail that he sounds human. John Smith may have been biased and, in his later writings, self-aggrandizing. But he wrote so voluminously about his time in Virginia that the people he had the most dealings with—Powhatan, among the native people—come alive. Opechancanough had no such scribe.

Not only do we get a narrower view of Opechancanough, but we also get fewer and less descriptive records with which to reconstruct what he and his people were doing. That will make the Real People's history move faster in this and subsequent chapters. Only a time machine would enable us to see all the many things that went on in Tsenacomoco when the foreigners weren't looking.

Powhatan was succeeded by his next younger brother Opitchapam, who took the throne name Itoyatin (or Otiotan). However, this mamanatowick was now "decrepit and lame."[6] His taking the paramount chief's position at all indicates that he must have been a fine warrior in his time, though one who was usually ignored by the denizens of Jamestown. But his prime was over, and from the outset of the new reign, Itoyatin was overshadowed in the foreigners' records by his active younger brother and heir. Significantly, Opechancanough did not take a new name in 1618, signifying that his new prominence was not official. In order for his rather sudden conspicuous position in the records to make sense, let's backtrack a bit at this point, and say more about his rise to de facto power.

The Tassantassas' initial attempts to set up satellite forts (in 1609) had been foiled by the efforts of the people whose territories were invaded. Neither Powhatan nor Opechancanough had had to do much organizing of resistance. In the following winter and spring, the aliens had starved and finally tried to go home, all without anyone's raising a finger. Then several shiploads of foreigners had arrived, followed in succeeding years by numerous others. A change had occurred. The Strangers no longer starved, though they were sometimes hungry, judging by the Patawomecks' reports of their eagerness to buy corn there. The Strangers also became more aggressive against the native people—and more to the point, they began to succeed in establishing some of their people in various parts of the James River basin. First the Kecoughtans lost their territory at the river's mouth, followed by the Paspaheghs, who apparently dispersed after their weroance, Wowinchopunck, was killed. In that same year (1611), squatters took over part of the Arrohatecks' domain, right across the river from their capital, and there they stayed in spite of all the Arrohatecks' efforts to dislodge them. The same thing happened to Opossunoquonuske's town about then, so that the Appamattucks lost the ability to control the mouth of their river, where it joined the James. They lost part of their lands on the other side of their river's mouth a couple of years later. In that same year the Arrohatecks lost land on both sides of the river, and the Tassantassas began moving in on the Weyanocks' territory at its upriver end.[7] The result was that the native people's holdings along the James River below the falls were now checkerboarded with squatter settlements—*squatter* being the operative word because no payments were made to the land's owners. The ability of Powhatan's people to control the river was seriously compromised by the time of Pocahontas's capture, a matter for concern even though the Monacans were no longer enemies.

Powhatan let all of this happen, to some extent. He had the prestige and the wealth to amass a large number of warriors, who could have routed the badly outnumbered newcomers—for a time—in a maneuver that would have been a precursor of the Great Assault of 1622. His people also knew how to execute military maneuvers requiring large numbers of men, as John Smith had observed some years before in the mock battle between "Powhatans" and "Monacans." Instead he had his people wage guerrilla war, which the newcomers felt as mere pinpricks compared to European warfare, and once Pocahontas was captured in April 1613, he stopped allowing even that.

Why the inaction? No one knows. The Tassantassas, who left the only records, did not question it; they simply took advantage of it. Two answers seem possible, though. One is that Powhatan had seen the squatters starve not long before, and he was hoping to see it again. After all, the seven-year dry spell (1606–12) was still in progress during most of this early expansion of the Strangers. And the aliens were not managing to hold onto all the settlements they started, either. John Rolfe would record in 1617 that only six satellites had stuck,[8] the others presumably failing due to causes such as drought and disease. The other answer is that Powhatan's health could have been declining already. An incident that points in that direction is his refusal to see the emissaries who came to negotiate Pocahontas's release in 1614. No explanation was ever given for that refusal—nor asked for, according Ralph Hamor's detailed report of his interview with the mamanatowick the next month. With a long and physically hard life behind him, Powhatan may have been afflicted with any of a variety of ailments that gave him "good days" and "bad days" and that would have sapped his energy and will to take action. Organizing a mass assault in a polity on the chiefdom level required a great deal of politicking, which took its toll on anyone's energy. Powhatan may no longer have been up to that task, although Opechancanough was. But whatever the cause, Powhatan refused to use his resources to prevent the spread of the squatters. And his immediate heir, Opitchapam, seemed not to be interested, either.

Many fighting men in Powhatan's domain must have felt alarm as the Tassantassas' expansion began to accelerate (in 1613). One of those men was Opechancanough. He appears suddenly in the records of 1614 as a man who "hath already the command of all the people" and "one that can as soon (if not sooner) as Powhatan command the men."[9] That appearance points to several things: first, many warriors agreed with his position, which was covertly hostile to invaders. Second, he had taken the time and trouble needed to build up that much support: he had gone around through the towns and established personal ties with potential followers—with his overlord's knowledge.

Powhatan must have known of his younger brother's activities before long, for his mind remained sharp, and he probably retained his conduits of information from around his dominions. If his physical health was failing, he may have supported his brother privately while outwardly putting on an aloof face for the foreigners. But too much grassroots support for a younger brother and heir could definitely be threatening, and the rumor that circulated in Jamestown and London in 1616 about Powhatan's withdrawal to a far-off place "southwards" may have been accurate. Nonetheless, Opechancanough seems to have treated his overlord with respect during his lifetime.

The last few years of Powhatan's rule were officially peaceful. Until the last year of the mamanatowick's life, only two more squatter settlements appeared. That probably slowed down Opechancanough's organizing efforts, for not seeing an increase of threats to their well-being, the warriors of Tsenacomoco may have been reluctant to cooperate. Whatever the reason, no mass attack was made on the foreigners in 1614–17, while they lived vulnerably in less than a dozen places.[10] There was, however, one fly in the ointment for the leader of the "war party": not long after Powhatan had made a peace with the aliens, the previously autonomous Chickahominies made a separate peace that seemed to put them on the outlanders' side, possibly in fear of having to stand alone against the combination of Powhatan and the Tassantassas.[11] Another possibility is that they simply preferred not to join Opechancanough's movement as yet. But for those militant men currently raising opposition to the Strangers' presence, it was a stiff blow. If the warlike Chickahominies had seen fit to knuckle under, then some of the men in the "war party" might be tempted to align themselves with Powhatan's policy of peace. Something had to be done, but it had to done subtly so that the complacent squatters would not comprehend what was really going on until it was too late.

Opechancanough's solution was twofold. First, he encouraged his followers to take full advantage of the outlanders' complacency, which was enormous in 1614–17, when it seemed to the denizens of Jamestown that everything was going their way. Their writings prove their mistaken feelings of being invulnerable. They thought they had "the natives of the country in so awfull an alliance and amity . . . that many of those heathens voluntarily yielded themselves subjects . . . of King James, and did together with most of the rest pay a yearly contribution of corn [to sustain] the colony." The foreigners were proud that "all the bowmen of those that bordered upon the English paid a tribute of corn and those governors [at Jamestown] husbanded the business [so] that the Indians were forced to borrow corn for seed of the English and to repay it at their harvest with great advantage [to the creditors]."[12] That indebtedness occurred in poor crop years: 1614 was a year of average rainfall, and 1615 was a little better. But 1616 saw a fairly serious drought, and in 1617, a year of above-average rainfall overall, the summer was so dry that the crops failed. That was the year in which a governor wrote specifically, "Indians so poor can't pay their debts & tribute."[13] Life was not so good among the Tassantassas that year, either: some of them ran away to the native people,[14] a repeat of the early years of the Jamestown settlement. The native people may have been in debt, but some of the Strangers' settlements were fading away as well.

One of the runaways took his arms and ammunition with him, but that was not the major source of alien weapons for Opechancanough's purposes. The outlanders remained poor hunters, thanks to their increasing concentration on raising and exporting tobacco. So they took the easy, heedless way of getting meat: even the governor himself hired "friendly" native men to hunt—and provided them with firearms and taught them to shoot and reload.[15] By the time a new governor arrived at Jamestown in mid-1617, some of the Real Men were taking part in military drills in the fort! All the squatters were so intent on raising tobacco and getting rich that everything else had gone by the board. John Smith, hearing about it back in England, summed it up vividly. The new governor was met by "a martial order, whose right hand file was led by an Indian," and Jamestown was a shambles: "but five or six houses [left standing], the church [fallen] down, the palisade broken, and bridge [wharf] in pieces, the well of fresh water spoiled, the store-house they used for the church, [and] the market-place, and streets, and all other spare places planted with tobacco, the savages as frequent in their houses as themselves, whereby they were become expert in our arms, and had a great many in their custody and possession, the colony dispersed all about, planting tobacco." Smith also spoke of "our men rooting in the ground about tobacco like swine" (meaning with a hog's intensity).[16]

Hindsight shows that although the foreigners seemed weak at that moment, they had just proved that tobacco would grow well in Virginia soils, and their mania for the plant soon would cause them to begin a tremendous expansion into the farmlands of Tsenacomoco. Neither Opechancanough nor anyone else could see it coming for the time being, so his men went on acquiring firearms from the foolish intruders until that arriving governor (Samuel Argall) put a stop to it.

Opechancanough's second strategy to confound the Tassantassas after 1614 was to maneuver the Chickahominies into breaking their treaty and making an alliance with him instead. That proved easy to do after two years had elapsed, thanks to the kaleidoscope of governors at Jamestown. The Chickahominies had made the treaty with Sir Thomas Dale during his tenure as governor. But Sir Thomas returned to England in June 1616, in the company of Pocahontas and her entourage, and George Yeardley succeeded him. Although Yeardley was just as easygoing as Dale had been about hiring native men to hunt for him and letting local people come and go freely in his disintegrating fort, he was still a different governor from the one with whom the Chickahominies had made the treaty. Opechancanough, and probably other native people as well, seems to have considered peace treaties to be at least partially personal in nature. The parties to the agreement vouched for themselves and their followers, but if the followers took a new leader, all bets were off. Opechancanough assumed that was how the foreigners operated as well. His opinion on the subject was recorded in 1619: he marveled "why so many governors were sent [one after the other] . . . which made the Indians uncertain what to trust[, each] new governor being ready to alter what . . . [his] predecessors had decreed."[17] The Chickahominies may genuinely have considered their treaty null and void when Dale left; at least, that was the reason they gave. Alternatively, they may simply have been vulnerable to barbed suggestions from Opechancanough or his emissaries about what the new governor was like. In any case, the alliance came apart in 1616, when another drought hit the region.

There are two accounts of the alliance's demise, both written several years later. One is straightforward: the Chickahominies were late paying their "tribute" of corn, as promised in their treaty. The Tassantassas, who were running low on food themselves thanks to poorly supplied provision ships, sent a demand for it, which the Chickahominies refused to honor. The other account has Opechancanough informing the governor that the tribe had killed livestock, in violation of the treaty, and then persuading him to bring 100 armed men to a "parley" about it. At any rate, the new governor, George Yeardley, promptly sailed up the Chickahominies' river with a hundred armed men, to be greeted by signs of scorn, "telling him he was but Sir Thomas Dale's man [servant]" and that therefore they would neither pay him nor obey him. Amid mutual shouted threats, the foreigners in their boats and the tribesmen on foot proceeded up the river both that day and the next. Every town they passed had already harvested—and hidden—its corn. At last the showdown came: the outlanders rowed ashore, where they and the warriors mingled and threatened each other. But suddenly the aliens shot off their firearms, killing numerous people, and grabbed several hostages, including two of the eight ruling elders of the Chickahominy tribe. These people had to be ransomed, of course. The townsmen promised to give up a hundred bushels of corn, but they later reneged on the agreement. That is not surprising, for in the Real People's world the killing of their compatriots was enough to cancel any alliance and call for revenge.

Taking the townsmen's promises at face value and thinking they had ensured the payment of tribute for that year, the Strangers returned downriver with their hostages. But at Ozinies, one of the downriver towns, Opechancanough intercepted them and proceeded to take credit for persuading the Chickahominies to agree to the "truce" that had just been arranged. This he did in spite of a former promise of his to Yeardley that he himself would never make peace with the Chickahominies without consulting the governor first. That promise, probably false to begin with, was certainly obsolete now. The tribe hailed Opechancanough now as "the King of Ozinies"—Henry Spelman was present, to hear and translate accurately—"and brought him

from all parts many presents of beads, copper, and such trash as they had."
Those luxury goods were part of the traditional tribute to a paramount chief,
and thus was Opechancanough installed as the Chickahominies' overlord.
Where his brother Powhatan had failed to gather them in, the younger brother
had finally succeeded.[18]

After bringing the Chickahominies into his fold, Opechancanough's personal power was enough to justify the rumor the English heard about Powhatan's having "gone southward" out of fear of him.[19] He was a major power
now, albeit still an unofficial one.

The Tassantassas remained unaware of the coup, for the native people
went on acting like friendly allies even though yet another governor (Samuel
Argall) had arrived in mid-1617. In that year they appeared also to be dependent allies, for by late summer the crops failed due to hail and drought,
and the ships bringing the governor also brought an epidemic. The disease
was bloody flux,[20] and it was the worst epidemic recorded for many years:
"a great mortality among us, far greater among the Indians, and a murrain
[plague] among the deer." Two years later another epidemic struck, a fever
of some sort occurring not only in the aliens "but chiefly amongst the Indians."[21] The native people may or may not have blamed their misfortunes on
the Strangers, but if they did so, they were partially right. Ironically, one
probable conduit for the disease to the indigenous towns in 1617 was Uttamatomakkin, who came back from England.

The new governor sent the priest home with a message: Opechancanough
was invited to come to Jamestown to get a present. Unlike Powhatan in 1608,
this mamanatowick's heir went, apparently willingly, and received the present, whatever it was, "with great joy." The condescending Tassantassas were
correspondingly gratified. In reality Uttamatomakkin had made a vitriolic report about the arrogance he had observed on his voyage, and he warned his
master about how big the population really was in the foreigners' country.
Opechancanough—or perhaps just his followers—believed the former but
not the latter. If they had really taken in how many Englishmen there were,
the war immediately after the Great Assault would have been carried out very
differently, with further concerted attacks rather than mere sniping. The governor's message inviting him to Jamestown also tried to rebut whatever the
priest had said. So during the messenger's visit, Opechancanough cannily pretended to believe the governor's words, and he and his great men put on a

show that convinced the emissary that "Tomakin is disgraced." As for Powhatan, he once again kept himself far out of the picture, for the same messenger reported that the paramount chief was now "gone to the King of Mayumps [Tauxenent, or Doeg] in Potomac River and has left the government of his kingdom to Opechancanough and his other brother."[22] That may have been the "progress" he was on when the young man at Patawomeck used his wits to such good effect with his overlord. It is also possible that the wary old man was covertly aiding his younger brother, urging the Potomac River tribes to join him in opposing the invaders.

Second in Rank, First in Power

It was in the last few months of Powhatan's life that the Tassantassas began a massive increase in their evangelistic pressure on his subjects, thanks to the return of John Rolfe and others. Rolfe and his cohorts were determined, among other things, to rear the native people's children "correctly." Soon after his return to Virginia, Rolfe wrote with misguided optimism that the local people were "very loving, and willing to part with their children."[23] Rolfe had mostly taught Pocahontas, and it seems he had learned little from her in return. He and his well-meaning ilk were completely unaware of the terrible insult they were dealing out to the children's parents by implying that they did not know how to care for their own offspring. That was not exactly how Rolfe and the others meant it. Since at least 1500, English families (except for the poor) had been accustomed to placing their children in "better" (i.e., higher-status) households, so that they would have a rigorous, if cold-hearted, upbringing and make contacts to advance themselves socially. Social rank mattered terribly in England, even in small matters. People of higher status, including one's own parents, were to be abjectly obeyed at all times (not just on ceremonial occasions), and any resistance to orders was apt to bring physical punishment.[24] All of these elements were alien to Powhatan parents, who were gentle with their children and let the harder lessons of life be learned from experience or from the pressure of society in general. Any mother or father who tried letting a child live in such a harsh foreign household would soon have heard about it from the child, yanked the child back home, and spread the word far and wide. In the coming years few parents would part with their children, and with good Native American manners, they would simply listen politely and stoically when anyone attempted to missionize them—which misled the optimistic evangelists into seeing acceptance of their outlandish ideas.

It was Opechancanough who proved most adept in leading on the proselytizers, to keep them from looking too closely at his politicking among his people. He set right to work. Knowing that his brother's subjects would not want their children living on the scattered squatter plantations, he encouraged the leaders at Jamestown in 1619 to plan to receive whole families into those settlements.[25] However, further reflection made the Strangers realize the inherent dangers to themselves in the scheme, which were not only military but also cultural, stemming from intimacy with "heathens."[26] The outlanders resumed their futile pressure on local parents to give up a few children. And the pressure grew after 1619. By 1620 a missionary from Jamestown, George Thorpe, was making visits to Opechancanough himself.

In Powhatan's very last year of life, the Tassantassas began expanding their squatter settlements again. More and ever more ships arrived each year,[27] bringing intruders across the ocean. As both history and archaeology attest, many of the new arrivals died from the climate, epidemic diseases they brought with them, and the local "bugs" to which they had no immunity.[28] The native people, however, would have been primarily aware of how many foreigners were coming in and spreading out, however thinly. Before five years had passed, they posed a serious threat to the native people's hold on their territory in the James River basin.

Three new squatter settlements popped up the year Uttamatomakkin returned from England. Another, unsuccessful attempt was made in the early planting season of that year to take land at Warraskoyack, which made Opechancanough angry enough to refuse to deal with Jamestown for a time.[29] Two more settlements were made the next year. These five landgrabs took most of the rest of the Paspaheghs' old territory (another bit would go in 1622) and also a significant chunk of the Weyanocks' corn-growing ground south of the James. The year of a real explosion of incursions onto the people's farmland, though, was 1619. The Weyanocks lost most of the rest of theirs, leaving them mainly their foraging territory south of the river. The Appamattucks lost the downstream side of their river's mouth, though their capital a few miles upriver and their inland foraging territory remained unthreatened for the time being. The Arrohatecks had disappeared from the foreigners' records, probably moving in with the Powhatans. And now the Powhatans near the falls began losing their riverfront land; they would lose more in the next two years.[30]

The Tassantassas also began moving downriver in 1619 into the districts of the Quiyoughcohannocks, Warraskoyacks, and the foraging area the Chiskiacks had shared with the long-gone Kecoughtans. More was taken in the next two years from the Chiskiacks, the Warraskoyacks, and now the Nansemonds, leaving them, too, with reduced farmland but with their foraging grounds still intact. A similar explosion of settlers—these at least being foreigners who stayed with the permission of the local people—occurred in the Accomacs' territory. Thomas Savage the interpreter had led the way after being given Savage's Neck in 1619 by the Accomac chief himself.[31]

The Tassantassas simply seized the western shore lands. Only one record indicates an attempt at payment: George Yeardley, during one of his two terms as governor (1616–17, 1619–21), had granted land to a compatriot "with a proviso to compound with Opechancanough" to make the grant aboveboard. The Virginia Company heard about it simultaneously with the news of the Great Assault, and the company's officers were outraged that "a sovereignty in that heathen infidel was acknowledged, and the Company's title thereby much infringed."[32] Before the Assault, the company might have been a little more amenable to paying a native ruler for his land, but not much.

These inroads into native territory, poorly manned as they were in their early stages,[33] gradually consolidated the invaders' hold on the middle reaches of the James River within the tidewater. They also took over all of the prime corn-growing land, where naturally fertile Pamunkey loams occur, in that river's entire basin.[34] All the surviving James River chiefdoms—Powhatans, Appamattucks, Weyanocks, Quiyoughcohannocks, Warraskoyacks, and Nansemonds—suffered losses. Among them, the major losers were the Weyanocks. Significantly, it was the Weyanocks, tribute payers and also the middlemen between Powhatan and the puccoon-trading Iroquoian tribes to the southwest, who had long played a crucial role in the paramount chiefs' maintaining their wealth of luxury goods and therefore their prestige. Now it was much harder for Powhatan's successors, living on the Pamunkey River, even to meet with Weyanock people, whose remaining settlement was south of the James, thanks to unfriendly settlements of trigger-happy invaders occupying both banks of the river between the two. And not meeting meant an end to trade in prestigious goods. Therefore, a serious blow to the Weyanocks, among all the others, was a serious blow to Opechancanough and Opitcha-pam's power base. It could not be tolerated.

Even if the Tassantassas had not shut down much of the friendly relations between themselves and the native people in 1617–18,[35] and even if Powhatan had lived longer, keeping him in third place, Opechancanough would have stepped up his organizing of resistance in 1619. As it was, several matters came to a boil during that year.

First of all, the newest governor in Jamestown (George Yeardley again) ran a tighter ship than before, and that was unpopular with both the native people and one of the foreigners' interpreters, Henry Spelman. Two official interpreters now took messages back and forth between Opechancanough and the governor. Interpreters are often marginal people, caught between two nations because of their understanding of two languages and cultures.[36] Spelman had few problems with that, but the other man, Robert Poole, seems to have been unhappy with everyone. And like many unhappy people, he was eager to spread the misery to others, including both Yeardley and Spelman. Within a few years, nobody would trust him. In 1619, however, he was a new face to the governor, and he was able to get Spelman censured for something he was overheard saying to Opechancanough. This report of Poole's is the only eyewitness account of any length that we have of someone conferring with Opechancanough.[37]

According to Poole, Spelman was living at Jamestown when he induced a messenger of Opechancanough's to have the great weroance send for him. Once there, Spelman stayed and worked for the mamanatowick's brother. It is uncertain exactly where Opechancanough was living at the time, but it was somewhere on the Pamunkey River. Poole arrived at the "court," wherever it was, and found that Spelman was far from glad to see him: he would not even look at him, much less speak to him. When Opechancanough asked Spelman to explain the snub he had given his countryman, the young man said Poole should speak first, a rather petulant reply. The next day Spelman and the chief had a long, private conference, with a sentry at the door to prevent anyone else from entering. The conference ended, Opechancanough summoned Poole and, presumably based on what Spelman had told him, demanded to know what "great king" (Tassantassa official) was about to leave England to come to Virginia as the new governor. This demand was made in midsummer of 1619, only two or three months after Sir George Yeardley had succeeded Samuel Argall in the office; but the turnover of governors at Jamestown had been so rapid up to then that Opechancanough was willing to believe that a replacement for Yeardley was already on the way across the Atlantic. Spelman had further led him to believe that the incoming governor was somebody much more important and powerful than Yeardley was, and therefore somebody even harder for a weroance who was only the brother of the mamanatowick to influence. Poole said he had no idea who this luminary might be; ask Spelman. Spelman replied—in the Powhatan language, understood by everyone present—that it was Lord Rich, a man who did indeed outrank the Dale-Yeardley-Gates-Argall contingent that had run Jamestown for the past seven years. Not only that, but Rich intended to make a settlement at Chiskiack on the York River, and Spelman was to live there with him.[38] Spelman then added in English, which Opechancanough did not understand, that he wished Rich had already come, so that Spelman could "triumph over all his enemies."

Opechancanough demanded to know if this Rich was more powerful than the Yeardley he already knew how to deal with. Spelman replied that Rich (a baron) outranked Yeardley (recently knighted)[39] as much as the late Lord De La Warre had done, adding that such a powerful man would break any treaties his inferior had made and would relegate Yeardley to the position of a tanx weroance. Poole chided Spelman for these words, saying Yeardley would not be pleased when he heard about them. Spelman replied offhandedly that Poole could tell him if he liked.

Spelman plainly had his differences with Yeardley, but Opechancanough preferred to deal with Yeardley, a known quantity whom he liked, rather than a higher-ranking stranger. So he set up a private meeting with Poole, to give him a message for Yeardley. Having promised the governor, back before Yeardley made his trip to England (May 1617 to April 1619), that he would send a present of corn, he said he would now bring it to Jamestown personally, before the "new" governor arrived. Would Yeardley kindly let him know how soon he should make the trip? He "marvelled" at how quickly one governor succeeded another among the Tassantassas. And he told Poole to tell Yeardley that when he visited him, he would tell him some other things Spelman had informed him about.

Poole now added, in his deposition in Jamestown, that Spelman had "required" (insisted) that Opechancanough hand over King James's picture to him. This picture was a token that according to the peace of 1614 was to pass only from the mamanatowick to the governor and back again, signifying official messages. Its opposite number was the chain of pearls that the governor was supposed to have given poor Ralph Hamor to wear. Poole alleged that Spelman intended to use the portrait, as if it had been sent officially, on the frivolous errand of inviting someone else to "an Indian dancing." The great weroance initially refused to let go of it for this kind of thing, but Spelman eventually wheedled him out of it, saying that the current governor would not be around much longer anyway. What is interesting here is that in mid-1619 the portrait was in Opechancanough's hands, not Opitchapam's.

The next time Spelman went to Jamestown, he was hauled before the governor and council to be interrogated. He denied everything except saying that a new and more powerful governor would soon arrive. That untruth was enough to convict him of malfeasance. For according to Poole and others, "it seemeth he hath alienated the mind of Opechancanough from this present governor, and brought him in much disesteem, both with Opechancanough and the Indians." Poole's and Spelman's malice against each other was evident in the proceedings, but both remained on duty as interpreters, albeit with diminished reputations. Spelman was sentenced to serve the governor for seven years as his personal interpreter, and his contacts with the Powhatan leadership at Pamunkey were severely curtailed. Poole was now suspected of telling "false tales" to Opechancanough as well as to Yeardley, but he seems to have made a hasty departure for the court at Pamunkey after testifying. On his next visit to Jamestown, he was saved from punishment only because Opechancanough sent King James's picture with him along with a message to the governor. That meant that the great weroance still trusted the interpreter—on the surface. Of necessity, then, Poole was labeled a "neutral" person and was allowed to go on functioning.[40] Neither Opechancanough nor any governor would ever get a completely straight story from Robert Poole.

Trouble in Outlying Districts

It is very likely that Opechancanough had been trying for some years to keep the fringe areas of his elder brother's domain firmly within the paramount chiefdom. That was not easy, for the Tassantassas had been going to the

Potomac River and Eastern Shore chiefdoms to buy corn since well before
the capture of Pocahontas in 1613. All of those chiefdoms had remained officially allied with the mamanatowick. In 1619–20, though, the people of both
regions did things that must have hinted to Opechancanough that he could
not really count on them if a genuine war broke out with the invaders. The
Patawomecks made their move in the fall of 1619. Opechancanough may have
heard about the prelude to it if he had spies operating in or around
Jamestown. He certainly would have felt the brunt of the ploy when Iopassus, brother of the Patawomeck weroance and abettor in the capture of Pocahontas, came striding through his territory, heading home from Jamestown.
Iopassus had lured the foreigners with a promise of corn for sale. He not only
had managed to get two ships sent to Patawomeck, where everyone would see
them and word would filter back to Opechancanough, but he also had succeeded in getting an armed soldier to accompany him home by a landward
route through Pamunkey that was as ostentatious as it was inefficient.[41]
Opechancanough can scarcely have missed the point: the Patawomecks were
firm friends with the squatters. Word probably trickled back later that the
friendship was less than firm: once back home, Iopassus broke his promise
and traded with the foreigners only when forced. Nevertheless, the tip of the
wedge was in.

Quarrels soon developed between Opechancanough and Esmy Shichans,
the "Laughing King" of Accomac. The Eastern Shore chiefdoms may have
been resisting the former's blandishments for some time, since in general their
geographical isolation tended to make them less warlike than the people on
the mainland. That isolation also made them more amenable to receiving foreign settlement peacefully. In 1619 Esmy Shichans gave a sizable part of his
domain to Thomas Savage, whose widow later patented it according to the
laws of her own country.[42] Savage would prove to be a major factor in the
next few years in the steady flow of corn from Accomac to Jamestown.

In late 1619 or early 1620, one of Opechancanough's sons, name unrecorded, and thirteen others went to Accomac territory and tried to kill a
Tassantassa neighbor of Savage's for unspecified reasons. Savage and three
others interfered, challenging the fourteen men to fight in front of a hundred
or so Accomac onlookers. The fourteen backed down, and the Accomacs derided them as cowards, making them into a laughingstock—and Opechancanough, too, by extension. That kind of shame was not to be borne in the

native people's world. Opechancanough then sent another warrior, Onian-imo, to Accomac to kill Savage, but he returned a failure, too. When another foreigner (John Pory) went touring around the Eastern Shore in mid-1620, he was given a warm welcome.[43] The aliens seemed to be winning over there. Things would get worse the next year.

On the other hand, in 1619–20 the Chickahominies proved that they had become the point men for loyalist maneuvers that upset the Tassantassas. When some foreigners ignored their own nation's current law and came trading among them in the summer, some of the tribesmen killed them, partly for the goods and weapons they had and partly to revenge the deaths of their people at the governor's hands back in 1616. However, the killers went further and made themselves outcasts, according to the local people. They raided their own *quioccosin* house (temple) for "treasure," which was a sacrilege, and then they disappeared. The next Sunday the renegades killed some more Strangers, three of them children left alone in a house. Opechancanough now received complaints from both sides: the Tassantassas aggrieved over the Sunday killings and the Chickahominy townsmen afraid of being blamed for what their less scrupulous fellows had done to the traders.

The mamanatowick's brother sent word to the governor that the peace would never be broken by him. He added that the robbers' town was to be turned over to the Strangers by way of recompense, and the robbers' heads would be sent to Jamestown as soon as they could be caught. He kept neither promise. The town remained in Chickahominy hands, and the renegades went their way, eventually making up their differences with the paramount chief. In 1620 or 1621 the outcasts attempted to do unspecified harm to Esmy Shichans, the Laughing King of Accomac, presumably on Opechancanough's behalf after his unsuccessful quarrel. But they were found out before they could strike, and after fleeing to Smith's Island and destroying Tassantassa livestock there, they settled somewhere "betwixt Chesapeake and Nansemond . . . under the command of Itoyatin" and therefore also of Opechancanough.[44] Predictably, the Strangers were now plotting revenge upon all the Chickahominies, if they could do it without causing a general war.[45]

Opechancanough already had executed a couple of ploys of his own. One occurred at the same time that Iopassus tried to unsettle him, perhaps by coincidence and perhaps not. In the late summer or early fall of 1619, he had Robert Poole tell the governor that he himself would visit Jamestown if the governor would send two men to escort him. Although Yeardley distrusted Poole by now, the men were sent—and returned to Jamestown with the message that Opechancanough wondered why they had come, because he had no intention of making such a trip. (Shades of his brother Powhatan!) The governor then sent John Rolfe, the nephew-in-law of whom the great weroance was still fond, to Pamunkey to get to the bottom of the matter. Rolfe's boat got within five miles (8 km) of the town where the chief lived (name unrecorded) and sent Henry Spelman ahead. Meanwhile the two ships heading up to Patawomeck at Iopassus's insistence detoured up the York River and joined Rolfe. That rendezvous looked like a large armed force to Opechancanough and his people. He already had given Henry Spelman a harsh reception, partially because his rival, Robert Poole, was in residence. But now, hearing that Rolfe had come to see him, he changed his demeanor, treating Spelman kindly and sending him back to Rolfe with a statement, which may have been partially sincere, condemning Poole for trying to break the peace between the two nations. He asked to see Rolfe, but for reasons unknown Rolfe sent back word that he was "sick of an ague" and could not come. Opechancanough pronounced himself satisfied, and the ships left. Poole remained, because Rolfe had no orders to remove him. That may have disappointed Opechancanough, for "they seemed also to be very weary of him."[46]

In November 1619 the mamanatowick's brother sent one of his greatest warriors, Nemattanow, to Jamestown to offer the Strangers a deal. Eight or ten Tassantassa soldiers would join his forces and "assist him in battle against a people dwelling about a day's journey beyond the falls . . . for murdering certain women and children of his contrary to the law of nations." The miscreants' name was garbled (it appears nowhere else in the surviving records), and it is unlikely to have been a Monacan town, a real day's march away, for the Monacans were presumably still his allies. But, then, the whole offer was bogus to begin with. Nemattanow continued: Opechancanough would supply the soldiers with moccasins, and his men would carry their armor for them until they were ready to fight. After a successful battle he would share the booty with his allies: "of male and female children, of corn and other things, and to divide the conquered land into two equal parts between us and them." The council at Jamestown found the plan to be a good one, among other things, because it would palliate Opechancanough, who had "stood aloof upon terms of doubt and jealousy" since the beginning of Yeardley's term as governor the spring before "and would not be drawn to any treaty at all notwithstanding all the art and endeavor the governor could use." (Spelman's poison had worked well.) If Opechancanough would not change his attitude, perhaps cooperation "might win amity and confidence from Itoyatin the great king" and drive a wedge between him and his powerful brother.[47] The project came to nothing, however.

In the early spring of 1620, Opechancanough tried something else. The previous year's harvest had been a very good one. But the native people, as was their habit, had raised only enough to pay their tribute to their weroances and see themselves through the winter. Normal practice was for the women to get the materials for bread making out in the marshes, by digging tuckahoe roots; it is unlikely that anyone really planned to do any differently that spring. But Opechancanough decided to test the Tassantassas by sending word to Jamestown that he and his people were out of corn and wanted to buy some from the Strangers. The mamanatowick's brother may have found out from some of his people visiting the aliens' plantations that many settlements were running low on supplies and that the governor and council were waiting for ships and hoping they were well laden. The foreigners decided not to let go of any foodstuffs, and a proclamation was circulated forbidding anyone on any plantation to sell any corn.[48]

Opechancanough probably did not care. He accomplished his mission, which was to convince his enemies of his people's weakness while putting the finishing touches on an assault that would wipe the squatters out.

16

The Great Assault of 1622

IN 1620 AND 1621 Opechancanough was preparing to carry out the plan that would remove the foreigners from his and his brother's land. At the same time the foreigners were spreading out farther, though not so rapidly as in 1619, and they were attracting some young people from the native towns to live and work on their intruding plantations. We hear only of young people in those times, and not many of them. They were of an age to be malleable in new cultural surroundings, and it is likely that at least some of the boys had chosen to live among the aliens rather than undergo the rigors of the huskanaw process. Access to European goods may also have been a motive for making the move. Metal cutting tools were still attractive, and woven cloth for garments would gain in popularity in the 1620s among the inhabitants of the native towns. People who worked on a plantation could have these things all the time, if they could put up with the denigration of being thought "heathens" and given orders. Those who went to work for kinder foreigners became emotionally attached to them, which is not surprising. Several such people would give away Opechancanough's plan when the time came.

The time was supposed to come in 1621, not 1622, and it was not a young person who gave the plot away. The Assault was originally planned to take place soon after "the taking up of Powhatan's bones at which ceremony great numbers of [people] were to be assembled." Men from all the towns would be there and could be given the upcoming date on which to attack the Tassantassas living nearest them.[1] It was an elegantly simple way to synchronize the warriors' movements while paying proper respects to a dead mamanatowick.

However, Opechancanough overreached himself by adding a complication that backfired. He planned to invite foreign dignitaries to the ceremony as well, and there he wanted to poison them. He knew, as modern botanists do, that the plant most poisonous to human beings within the Chesapeake region is spotted cowbane (*Cicuta maculata*); a thumbnail's worth can kill a fully grown cow. The plant grows throughout the region, but it is more plentiful on the Virginia Eastern Shore. He therefore sent to Esmy Shichans, weroance of the Accomacs,[2] asking for a supply of it and offering payment in beads, probably copper ones because the Accomacs had plentiful shells in their territory. When Esmy Shichans balked, the messenger explained why it was wanted, at which point the chief refused altogether to have anything to do with the project. Not only that, but he sent a warning about a plot to the governor in Jamestown. Interestingly it seems to have been a year later, after the Great Assault actually came off, that Esmy Shichans told his Tassantassa friends about the poisoning part of the plan. But his break with Opechancanough was complete nonetheless. That fall he gave another large chunk of land to his foreign friends, this time the land right next to his capital.[3] His warning caused the governor to order all the plantations to be on guard, so the assault had to be postponed.

When an explanation was demanded of him, Opechancanough "earnestly denied" any conspiracy, and nobody else among his people admitted it either, so that the enemy lacked concrete proof of one.[4] He then resumed his active lulling of the Strangers' suspicions. The best way of doing this, he had found, was to welcome the missionary George Thorpe. Poor, well-meaning Thorpe had no idea he was being played for a fool; but then, neither did he have any idea how insulting his proselytizing was to a dignitary who belonged to a long-established religion. By May 1621 Thorpe thought he saw a softening in the attitude of the great weroance and his people, writing that "they begin more and more to affect English fashions," and he asked the Virginia Company to send over some "householdstuff" to give to Opechancanough and other chiefs. The mamanatowick's brother began sending for him frequently, saying he wanted to be "further informed" about the Tassantassas' religion.[5] Before much longer, thanks to Thorpe, he was the proud possessor of a foreigner-built house erected at the capital of the Pamunkeys, and the locks on the house's doors are supposed to have intrigued him greatly. Thorpe even had some of his compatriots' dogs—immense mastiffs—killed, to demonstrate that although their looks frightened Opechancanough's people, the animals were still mortal.[6]

Someone else was proved to be mortal in the summer or early fall of 1621, and that was Nemattanow, whom the aliens had begun calling "Jack of the Feather" in 1611 because of the garish feather decorations he wore to attract enemy fire.[7] No arrow or bullet had ever touched this *cockarouse* (great warrior), and he had the reputation among the chiefdoms of someone who could not be killed by any weapon. What had worked for him a decade before, when on Powhatan's orders he hectored the Tassantassas trying to settle at Henricus, ceased working for him now, for like his new overlord, he overreached himself.

Nemattanow approached a Stranger named Morgan, whom he persuaded to accompany him on a trading expedition to Pamunkey. He then murdered Morgan on the trail and took his large supply of trade goods; he also took Morgan's cap and began wearing it as a trophy. A couple of days later, the cockarouse brazenly returned to Morgan's homestead with the cap on his head, and when two serving boys asked him where their master was, the warrior told them he was dead. Spotting the cap, the boys guessed the truth and tried to talk him into going with them to George Thorpe's, Thorpe being a magistrate. When he resisted, the boys got physical with him, and in the ensuing scuffle they shot him. They then hauled the mortally wounded man into a boat, intending to take him to the governor in Jamestown, several miles away. But Nemattanow, realizing that he was dying, asked the boys to promise him two things: that they would bury him among the Tassantassas and that they would not let anybody know he had been killed with a bullet. Right to the end, he wanted his reputation to remain intact. The word got out, of course, and reached Opechancanough and his people.[8]

The cockarouse's death would have been a blow to everyone's morale and a warning to the aliens. But Opechancanough had to keep the peace with the Strangers until their guard was relaxed enough once more for his warriors to be most effective. So he sent word to Governor Yeardley that the death was of little account. In fact, he said, Nemattanow had been out of favor when he died. He himself claimed to remain a firm friend of the Tassantassas, to the extent that he would rather have his own throat cut than see a breach made in the peace between the two nations. He even pretended that he had sent people to search for "the bodies," in hopes of proving that Nemattanow was not guilty of such treacherous behavior. Lastly, he asserted that "the sky should sooner fall than the peace be broken" by him, and he had ordered all his people to keep the treaty.[9]

The foreigners were noticed to be on their guard nonetheless, so the Great Assault, if it had been coming that fall, was postponed again. In October, Opechancanough welcomed George Thorpe as emissary from the new governor (Sir Francis Wyatt), who had sent him a message of goodwill and a present. The mamanatowick's brother went so far as to ask that the articles of the peace be "stamped in brass, and fixed to one of his oaks of note."[10] Thorpe took the opportunity to preach, as usual, and in his conversation with the great weroance he was surprised—as modern people usually are about traditional Native Americans—to find that the Powhatans had astronomical knowledge.[11] Opechancanough led Thorpe even further down the garden path this time, by admitting that his religion "was not the right way," that "God loves [the aliens] better than [the locals]," and that perhaps the reason God was angry with the native people—1620 and 1621 both having been dry years[12]—was the "heathen custom of making their children black boys" (referring to painting during the huskanaw). Thorpe was immensely gratified by these apparently artless disclosures.[13] Opechancanough, via Thorpe, gave the new governor the impression that his people were "weaker" than the Tassantassas and that they wanted to be "safely sheltered and defended" by them.

Neither Thorpe nor Governor Wyatt were sufficiently versed in Powhatan culture to notice a bit of information from this visit that was probably ominous: both Opitchapam/Itoyatin and Opechancanough had changed their names. Thorpe reported back that the mamanatowick was now called Sasawpen, and the younger brother was Mangopeesomon, names that nearly all later record makers neglected to use. Powhatan men changed their names multiple times in their lives, according to the great deeds they performed.[14] It is likely that Opechancanough and his brother had changed their names that fall for a reason, perhaps connected with a ceremony intended to imbue them and their followers with a new determination to bring off the Great Assault.

The squatters, for their part, relaxed their guard again and went on preparing to plant the year's tobacco crop on (in the native view) their ridiculously scattered-out plantations, where a very few families and laborers would sit, like a dog in the manger, in the middle of each tract they claimed was theirs.

They unthinkingly welcomed the "friendly" real owners of the land into their houses when they came to trade. They loaned out their boats when asked, and they even allowed their visitors to lighten their workload by sharing in the labor and using their tools, including tools with sharp edges. The Tassantas-sas had, in fact, become sitting ducks once again.[15]

The Day of Retribution

The Great Assault was carried out on all the squatter settlements with great precision on March 22, 1622. Why the choice of a day in March? The worst of winter would be over, to make traveling a bit less rigorous. The summer, with its heat and foreign epidemics, would not yet have begun. A more co-gent reason was that the season of cattapeuk was a time when the enemy could not retaliate against the warriors' loved ones. Powhatan families dispersed out of the towns in the early spring to take advantage of fish runs and to forage for other wild foods. They made visits back to plant crops and, at intervals, to weed them, but that was all. (The Assault was probably originally planned for taquitock, the late fall 1621, for the same reason of dispersal.) What safer time, for the women and children, to attempt a general attack and escape angry survivors with ease?

Why that day in March? No record maker ever speculated, and no one seems to have asked Opechancanough in later years. It is unlikely to have been anything to do with the phase of the moon, which on the night of March 21 was two nights short of the last quarter.[16] More likely, the priests had con-sulted with their deity and been told which day was most propitious. To co-ordinate the attack itself, Opechancanough would have followed the proce-dure described by William Strachey a decade before. He sent out several messengers ("officers") on one day. It is likely that each would have had or-ders to visit certain towns along an itinerary (for example, one to going to Powhatan town, the Appamattucks, and the Weyanocks in turn, another going to the Quiyoughcohannocks, the Warraskoyacks, and the Nansemonds in turn, and so forth). Each messenger would approach the warriors whom the paramount chief wanted, "strike them over the back a sound blow with a bastinado [a stick], and bid them be ready to serve the great king, [telling] them the rendezvous[,] from which they dare not at the time appointed be ab-sent."[17] The message in this case would have been to go into action a certain number of days after Opechancanough sent out the messengers, which allowed for the messengers' travel time to the farther districts. The warriors were to leave off their usual warpaint, to lull their victims, and proceed to the nearest plantations under the guise of friendship, either staying overnight or appearing there in the morning of the day the mamanatowick had decreed. Then as work was beginning, they were to turn on the Tassantassas and do as much killing and damage as possible. And so it happened, with clockwork precision.

Leaks occurred, however—and from more than just the single composite character called "Chanco" who appears in the popular literature. Several native people gave warning to the enemy,[18] usually to individuals of whom they had become fond. One, the prototype for most of the "Chanco" legend, was a young man whose name was never recorded; in the contemporary records he is called only "Perry's Indian." He was employed at William Perry's plantation across the river from Jamestown, but he lived with a neighbor named Richard Pace, who had treated him with great kindness. On the night of March 21 he was joined in bed by his brother, who whispered to him of the attack planned for the next day, in which he would kill Perry, and who urged him to kill Pace, after which other people would come and finish off the survivors. The youth was unwilling to harm someone who had been like a father to him. So either that night or the next morning—the accounts written closer to events indicate he mulled it over for some hours—he alerted Pace. At first light Pace jumped into a boat, rowed across the river, and gave the alarm, which was then spread to nearby settlements.[19] That much of the legend in true.

The name in the legend, however, came from someone else, an adult of uncertain age and sex, gave warning in the Pamunkey River area, right on Opechancanough's doorstep. Specifically, that person alerted "the pinnace trading in Pamunkey" at the time. It may or may not have been the same man as Chauco (source of the name "Chanco"), who was mistakenly trusted enough by Opechancanough to be sent as a messenger to the enemy the next year. Chauco "had lived much amongst the English, and by revealing that plot to divers [individuals] on the day [of the Assault] had saved their lives."[20]

Yet another native person, this one living on a plantation with George Thorpe, had tried unsuccessfully to warn that eternally hopeful missionary only an hour before the first warriors appeared. Thorpe was killed, as so many were, without making much defense, and the killers, who came from a culture

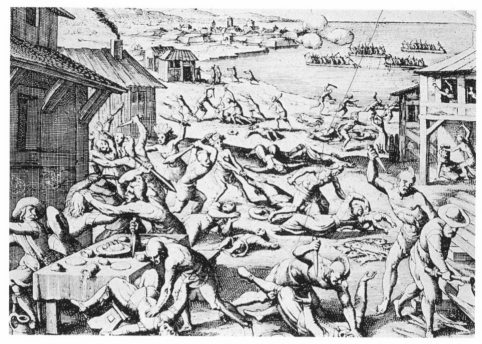

The Great Assault of 1622. Engraving by Matthaeus Meriam, plate 7 in Theodor de Bry, *Dryʒehender theil Americae*, pt. 23 (Frankfurt, 1628).

in which trophies were taken, mutilated his body especially horribly, presumably to express their revulsion for his aggressive evangelism.[21]

The Assault itself was carried out in traditional Powhatan style: a friendly approach followed by a sudden ambush in which warriors killed anyone easily dispatched, wounded as many others as possible, and wasted little time in attacking those who put up a serious fight. Where they could do so without danger to themselves, they took trophies and various belongings from the dead and smashed what they could not carry away.[22] They also took living prisoners: some were known later to be among both the Nansemonds (this married couple soon escaped)[23] and the Pamunkeys. Then they retreated into the forest and returned home in triumph to their families. Most of the men involved were from James River chiefdoms, judging by who received vengeful raids later on: on the south bank of the James, the Nansemonds, the Warraskoyacks, the Quiyoughcohannocks (still misguidedly called "Tappahannas" by Jamestown), the Weyanocks, and the Appamattucks all participated. So did the people of Powhatan town, the only chiefdom remaining intact at that date on the north bank of the James. The Chickahominies were also active, of course, as were the "Pamunkeys" (probably the combined Youghtanunds and Pamunkeys of earlier times).[24] The Chiskiacks seem to have abandoned their town temporarily, as being too close to the enemy, and they may have fought under another name. Other chiefdoms known to have been sympathetic to Opechancanough and willing to attack any Tassantassas to came within range were the Rappahannock River peoples and the Wiccocomicos on the Northern Neck. Their neighbors the Sekakawons were invited to join the alliance but chose not to be active. The Patawomecks sat on the fence, which brought them a lot of trouble later.[25] It was a fairly impressive lineup for Opechancanough, in spite of the aliens' efforts to woo away his "fringe" chiefdoms.

The intent behind the Assault was equally in accord with traditional Powhatan warfare: show them that you are stronger and that they are unwelcome, and if they value the lives of their limited personnel, they will withdraw. Opechancanough specifically assured the Patawomeck weroance (who later tattled to the Tassantassas) that "before the end of two moons there should not be an Englishman in all their countries."[26] The Tassantassas did indeed withdraw, but after discarding the idea of refugeeing to the Eastern Shore,[27] they chose instead to consolidate their survivors into a few better-defended plantations on the Lower Peninsula: an English reservation, in fact. Its boundaries, as John Smith perceived them, were the James and York Rivers, the Chesapeake Bay, and to the west, the Chickahominy River, its tributary Diascund Creek, and an imaginary line over to the Pamunkey River.[28] But the Strangers did not intend to leave for England, as the paramount chief and his brother hoped. The outlanders came from a country with a huge population compared to the Powhatan one, and they had a cash crop that could entice plenty of replacements for those who had died. From this reservation, then, established in their minds as irrevocably "theirs," the Tassantassas intended to pursue Opechancanough and his people to the death.[29]

17

A War of Attrition, Including an English Massacre

THE NEXT FEW YEARS were miserable, hungry ones for everybody, even though they had above-average rainfall.[1] Hostilities interfered with the planting of crops, as well as seeing the ones that did get planted through to the harvest. Both sides were involved in skirmishes, and each side suffered the consequences of the other's enmity.[2] John Smith reported that the native people withdrew, sitting back to watch the enemy, until they recommenced raiding on September 9. Yet records sent from Virginia at the time indicate that the local people resumed sniping again almost immediately.[3] In the next year the foreigners tried to buy corn from the fence-sitting Patawomecks, among others, but Opechancanough need not have worried: the Arrogant Ones were so heavy-handed that their behavior was more alienating than inviting. Only the Accomacs, now permanently detached from the paramount chiefdom's fringe, managed to trade peacefully with the jumpy outlanders.[4]

It is likely that the native people suffered less than the Tassantassas did. For one thing, unless they were actually being raided at the time, the inhabitants of Tsenacomoco could move fairly freely about their remaining territories, while the aliens holed up on their reservation. Not only that, but their contacts with the foreigners, now very limited and mostly at shooting range, would have served to protect them against the epidemics that were sweeping the plantations. More importantly, they knew how to survive droughts, which produced the same deficit in corn as warfare did, and they could turn to living entirely off wild plants and animals when they had to. Attacks on corn-

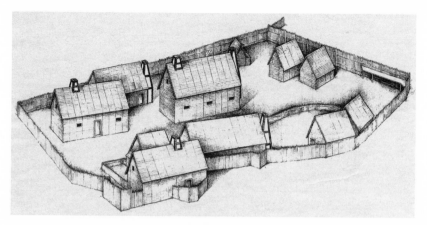

Artist's rendering of 1620s fortified homestead at Jordan's Journey.
(Courtesy, Virginia Department of Historic Resources)

fields were to be expected, the people felt, but an enemy would have little luck trying to root up the people's supply of tuckahoe. With their knowledge of the land, it was impossible starve out the Real People; what actually defeated them in the end would be a tidal wave of immigrants washing over them. Meanwhile, if the rumor was true, Opechancanough was trying to produce gunpowder for the weapons his men had captured on March 22. The trouble was that he had no one to tell him how it was made. Instead, assuming it was some sort of plant material, he had it sown in the ground the next cohattayough (of 1622), presumably in hopes that it contained seeds that would sprout.[5]

Opechancanough had Tassantassa prisoners with him at Pamunkey after the Great Assault; they may have been most of the prisoners taken by the various district chiefdoms. The brother of the mamanatowick was well aware of their value as hostages, but that did not necessarily keep them all alive. In accordance with Powhatan tradition, "the men that they took they put them to death." Females were kept and put to ordinary women's work under careful guard, which one of them later described as "slavery." The captives totaled twenty in June 1622, but by the following spring the number was down to nineteen (or fifteen, according to another account).[6] No record survives to tell us what happened to those who died over the winter: whether it was one last male to die under torture or one or more females who died of natural causes, the health of foreigners being rather fragile in the "New [to them] World."

In nepinough (late summer of 1622) ships came, bringing more aliens and some supplies. The native people would have taken note of this, and perhaps also of the fact that those disembarking were already sick, so that disease spread up and down the James River thereafter.[7] But the arrivals' major effect on the region's inhabitants was that the enemy now had the wherewithal, in guns and ammunition, to make serious moves against the native towns. They had made feeble attempts against the Appamattucks and Weyanocks before the ships came, but now the raids could carry a real sting.[8] People had to move fast to salvage their crops. The Nansemonds, for instance, carried away what they could of their newly gathered corn and burned their own houses rather than let the raiders get the remnants. The invaders then went to Opechancanough's town on the Pamunkey River and demanded the return of the surviving prisoners. The mamanatowick's brother stalled for "ten or twelve days," during which everybody upriver hurriedly gathered and hid their corn. Eventually the Tassantassas lost patience, came ashore, and took the corn they found in the immediate area, in spite of ambushes laid for them, before burning the town.[9] From the violence of their behavior, Opechancanough could have guessed, if he did not know for certain, that the governor in Jamestown had put a bounty on native people's heads, especially his.[10] Another boatload of foreigners went up the Chickahominy River, where the tribesmen withdrew rather than offer resistance; they lost some of their property, too. The remaining James River chiefdoms were hit as well, losing both houses and fishing weirs.[11] Their men did not sit passively by: they continued their sniping activities.

In cattapeuk (of 1623), after the native people had passed a hardworking winter and the outlanders had passed a famine-stricken one, Opechancanough pretended that his people were in as bad a state as the enemy, and he asked them for a truce so that the women of his towns could plant the year's crops. As an inducement, he offered to return the surviving prisoners. The governor, for his part, pretended to like the idea and agreed that his people would not interfere with the native inhabitants of Chiskiack and Pamunkey. Both sides knew that war would come again when the corn was ripe.[12] An unhappy complication for everyone then occurred (on March 30), when interpreter Henry Spelman was killed while trading on the Potomac River, apparently by the Piscataways.[13] That left only the unreliable Robert Poole, as far as the records show. Of course, ex-employees of the enemy like Chauco were available to Opechancanough; whether he fully trusted them or not was another matter.

It was the double-dealing Chauco and another man who had delivered the message from Opechancanough to the governor. No record tells us whether or not the mamanatowick's brother knew that Chauco had warned the Tassantassas the previous spring; logically he did not, or he would have had the traitor's brains smashed out long before. He probably simply chose the man as intermediary because he spoke the aliens' language and would be recognized as a noncombatant. That is probably why Chauco and his companion, Comahum, went first to Martin's Hundred rather than to Jamestown; the survivors there probably knew him by sight. As it happened, they also knew Comahum: he had done some of the killing on that plantation during the Great Assault, so they put him in chains.[14]

Giving Up the Prisoners — and Being Ambushed in a Massacre

Chauco took the governor's acceptance of the offer back to Opechancanough, and a week later one of the prisoners, Mrs. Boyse, was escorted to Jamestown. Although she had been put to ordinary work—i.e., hard, physical labor— among the Pamunkey women, on this occasion she had been dressed up like the wife of a weroance, in a long fringed mantle with copper and shell jewelry. However, the other prisoners were not released as yet, and it was Robert Poole's fault. That contentious man had made "threatening speeches" to Opechancanough, apparently to the effect that if the women stayed in town to begin planting, the invaders would come and kill them. The great weroance sent a request with Mrs. Boyse that Poole be recalled to Jamestown and another foreigner sent with an assurance that the truce was genuine. Poole returned on his own soon afterward, but an (unnamed) emissary arrived in Pamunkey as requested. He brought with him a stock of glass beads to "pay" for the release of the prisoners.[15] (One of those prisoners would later be held in servitude by the physician at Jamestown to "pay off" her "debt" of beads.)[16]

"The great king" (meaning Opitchapam) next invited the Tassantassas to send a boat to his town to collect the ransomed prisoners. With or without his brother's knowledge—probably the latter—he added an offer: when they came, he would deliver Opechancanough into their hands "either alive or dead." That was too good to pass up, so a captain and a dozen soldiers went to Pamunkey. They left Jamestown by boat (on May 22, 1623) while "the interpreter" (probably Robert Poole) and a native man took the faster route by land to inform Opechancanough.[17] The precise place of the meeting was not recorded.

The parley seems to have gone off in the ordinary manner, presumably with a formal welcome, a pipe smoked, and a meal eaten. After the captives were turned over to their compatriots, both sides made "many fained [insincere] speeches." At length the Strangers harked back to a custom of their own and proposed a toast, consisting of sack that they had brought. Unknown to Opechancanough, some of it had been laced with poison.[18] The foreign captain and the interpreter drank first, of wine that had been poured from another source, and then Opechancanough, the weroance of the Chiskiacks, "their sons," and other leading men drank. Whatever the poison was, it took hold fairly quickly, making the Real Men "drunk." The Treacherous Ones made a hasty exit at that point, which is why the one eyewitness account is not clear about who died from the poison and who did not. But to make sure of their "victory," once they had reached their boat, the soldiers suddenly turned and fired a volley of shot into the staggering people, killing several dozen. Some of them then rushed back ashore and cut off some scalps (we "brought home part of their heads").[19]

Opechancanough was the central figure in the attack, and he was observed to have been both poisoned and shot. The Strangers were positive that his injuries were mortal.[20] But he did not die, nor did his brother. He disappeared from the written records for several years, indicating that he was a very sick man for a long time. But he ultimately outlived his brother and became mamanatowick in his own right.

More Misfortune

The people of Tsenacomoco did not prosper in the next few years while their war captain was out of commission. Everyone, including the foreigners, was jumpy about planting crops, so little was planted; sniping by the men prevented the enemy from doing much hunting, either.[21] Hunger then drove the enemy to go trading and also to go on the attack.

The people's towns were raided again that nepinough, so that once more they lost most of their crops and houses and some of their family members. Those hit were the Chickahominies, the Weyanocks, the Appamattucks, the Powhatans (the town), the Warraskoyacks, and the Nansemonds (all on July 12, 1623). Several days later the Weyanocks and Nansemonds were attacked again.[22] Sporadic trading, which sometimes turned into robbing of native people, continued for some time, as did the mutual raids, and the Tassantassas relied on the Patawomecks, among others, for foodstuffs. Without the charisma of Opechancanough to keep them at least on the fence, the Patawomecks became firm allies of the invaders.[23] They felt that Jamestown was so far away that their country would not be threatened. As Opechancanough could have told them, their "isolation" would not last indefinitely.

The next cohattayough (of 1624) was just as dangerous for the women and children planting fields as it had been the previous year, although they knew that the major threat would come in nepinough when the corn was ripe enough that the enemy could either harvest it or at least cut it down and make it useless to the Real People.[24] Of course, the men would pose a threat to the enemy's farmers, for the growing crops of the Strangers would conceal snipers.[25] This year the Pamunkeys planted more corn than usual, so that if their allies on the James River lost theirs, they could make up the difference. Those plans proved to be futile.

Nepinough came on time, that year being a wetter-than-average year.[26] The cornfields that had been planted first were becoming ripe, and the later-planted ones were well grown; the crop looked promising. Because Opechancanough was still apparently very ill, Opitchapam ("Otiotan") was governing the people, and in a fit of bravado he had done some bragging. Not only would the Pamunkeys feed their allies if needed, but when the enemy raiders came, as they inevitably would, his men would give them a fight they would never forget. Word of that boast reached all the way to the Patuxent River in what is now Maryland, for the Patuxent chief actually sent an observer southward to see the fireworks.

Sure enough, the governor of the Tassantassas led sixty soldiers up the Pamunkey River to the mamanatowick's town. A huge force of warriors stood ready for them, if the governor can be believed: "eight hundred ['Pamunkey'] bowmen, besides divers nations that came to assist them," all being intent upon defending not only the winter's supply of corn but also their own reputation as fearsome fighters. Once ashore, two dozen of the enemy (presumably armed with swords) headed over to the cornfields to begin hacking down the plants. The other three dozen, armed with their guns, engaged the defenders who were trying to get the corn cutters to cease operations. The open-field skirmishing went on for two whole days, and by the end of it, so many of Opitchapam's men had been killed and so much corn had been cut ("sufficient to have sustained four thousand men for a twelvemonth") that the people quit struggling and let the enemy cut down the rest of the crop while they "stood most ruthfully looking on." It was a smashing defeat for the Pamunkeys.[27] No more raids on native towns took place that summer, but no more were needed. The people's corn was gone for that year, and their men's reputation was ruined for a long time to come. Opechancanough, wherever he was lying and trying to recover, must have been fuming helplessly.

An Ill-Reported Aftermath

The surviving Virginia records become scarce after 1624, for a variety of reasons: the Virginia Company becoming defunct, the royal administration records being lost, etc. In fact, the remainder of time covered by this volume is something of a "dark age" in the records about anybody in Virginia. Counties were established in the 1630s and began dealing with the tribes near them, but many of their records were destroyed during the subsequent centuries. Thus what is known about Opechancanough's life from this point on is even sketchier than what went before.

Hostilities with the Tassantassas continued for several more years, but at an attenuated rate. Opitchapam's people seem to have continued sniping at squatters, but their morale appears to have been too low for them to attempt any major move. The invaders' ability to conduct raids was limited as well, and their surviving records tell us that it was because of the niggardly shipments of supplies (including ammunition) from their homeland. In fact, in the year after the defeat of the Pamunkeys no raids at all could be carried out, because the necessary powder did not arrive before harvesttime. (The native leaders would have discerned that fact and rejoiced over it.) The interpreter Robert Poole returned to England in that year, and if someone replaced him, that person is unknown; Henry Spelman was dead and Thomas Savage was acting as the official interpreter on the Eastern Shore. Still, the native people got the impression across to their enemies that they would prefer not to be on fighting terms anymore. They may or may not have been sincere, but the foreigners' amenability to peace was definitely a ruse.[28]

No one seems to have undertaken a raid in the following year (1626). But two Tassantassas went to Pamunkey accompanied by native men, and one did not return. Other squatters were letting down their guard about local people who came to them to trade, something the governor in Jamestown forbade.[29] As of September, neither native guides nor experienced interpreters who could double as guides for the governor were available. So the first native man who visited a squatter plantation found himself detained and sent to the governor, who handed him over to someone (William Claiborne) who had devised a plan to "keep" native people on hand to use as guides. The next month a Weyanock man was captured and kept, his captor getting permission to take him to England.[30] Some active hostilities then took place during taquitock and popanow (the cold months of 1626–27). The Nansemonds took prisoners (there are no details), and snipers killed some of the foreigners' livestock. By the spring (of 1627), Opitchapam's people had recovered enough that they were planning another assault on the invaders' plantations, or so the rumor went.[31] The assault seems not to have come off, for whatever reason, but plenty of sniping probably went on in its place. The Tassantassas retaliated in raids (on August 1, 1627): on the people of Powhatan town, the Appamattucks, the Weyanocks, the Chickahominies, the Quiyoughcohannocks, the Warraskoyacks, the Nansemonds, and the "Chesapeakes" (Nansemonds living in the old Chesapeake territory). The paramount chief's attention was diverted at the same time by an attack on the Pamunkeys, who endured a second raid later on.[32] As it happened, the Pamunkeys may have had an addition to their forces. Several Carib Indians escaped, before they could be sold, from a slave ship that had called in at Jamestown. They promptly made for the native towns, where they knew they would be given sanctuary.[33] Nothing more is recorded of them.

By the next cattapeuk the Pamunkeys had some Tassantassa prisoners in their possession, taken either during the raids on their country or by their allies in other, unrecorded, hostilities. Significantly, the captives this time were male. They had not been killed in the traditional death meted out to enemies, probably because their value as hostages was much greater than considerations of revenge—a telling sign of weakness on the part of the Real People.

One of the prisoners sent out a message on a piece of bark, probably with Opitchapam's permission, and sure enough, a somewhat more peaceful time ensued. By nepinough a proposal of peace had arrived at Pamunkey and had been accepted. Once again, at least one side (the invaders) was insincere.[34]

The text of the treaty, which went into effect in early August 1628, has not survived; judging by the few pieces of it mentioned in contemporary records, it probably had many elements of the treaty of 1614 with the Chickahominies.[35] However, priorities had changed. The "first and principal article" of the 1628 agreement was that no native people were to come to the squatter plantations and try to enter the houses; they were to approach plantations only on official business from "the great King" and then see only the governor or the militia commander at "Paspahegh" (the real Paspaheghs' old lands near Jamestown). Another condition was that the Real Men were not to harm the Strangers' livestock, which often was allowed to roam, or anyone they met in the woods.

The native people broke both of these articles almost immediately and went on doing what they had always done: treating the land and the animals on it as their own and treating the foreigners as intruders. Why shouldn't they? It was their country, where their ancestors had lived since time immemorial. The customs of their ancestors said that men should hunt animals roaming in the forest and that people of both sexes could go trading. It was the way the Real People lived. So why were the aliens outraged? But the Tassantassas refused to understand, and they broke off the treaty the next popanow (in January 1629). Yet another Powhatan man who had gone among the aliens at the wrong time, this time just after the end-of-treaty message was sent to Opitchapam, was released and sent with another message: you have this man back because you haven't killed any of us lately.[36]

It was Opitchapam alone who dealt with these messages. Opechancanough was still out of the picture, and the invaders still did not know that he was even alive. The interpreter employed was Robert Poole, who had returned from England.[37] Even Poole seems to have been kept in the dark about the mamanatowick's brother.

That summer of 1629 raids were launched on the native towns again, and yet again in the fall and in the following spring.[38] The native people probably retaliated; their sniping may have become so ordinary as not to be mentioned in the Strangers' records. But more foreigners began pouring into Tsenacomoco, intent on getting rich raising tobacco. And the raids began damaging Indian towns that had not seen action before. One skirmish in 1629 wiped out the corn of the people at Cantaunkack, on the north bank of the York River not far from the old site of Werowocomoco. The Tassantassas tried the next year to settle in the Chiskiacks' town. The reason given this time, so that they could "face their greatest enemy, Opechancanough," indicates that word had now reached them that he was alive—and still inimical to them.[39] They probably had found it out because of Opitchapam's death; that lame man disappears from the records after 1629, and Opechancanough appears in his place. Opechancanough was finally, at the age of eighty or so, the mamanatowick.

Hostilities continued thereafter, though next to no records survive that specify which native people were raided or what they did in return. The enemy finally succeeded in settling in the Chiskiacks' town, which was imprecisely described as "bordering upon the chief residence of the Pamunkey King the most dangerous head of the Indian enemy."[40] Then in the summer of 1632, in which everyone suffered from a drought,[41] someone made a move for peace. Only one lone passage—noted down by a nineteenth-century lawyer before the General Court records burned in 1865—tells us: "governor to parley with Chickahominy Indians." The Chickahominies had broken their sixteen-year alliance with the mamanatowick and were suing for a separate peace. Opechancanough himself had not yet knuckled under, for a law the foreigners passed among themselves on September 4 orders the war to continue. By month's end, though, it was all over: another terse notation by the lawyer reads "a peace with Pamunkeys and Chickahominy Indians but a proclamation [by the governor] not to parley with or trust them."[42]

Opechancanough's people did not suddenly begin liking or trusting the invaders, either. In spite of this treaty, all details of which have been lost, some native people still committed "mischiefs" in January 1633,[43] and because oftentimes those "mischiefs" involved hunting free-roaming livestock in the woods, they would go right on occurring for several decades longer. The treaty of 1632 meant primarily that raiding by both sides would cease. And security from raids would mean squatters moving in on the Real People again.

18

Running Out of Time

THE LIMITED records of the period tell us next to nothing about Opechancanough's activities, nor even about his surviving family. As a man of about eighty and one who had come through many wars as both raider and raidee, he probably had outlived a great many members of his family besides his brothers. The only sibling on record—and that one is mentioned in a one-sentence abstract made by the nineteenth-century lawyer—was a sister, whom the foreigners called "Cleopatra." In December 1641 their great-nephew, Pocahontas's son Thomas Rolfe, got permission from the governor to visit them. The whole sentence is this: "Thomas Rolfe petitions governor to let him go see Opechancanough to whom he is allied [is a kinsman] and Cleopatra his mother's sister."[1] Aside from that, the records are silent.

The decade after 1622 had seen a moderate trickle of invaders continue to cross the Atlantic to lands they considered empty. The 1630s saw it become a flow and then the beginnings of a flood. More and more inhabitants of an ever-smaller Tsenacomoco came more often into contact with the foreigners and learned something of their language (and vice versa). The native people then realized—to their outrage—that they were considered the squatters, not the Tassantassas.

Their ancient ways of using the land got no respect from the incomers. They knew to shift their houses and fields at intervals, rather than wearing out the land by overfarming (supposedly that was "using it properly"), so they were labeled "nomads." When the intruders wore their land out, they demanded new lands and thought of it as "good" business practice in a competitive world. Fools! As for the squatters' grabbing land and then insisting that they owned it forever, even after they stopped farming it, that was ridiculous. The Real People did not claim ownership of animals, either, much less keep them penned up. The outlanders kept mainly hogs and let them range the woods freely; but illogically they insisted on the principle of "proper" ownership, so woe betide you if you killed one of those hogs. What was worse, opportunistic hunting—on behalf of one's family, not for sport—led the Arrogant Ones to accuse the native people of "living from hand to mouth." Comparisons of that sort were not flattering to native pride, which was still considerable. The Old Inhabitants' ability to live decently even during droughts, when the crops failed, was thus downgraded by new neighbors who would starve at such times. When too many such ignoramuses landed in Tsenacomoco and moved in on the native people, it became intolerable—again.

Tensions Building

Opechancanough and his people had only made an outward peace with the invaders of their world. The governor in Jamestown wrote in 1634 that the two nations were on "fair terms" but that wariness was still the order of the day.[2] Indeed, both sides were wary enough of each other that the governor's permission was needed for any interaction with the native people, not that it stopped both the Real People and the Tassantassas from meeting, trading, and occasionally fighting each other if they were well away from Jamestown. The aliens' repeated forbidding of selling guns and ammunition to the native people indicates that Real Men were beginning to carry firearms, as well as bows and arrows, when going about their daily work. That custom was strengthened by the foreigners' penchant for concentrating on raising tobacco and then going to the local people—or the Dutch ships that came trading in the lower Chesapeake—to try to buy food.[3] If the local people were Accomacs, accustomed to a region without tuckahoe[4] and thus to raising large amounts of corn from traditional times, that practice worked. If the locals were mainland people, who had always been less intensively agricultural, it was less successful. And the more aliens who moved in on the native people, the more likely there were to be awkward incidents.

The Real People were now a reduced population, although by how much is unknowable. But if the land appeared empty to the invaders of 1607, it appeared even more so to the incomers of the 1630s. Jamestown now allowed

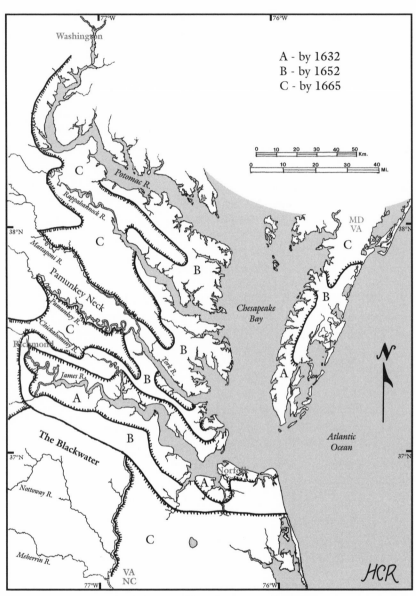

Settlers' claims in the mid-seventeenth century

them to patent (i.e., claim) land, and records of the claims are most of what has survived from that time. Thus the greatest volume of Virginia records we have from the 1630s and much of the 1640s relates to where the invaders were staking out their claims. It should be needless to state that no permission was asked of the native owners before their foraging territories and fallow lands were taken.[5]

Both the Warraskoyacks and the Quiyoughcohannocks lost their land and disappeared from the written records in the mid-1630s, though aliens initially had tried to patent parts of their territory as early as 1627–28. The Nansemonds began losing the old Chesapeake district to the east in the mid-1630s, but they held onto some land along their river. The Chickahominies were in the same position, being forced out of their upriver towns and holding onto Ozinies (Oraniock, later called Warreny) near modern Diascund Creek. That town began to be surrounded by squatters in 1638. The one remaining Appamattuck town began being impinged upon in 1635.

In the York River basin, the Tassantassas began settling the north bank, downstream from Poropotank Creek, in the early 1640s; because of Opechancanough's resistance, they would not go upriver for several more years. Settlement had begun earlier on the York's south bank. The Chiskiacks, now living on the Piankatank River, began to see unwanted neighbors in 1642, the same year that claims were laid on both sides of the lower Rappahannock. The next year the Wiccocomicos and the Sekakawons began to feel the effect of outlanders moving into the Potomac River basin. The Chiskiacks, at least, did something or other that was violent about the squatters near them, but the records with the details have been lost.[6]

Though the records are silent on the matter, the young Powhatan adults of this period were people who did not remember a time when pale-skinned foreigners had not been settled in their country and trying to take more of their land. The stories that Opechancanough and other elders told them about earlier times would increasingly have seemed to be a distant "golden age," free of the Arrogant Ones. The threats from Native American enemies like the Massawomecks (who were not active in the Chesapeake region after the 1630s) would have receded into the mists of memory by comparison.

Some of the Nansemonds lowered their defenses sufficiently against the squatters at Basse's Choice that one of the Basses, John, who was a minister, won them over and even married one of them in 1638.[7] No record remains of what Opechancanough thought of this surrender, but he probably did know about it, because native people kept in touch with one another. For him, it meant another batch of people detached from his paramount chiefdom. Other chiefdoms also had a few young people siphoned off by evangelistic foreigners in these years. Funding was available for plantation claimants to rear such children in the foreign manner after 1640, and at least one child was taken in, presumably with the parents' permission.[8] One youth, probably from among the Weyanocks, had lived with the same Perry as did "Perry's Indian" of 1622, although he had not gone to that plantation until 1630.

Another native person, of undisclosed age, was working on a plantation near the Piankatank River in June 1640 when he stole a neighbor's gun "and a shirt and a pair of breeches." He apparently disappeared into the woods, heading for home, for instead of going after him, the Tassantassa victim complained to the governor. The governor's solution was clever and required no woodsmanship at all: the next native person who visited the victim and was found to know the culprit was to be held there as a hostage until the culprit returned what he had stolen. No punishment of the thief was specified.

It may have been this relatively mellow approach toward Opechancanough's people that led the mamanatowick to be equally lenient after a nasty incident occurred a few months later. An outlander (John Burton) working on a plantation found some of his belongings missing thanks to one of the native youths who were his coworkers. Instead of tracking the culprit or complaining to anyone, this victim killed the next native man he encountered, having mistaken him for the thief. (It was either a case of "all savages look alike," or else the victim was not sure who had robbed him.) Word got back to the Real People's towns, of course, and Opechancanough knew as well as the foreign authorities that this incident endangered the peace. He was prepared to be lenient, but he was very probably already organizing another Great Assault and wanted to propitiate the enemy as much as possible. That is the best explanation of his going further than the governor ever had: the paramount chief urged the governor, who had fined the killer, to remit the fine and consider the killing a case of mistaken identity. The next year it became a matter of law among the foreigners that anyone wronged by a native person should go to the nearest militia commander rather than acting on his own.[9] Meanwhile, the mamanatowick had violated his people's own code, which speci-

fied that wrongful deaths were avenged, in order to keep the increasingly fragile peace.

In 1643 considerable trade still occurred between Opechancanough's
people and the squatters, especially for guns and ammunition. The Jamestown
government seemed unable to stop it, which was to Opechancanough's advantage. In March of that year another effort at prevention encouraged the
squatters to confiscate the firearms of any native person they met. The law
actually said that only arms that had been illegally lent to that person by a foreigner were to be taken,[10] but plenty of incomers were willing to bend the law
in their own interests. It is a pity that the records of many counties claiming
the territory of Opechancanough's people (i.e., Nansemond, Charles City,
James City, New Kent, Gloucester) were burned in the American Civil War
and at other times; had they not been, concrete evidence might exist of what
probably happened: an escalation of awkward and even bloody incidents.[11]

The Great Assault of 1644

Opechancanough was now somewhere in his nineties. An oral tradition
recorded by Robert Beverley in 1705 indicates that he was very frail physically. But his mind was as sharp as ever, and so was his organizing ability. He
still had chiefdoms that were loyal to him: the Weyanocks, the Appamattucks,
part of the Nansemonds (the part not Christianized), the Chickahominies, the
Pamunkeys, the Mattaponis, and some of the Rappahannock River tribes,
probably including the Chiskiacks, though not the Rappahannocks themselves.[12] It is doubtful that by this time the mamanatowick actually thought
he could induce the invaders to leave by attacking them. However, a rumor
among the Tassantassas said that he had heard about the outbreak of civil war
in England and had decided to strike while that government was in disarray
and unable to help its battered subjects across the Atlantic.[13] That rumor could
well have been accurate. It is just as likely, though, that in his extreme old age
and with his people's resentment against the encroaching, abrasive aliens
ready to boil over, Opechancanough wanted to organize one last, grand
protest against the disruption of his entire world.

Few or none of the foreigners realized at the time exactly why the native
people were making this strike. For them, it was just one more proof that the
Powhatans were a treacherous people. It required someone who was personally

friendly with the local people to see even part of their side of things, even if he did not agree with it. Such a person was Robert Beverley, who wrote in 1705 after years of working with Chickahominy and Mattaponi people: "The subtle Indians, who took all advantages, resented the encroachments upon them by his [then-governor Harvey's] grants. They saw the English uneasy and disunited among themselves, and by the direction of Opechancanough their king, laid the ground-work of another massacre."[14] That was the closest thing to comprehension that the native people would get for three more centuries.

Once again, Opechancanough's forces struck in the spring (on April 18).[15] Once more the phase of the moon was irrelevant (being in the same between-phase as before),[16] and the priests probably used their divination ritual to set the date, which was then relayed to the loyalist districts in the traditional manner. Once again, the women and children were safely out in the remnants of their foraging territories, having planted their first fields of the year. Yet again, the Tassantassas were caught off guard, and many of them were killed by "friends" who had appeared on their doorsteps that morning. A large number of prisoners were taken this time,[17] presumably to use as hostages held for ransom.

This Assault, however, had an immediate aftermath different from the first one. Instead of following up the attack at least by sniping maneuvers, Opechancanough's forces withdrew into the forest altogether—against his orders, if the one chronicler of the proceedings can be believed. The Weyanocks and a faction of the Nansemonds fled their homeland altogether, the former group going as far south as the Roanoke River in what is now North Carolina. When Opechancanough sent for them, they killed the messengers. The two groups never returned to their James River homelands.[18]

If all the reported withdrawals did actually take place, then for the mamanatowick's subjects the Assault was even more of a symbolic gesture than it was for him, possibly because of the generation gap mentioned earlier: their youth prevented them from remembering a time when their country was really theirs.

The Strangers gathered themselves up and began fighting back, as everyone knew this time that they would. They took the fight directly to Pamunkey that summer, where they were apparently unsuccessful (it is more likely that Opechancanough and his tribesmen withdrew than that they repulsed the enemy). They raided native towns the next fall, and in the following winter, after discussing war against the Rappahannock River towns, they approached the Rappahannocks about joining their forces.[19] They also established new forts at strategic—and intrusive—places: one "on Pamunkey" (far up the river, on the south side), one at the falls of the James, and one "on the ridge of Chickahominy" (on the uplands overlooking the river, somewhere west of Diascund Creek).[20] These in turn became staging points for the raids on native towns that took place in July 1645, in which the Chickahominies lost their last town, Oraniock (Warreny), and moved northward to the Mattaponi River. The townsmen lost numerous adults and children in the raids. The prisoners over age eleven were taken by ship to "the Western Island" (identification uncertain) to prevent their rejoining their people; no record exists of their ever returning home. More attacks on the towns were made in late summer or fall in a barrage that must, to Opechancanough and his people, have seemed never to cease.[21] The foreigners now had so many people able to go on campaigns![22]

In the spring of 1646, another new fort, this one at the falls of the Appomattox River, interfered with the Appamattucks' fishing, as it was intended to do. It also became a staging point for raids against the "Nansemonds" (the hostile faction of them, which lived not far away). But at the same time, with Opechancanough's people all being dispersed to go foraging as usual at that season of cattapeuk, the Tassantassas sent emissaries suggesting a peace.[23] The paramount chief would have seen it as the ruse it was: at that season the enemy could not get at his people any other way.

Sometime that summer the Tassantassa governor himself (Sir William Berkeley) led one last attack on Pamunkey and captured Opechancanough, then aged "upon 100 years old." Because nearly all the contemporary records were destroyed in the nineteenth century, the earliest account is Robert Beverley's, written fifty-nine years later, in which oral tradition may have been included with the history.[24] According to Beverley, the mamanatowick "was now grown so decrepit, that he was not able to walk alone; but was carried about by his men. . . . His flesh was all macerated, his sinews slackened, and his eyelids [epicanthic folds over the eyelids] so heavy, that he could not see, but as they were lifted up by his servants."[25] He was "some distance from his usual habitation" when the governor and a mounted party heard of his presence, intercepted him, and made a quick capture.

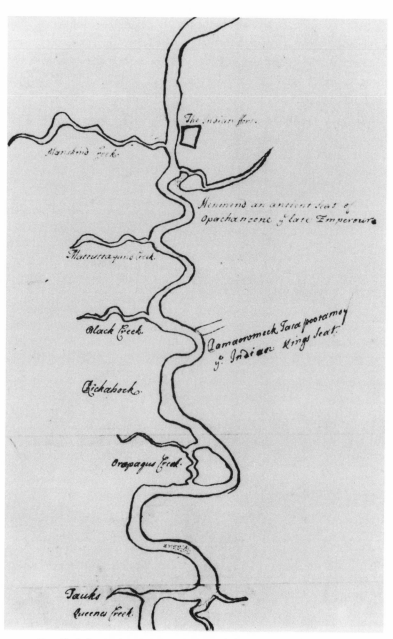

Detail of the Anthony Langston map of the York River, ca. 1662.
(Photo courtesy, Virginia Department of Historic Resources)

The prisoner was taken to Jamestown and kept in close confinement, although "at the governor's command, he was treated with all the respect and tenderness imaginable." Not all the jailors were of that mind, however. One of them shot him in the back, giving him a mortal wound. Before that, though, he had remained his usual feisty self. He had been an object of great curiosity, for flocks of aliens crowded in to see their former nemesis. Beverley described the helpless old man hearing the commotion, having a jailor hold up his eye folds, seeing the gawkers, and angrily sending for the governor. When the governor arrived, the captive mamanatowick "scornfully told him, that had it been his fortune to take Sir William Berkeley prisoner, he should not meanly have exposed him as a show to the people." Yet remembering how he himself had handled John Smith back in 1607, we may wonder if one last time, Opechancanough was not trying to score a point against his enemies.

Epilogue

THE WAR AGAINST the Tassantassas, already waning, collapsed after Opechancanough's death. By fall a new mamanatowick named Necotowance was in place, and he had agreed to a treaty that subjected all the native people of Virginia—including chiefdoms no longer within the paramount chiefdom, like the Rappahannocks—to the king of England. Another English reservation was set up, consisting of the main Virginia peninsula and the riverfront across the James River, but the boundaries of that reservation would be smashed in 1649 and the Real People flooded out thereafter. They did not die out, however. Their descendants survived, eventually adapted to their smaller land base, and remained—as Native Americans—among the law-abiding citizens of Virginia.[1] Opechancanough's successors ruled the Pamunkeys until the early eighteenth century, when a more general council of elders took their place. The Pamunkeys and their neighbors the Mattaponis still have reservation land, which they own in common while living on usufruct plots, in the traditional Powhatan manner.

The reputations of the three subjects of this biography have gone in divergent directions since their deaths, just as their careers went in such different directions after the founding of Jamestown. The image of Powhatan has changed the least: for four centuries he has been remembered as the father of Pocahontas and as the formidable "emperor" of Tsenacomoco, even though—or perhaps because—the coming of the foreigners eventually caused the eclipse of himself and his successors. He was the established leader whose threat proved to be temporary, when the "right" side prevailed. He wanted to go into a peaceful retirement, and he did so, along with his reputation.

On the other hand, Opechancanough is hardly remembered today. He had a fairly bright future in his youth, as the second in line for the paramount chief's position. It was his tragedy that by the time he even achieved de facto power, the foreigners had gained a very solid foothold in his brother's country, and it would be downhill from there. Making the best of it, he was in fact both a charming diplomat and a great "resistance leader."[2] He appears in the history books as a doggedly hostile man who was ultimately a failure. He undoubtedly did bring more trouble to his beleaguered people. By Robert Beverley's time his memory was so unpopular with the conquerors of Tsenacomoco that the native people had disowned him: "They say he was a prince of a foreign nation, and came to them a great way from the southwest, and by their accounts we suppose him to have come from the Spanish Indians."[3] I cited that oral tradition in chapter 2 to indicate that Opechancanough's (and Powhatan's) father may have come from among the Carolina Iroquoian speakers. If the Real People let Beverley believe that Spanish territories were meant, and if they still retained any feelings like those the Chickahominies had in 1614, namely, that the Spanish "name is odious among them,"[4] then the insult to Opechancanough's memory would have been deep indeed. Yet that distancing from him made them seem a less threatening minority to the conquerors, increasing their chances of survival as a people, so it was worth it.

Pocahontas, the girl who would never be chief and whose fate was altered the most by the coming of the foreigners, proved to be a flash in the pan, for though she eventually mingled with English high society, she was not vividly remembered in either Virginia or England after she died. She was not a celebrity during her lifetime, and after her seven-days' wonder experience in England, people lost interest in her except as the exception to the general rule (until the late eighteenth century) of native people who rejected Christianity. Even John Smith's embroidered accounts of her in his *Generall Historie*—the only published eyewitness source from early Virginia that was available to readers for 225 years—did not make her any more than a footnote to the scenario of supposedly heroic, righteous colonists conquering the "wilderness." At least readers' attitudes toward her were positive, unlike their feelings toward her father and uncle. But that was because she was a convert,

with all that such a decision represents: joining one group and forsaking another. For the people she had joined, she was a "savage" who had "seen the
light." For her own people, including the modern Virginia tribes, she left
mixed feelings behind.

Modern Americans' "knowledge" of Pocahontas is based upon what could
well be called a movement to canonize her that began in the 1830s. The people
behind it were southerners intent—correctly, in my view, if only they hadn't
overdone it—upon counteracting a still-popular opinion that American history began with the Pilgrims in Massachusetts in 1620. These writers pointed
out that the Jamestown colony was older, which it was by thirteen years. But
then they seized upon the exaggerated account of Pocahontas's doings in
Smith's book (William Strachey's more temperate view of her and her people
was not available until 1849), and they used her inflated relationship with John
Smith to attract readers' attention to an American story that took place before the Pilgrims landed on Plymouth Rock. Not coincidentally, in the 1830s
it became a plus rather than a minus to be descended from the now "royal"
lady, so that her many descendants—if they knew they were such—no longer
needed to be ashamed of being not wholly white. And on and on the legend
went, blossoming out in all directions and culminating in the truly fantasti-
cal Disney cartoon of 1995.[5] The lady has been mythologized out of all recognition. And that mythologizing is what most books about Pocahontas really
discuss, for historical records about her are scarce.

Professional scholars have not always done much better in presenting these
three people in a realistic light as human beings instead of stereotypes, until
the 1980s.[6] The difficulty is that reconstructing the lives of persons who lived
in a different time and in a different culture—one that did not leave the
records—demands training in two academic fields, not one: history and anthropology; in combination, called ethnohistory. Few scholars want to spend
the extra time and money to tackle a double load. But that is what it takes even
to have a chance of accurately reconstructing the lives of people who lived in
such different circumstances. The reality may not be as romantic as the myths.
But the people themselves, especially a sparkling personality like Pocahontas,
can then have a chance to come alive once more.

APPENDIX A

Annual Comings and Goings of Powhatan People

Ongoing things that took people out of town daily, year-round:

MEN: hunting for fresh meat, visiting fish weirs
WOMEN: gathering firewood, getting drinking water

Completion of the year was at "the fall of the leaf" at the coming of really cold weather; that meant the new year began anywhere from mid-December to early January.

Mid-December to mid-March (*popanow*, "winter")

Season of limited food available anywhere, so people lived mainly on stored food

MEN: in and out: intensive hunting of migratory waterfowl
WOMEN: in and out: major time for gathering now-dry reeds, cordage plants

Mid-March through April (*cattapeuk*, "spring")

Season of runs of anadromous fish; sap rising in trees made optimum season for cutting bark for house coverings

MEN: in and out: intensive fishing; clearing new fields for women
WOMEN: in and out: gathering saplings, bark (or making mats) for house building; early planting

May to whenever green corn was available
(*cohattayough,* "the earing of their corn")

Main season of planting. Stored foods were gone, so major food was wild tuckahoe tubers from marshes

M E N : mostly out: sturgeon runs continuing in May; hunting, other fishing
W O M E N : mostly out: foraging for tubers, greens, and berries, when not back in town planting and weeding

August (in a good year) to mid-October (*nepinough,* "the harvest")

Season of living on fresh garden crops

M E N : in and out: hunting, fishing, some helping with harvest
W O M E N : mainly in town, harvesting crops; later, gathering nuts

Mid-October to mid-December (*taquitock,* "fall of leaf ")

Season of intensive collecting of wild foods to store for winter

M E N : mostly out: intensive communal deer hunts
W O M E N : mostly out: nutting, processing deer carcasses to take home

Note: In a drought year *nepinough* would be late or would not occur at all. And after two or more consecutive drought years (e.g., 1607–12), many of the wild food plants—those with shallow roots that did not reach the receding water table—would not be available. Hence John Smith's emphasis on tuckahoe, which grows along streams and has very deep roots. It is one of the most drought-resistant nonwoody plants in the region.

Sources: Based on seasonal foods described in Smith 1986b [1612]: 147, 153, 155–56, 162–63; Strachey 1953 [1612]: 79–80; Haile 1998: 636–37; with additions found only in Strachey 1953 [1612]: 121, 127; Haile 1998: 678, 684. Completion of year: Strachey 1953 [1612]: 72; Haile 1998: 630.

APPENDIX B

Leaders Who Dealt with One Another

Powhatan *Mamanatowicks* (Great Chiefs)

Before 1596–April 1618	Wahunsenacawh (Powhatan)
April 1618–winter 1629–30	Opitchapam/Itoyatin or Otiotan
Winter 1629–30–1646	Opechancanough

Virginia Colony's Leaders

Presidents (unless otherwise noted) of the council (under the first charter):

May 13–September 10, 1607	Edward Maria Wingfield
September 10, 1607–September 10, 1608	Capt. John Ratliffe
September 10, 1608–September 1609	Capt. John Smith
September 1609–June 10, 1610	George Percy (Acting Pres.)

Governors (unless otherwise noted) of the colony (under subsequent charters):

June 10, 1610–March 28, 1611	Thomas West, Baron De La Warre
March 28, 1611–May 19, 1611	George Percy (Deputy Gov.)
May 19, 1611–August 2, 1611	Sir Thomas Dale (Deputy Gov.)
August 2, 1611–March 1612	Sir Thomas Gates (Acting Gov.)
March 1612–June 1616	Sir Thomas Dale (Acting Gov.)
June 1616–April 1617	Sir George Yeardley (Deputy Gov.)
April 9, 1617–April 9, 1619	Capt. Samuel Argall (Deputy Gov.)
April 9–19, 1619	Capt. Nathaniel Powell (Senior Councillor)
April 19, 1619–November 18, 1621	Sir George Yeardley
November 18, 1621–March 1626	Sir Francis Wyatt

Governors of the colony (royal rule beginning in 1624):

March 1626–November 1627	Sir George Yeardley (Deputy Gov. till April 19, 1626)
November 14, 1627–March 5, 1628	Capt. Francis West
March 5, 1628–March 1630	Dr. John Pott
March 1630–April 1635(?)	Sir John Harvey
April 28, 1635(?)–April 2, 1636	Capt. John West
April 2, 1636–November 1639	Sir John Harvey
November 1639–February 1642	Sir Francis Wyatt
February 1642–June 1644	Sir William Berkeley
June 1644–June 1645	Richard Kemp (Acting Gov.)
June 1645–April 1652	Sir William Berkeley

NOTES

Introduction

1. See, for instance, the "Who's Who" section of the Introduction to Haile's collection (1998: 42–67), which is not exhaustive.

2. Strachey: Culliford 1965. Smith: (among others) Barbour 1964. Much of the literature about Smith—and Pocahontas, for that matter—is about literature rather than history.

3. Strictly ethnohistorical reconstruction of the culture, based on eyewitness accounts: Rountree 1989. Reconstruction of Powhatan's political power based on ethnographic analogy with chiefdoms around the world: Rountree 1993a. Reconstruction of people's activities as travelers: Rountree 1993b. Reconstruction of women's lives based on history, living history, and ethnobotany: Rountree 1998. Reconstruction of people's use of ecological zones available in the region: Rountree 1996 and parts of Rountree and Davidson 1997.

4. Judging by the angry words she tossed at him when they met in England in 1617 (see chap. 14).

5. Based upon the Powhatan's language's sound system and grammar, as reconstructed by linguist Frank T. Siebert (1975). Instead of stringing separate words together, as English does, the Powhatan language tended to add syllables to stem words, making many-syllabled words and names. Although they were reluctant to use Englishmen's surnames (Strachey 1953 [1612]: 86; Haile 1998: 643), lacking the concept themselves, they could have felt that Smith's one-syllable first name was insufficient.

1. Setting the Scene

1. Tsenacomoco: Strachey 1953 [1612]: 56; Haile 1998: 613. Strachey's statement (1953 [1612]: 40; Haile 1998: 601) that the people "are conceived not to have inhabited here below much more in [than] 300 years" was probably gathered from the

Patawomecks through Henry Spelman. Archaeologists currently see their Potomac Creek ceramics (though not necessarily all the people themselves) as having come down from the Maryland piedmont ca. A.D. 1350 (Rountree and Turner 2002: 58–59). No similar tradition was recorded south of Potomac River.

2. Women using all parts of tribal territories: Rountree 1998. English marveling at their ability: Smith 1986b [1612]: 164; Strachey 1953 [1612]: 82; Haile 1998: 639.

3. A. White 1910 [1634] 40. This description is very probably exaggerated (Grace Brush, personal communication 2004). Smith 1986b [1612]: 162; not in Haile.

4. Strachey 1953 [1612]:79; Haile 1998: 637.

5. My own personal experience, thanks to the staffs of Jamestown Settlement near Williamsburg and the Mariners' Museum in Newport News.

6. Smith 1986a [1608]: 73; Haile 1998: 170.

7. Epidemics' lesser mortality: Alfred Crosby, personal communication 1991. Health status: Ubelaker 1993. Health status and lesser proneness to contagious disease: Ubelaker and Curtin 2001: 128–32.

8. Strachey 1953 [1612]: 79–80, 125–26; Haile 1998: 637, 682.

9. Alfred Crosby, personal communication 1991.

10. Smith 1986b [1612]: 116; Strachey 1953 [1612]: 77–78; Haile 1998: 635.

11. Learned from a runaway: W. White 1969 [1608?]: 145–46; Haile 1998: 141.

12. Smith 1986b [1612]: 159.

13. Names of seasons: ibid., 158; Strachey 1953 [1612]: 124; Haile 1998: 680.

14. Kecoughtan: Strachey 1953 [1612]: 67; Haile 1998: 626. Accomac: John Pory, in Smith 1986c [1624]: 291.

15. Smith 1986b [1612]: 156–57.

16. *Taquitock* completing the year: Strachey 1953 [1612]: 72; Haile 1998: 630.

17. Stahle et al. 1998: fig. 3-B.

18. Rountree 1998.

19. Bridenbaugh 1967: 91–98, 210, 355, 384–85.

20. Rountree 1990: chap. 7.

21. Stahle et al. 1998: 565 and fig. 3-B.

22. Smith 1986b [1612]: 162–63; Strachey 1953 [1612]: 80; Haile 1998: 637.

2. The VIP Lifestyle

1. Smith 1986b [1612]: 174; Strachey 1953 [1612]: 59; Haile 1998: 617.

2. For a more detailed definition of "chief," see Rountree 1993a.

3. Smith 1986c [1624]: 151 (work); Strachey 1953 [1612]: 56 (addressing him); Haile 1998: 239, 614.

4. For detailed analyses of his powers and influence, with some comparisons with others elsewhere in the world, see Rountree 1989: Epilogue, and Rountree and Turner 1998 and 1999.

5. Spelman, 1910 [1613?]: cxi; Purchas 1617: 955; Haile 1998: 491–92, 882.

6. Smith 1986b [1612]: 169–70; Strachey 1953 [1612]: 95; Haile 1998: 652.

7. Smith 1986b [1612]: 165; Strachey 1953 [1612]: 104; Haile 1998: 662. For a detailed analysis of Powhatan warfare, see Gleach 1997.

8. Williamson 2003: chaps. 4, 5.

9. Clayton 1965 [1687]: 23.

10. For specifics, with very detailed references pieced together, see Rountree 1989: 108.

11. Smith 1986b [1612]: 168; Strachey 1953 [1612]: 85; Haile 1998: 642. The identities of such women were never recorded.

12. For specifics, with very detailed references, see Rountree 1989: 102–9.

13. Smith 1986b [1612]: 173; Strachey 1953 [1612]: 80; Haile 1998: 637.

14. For a description, with photos (including a close-up of the embroidery on "Powhatan's Mantle"), see Rountree and Turner 2002: 115–19.

15. Rountree 1993: 47–49.

16. For more specifics, with detailed references, see Rountree 1989: 113.

17. Smith 1986b [1612]: 247; Smith 1986c [1624]: 196; Strachey 1953 [1612]: 77; Haile 1998: 299, 634.

18. Strachey 1953 [1612]: 64; Haile 1998: 622.

3. Introducing the Chiefly Family

1. Nyack Indians: Denton 1937 [1670]: 9. Strachey 1953 [1612]: 116; Haile 1998: 673.

2. Bridenbaugh 1981.

3. Archivo General de Indias, Seville: Contratación 5167, bk. 1, fols. 112–12v, cited in Hoffman 1990: 184.

4. Lewis and Loomie 1953: 36.

5. Hamor 1957 [1615] 13; Haile 1998: 811.

6. Either by an uncle's adoption, or in a kinship terminology system—the Powhatan one was not recorded—in which the father's brothers and (in some systems) also the mother's brothers were called and treated as "fathers."

7. Lewis and Loomie 1953: 16.

8. Sixty: Smith 1986b [1612]: 173. Eighty: Strachey 1953 [1612]: 57; Haile 1998: 615. Exaggerated: Purchas 1617: 957; Haile 1998: 884.

9. Strachey 1953 [1612]: 68; Haile 1998: 627.

10. Anonymous 1947 [1649]: 7.

11. Ruling: Lewis and Loomie 1953: 44; location: ibid., 38–39. See also Appendix A.

12. Beverley 1947 [1705]: 61.

13. Turner 1993: 84–88. See also Rountree and Turner 2002: 42–44.

14. Roanoke simple-stamped. Found at the Governor's Land Site (a Paspahegh village): Luccketti et al. n.d.: 193; most of the sherds found were of the more general Townsend series.

15. Strachey 1953 [1612]: 112; Spelman 1910 [1613?]: cvii; Haile 1998: 669–70, 488.

16. Rountree 199b: 51.

17. Two sisters: Smith 1986a [1608]: 61; Haile 1998: 164. Two sisters, two daughters: Smith 1986b [1612]: 247; Haile 1998: 299.

18. Smith 1986b [1612]: 256; Smith 1986c [1624]: 205; Haile 1998: 311.

19. Smith 1986a [1608]: 75; Haile 1998: 171.

20. Smith 1986a [1608]: 77; Haile 1998: 172.

21. The brother was named Chopoke; two creeks, an old plantation, and now a state park in his old territory still bear his name, corrupted to "Chippokes." Young chief: Strachey 1953 [1612]: 64; Haile 1998: 622.

22. Beverley 1947 [1705]: 61; brackets mine.

23. Smith 1986b [1612]: 173.

24. Strachey 1953 [1612]: 57–58; Haile 1998: 615.

25. Hunting: Smith 1986b [1612]: 165; Strachey 1953 [1612]: 83; Haile 1998: 640. Women: Strachey 1953 [1612]: 84; Haile 1998: 840–41.

26. Smith 1986b [1612]: 164; Strachey 1953 [1612]: 83–84; Haile 1998: 640.

27. Hairdo: Smith 1986b [1612]: 161. Hairdo and hair length: Strachey 1953 [1612]: 74; Haile 1998: 632.

28. Smith 1986b [1612]: 161; Strachey 1953 [1612]: 74; Haile 1998: 632; brackets mine.

29. Strachey 1953 [1612]: 33 (falls), 57 (frontier); Haile 1998: 595, 614.

30. Strachey 1953 [1612]: 61–62; Spelman (the interpreter) 1910 [1613?]: cvii–cviii; Haile 1998: 618–20, 488–89.

31. Strachey 1953 [1612]: 62; Haile 1998: 620.

32. Strachey 1953 [1612]: 64–65; Haile 1998: 622.

33. Smith 1986a [1608]: 63; Smith 1986c [1624]: 151; Haile 1998: 166, 240; brackets mine.

34. Hamor 1957 [1615]: 42; Haile 1998: 834.

35. "A child of twelve or thirteen years" in December 1608: Smith 1986c [1624]: 258; Haile 1998: 861. "Ten years old" in May 1608: Smith 1986a [1608]: 93; Haile 1998: 181. "11 or 12 years" in 1608: Strachey 1953 [1612]: 72; Haile 1998: 630. "Not past 13 or 14 years of age": Smith 1986b [1612]: 274; Haile 1998: 336.

36. Short: "being of so great a spirit, however her stature": Smith 1986c [1624]: 260; Haile 1998: 863. Portrait: published in many places, including Haile 1998: 852.

37. Henry Norwood would write in 1649, "The queens . . . do esteem it a privilege to serve their husbands in all kinds of cookery, which they would be as loth to lose, as any Christian queen would be to take it from them" (1947 [1650]: 37).

38. Strachey 1953 [1612]: 86; Haile 1998: 643.

39. Dr. Donna Boyd, personal communication, 1995.

40. Strachey 1953 [1612]: 72; Haile 1998: 630–31.

41. Date: deduced from Strachey's saying she had married two years before he wrote his 1612 book (1953 [1612]: 62; Haile 1998: 620). Girls normally became mar-

riageable when their breasts became large enough (Strachey delicately called it *sororians virgo:* 1953 [1612]: 113; Haile 1998: 670) and definitely marriageable when they began menstruating.

42. Strachey 1953 [1612]: 72; Haile 1998: 630.

43. Hairdos: Strachey 1953 [1612]: 114; Haile 1998: 672. George Percy wrote more tersely that "the Maids shave their heads all but the hinder part" (1969 [1608?]): 146; Haile 1998: 137). Shaving: Smith 1986b [1612]: 160; Strachey 1953 [1612]: 73; Haile 1998: 631. Irish: Strachey 1953 [1612]: 114; Haile 1998: 672.

44. Virginia: Strachey 1953 [1612]: 73; Haile 1998: 631; first brackets Haile's, second mine. Carolina: Hulton 1984: 63, 65, 67, 77.

45. Machumps, brother of Winganuske: Strachey 1953 [1612]: 62; Haile 1998: 620.

46. Strachey 1953 [1612]: 113; Haile 1998: 671.

47. Strachey 1953 [1612]: 72; Haile 1998: 630.

48. Nancy O. Lurie, personal communication, 1972.

49. Strachey 1953 [1612]: 60; Haile 1998: 617.

4. Expanding His Dominions

1. Smith 1986b [1612]: 173; Strachey 1953 [1612]: 57; Haile 1998: 615.

2. For a summary of what is known about them in the Early Contact period, see Hantman 1990 and 1993. Summer: Lewis and Loomie 1953: 161. Fall: Archer 1969a [1607] 88: Haile 1998: 109.

3. Browne et al. 1883–1972: 3:403.

4. *Tayac:* Jesuit Letters 1910 [1639]: 125. *Tallac:* Speck 1927: 49. If all three cultures' terms were cognates, then that would indicate a common, considerably older origin for both the words and the political positions.

5. Appamattucks: the Bland expedition of 1649–50 and the 1669–70 Lederer expeditions, as well as the boundary line survey of 1708–11 (Bland et al. 1911 [1651]; Lederer 1958 [1672]; Byrd 1966). Weyanocks: Strachey 1953 [1612]: 56–57; Haile 1998: 614. Enoes: Blair A. Rudes, personal communication, 2004.

6. Pendergast suggested (1991) that they came from the Lake Erie region, but more recent archaeology shows people making Susquehannock ceramics living in and around the panhandles of Maryland and West Virginia in the late sixteenth and early seventeenth centuries (Susquehannock segment: Potter 1993: 175–76; identified as Massawomecks: Wayne E. Clark, personal communication 2004).

7. Smith 1986b [1612]: 232 (hatchets from French), 166 (birchbark canoes); Strachey 1953 [1612]: 108 (canoes only); Haile 1998: 268, 666.

8. Smith 1986b [1612]: 247; Smith 1986c [1624]: 196; Haile 1998: 299.

9. Martin Quitt also adds (1995: 239) that if epidemics had struck the Virginia natives after prior European visits, the survivors initially would have avoided the Jamestown newcomers rather than trying to befriend them.

10. Rountree 1993b.

11. Stahle et al. 1998: fig. 3-B.

12. Lewis and Loomie 1953: 39.

13. Smith 1986b [1612]: 266; Smith 1986c [1624]: 215; Haile 1998: 323.

14. Eastern Shore: Rountree and Davidson 1997: 41, 46, chap. 2. Hiring: Strachey 1953 [1612]: 68; Haile 1998: 627. North of river: Mook 1944: 200; Rountree 1989: 15. Methods: Strachey 1953 [1612]: 57; Haile 1998: 615.

15. Strachey 1953 [1612]: 68; Haile 1998: 627.

16. Smith 1986c [1624]: 175; Haile 1998: 275.

17. Strachey 1953 [1612]: 44; Haile 1998: 604.

18. Smith 1986b [1612]: 166; Strachey 1953 [1612]: 109; Haile 1998: 667.

19. Towns: Hulton 1984: 86; Smith n.d. [1612]. Enemies: Archer 1969a [1607]: 85; Haile 1998: 106. Destruction: Strachey 1953 [1612]: 104; Haile 1998: 662; italics and brackets mine. Repopulation: Strachey 1953 [1612]: 108; Haile 1998: 666. For a discussion of timing, according to both me and David B. Quinn, see Rountree 1990: 20–21.

20. Strachey 1953 [1612]: 68–69; Haile 1998: 627.

21. Fringe the Patawomecks may have been, but they were definitely part of Powhatan's organization. Powhatan is known to have visited both them and the more northerly Tauxenents in the last years of his life (see chap. 15), and Henry Spelman, who lived with both the *mamanatowick* and the Patawomecks, wrote that Powhatan would only "visit another King under him (for he goeth not out of his owne country" (Spelman 1910 [1613?]: cviii; Haile 1998: 489).

22. Strachey 1953 [1612]: 56; Haile 1998: 614.

23. Lewis and Loomie 1953: 38 ff. (settling), 44 (repatriating).

24. Ibid., 45–47. One later Spanish writer (ibid., 111–12) has a silver chalice supposedly given to "an important chief in the interior" who may have been Powhatan. Making presents of valuables was part of Native American tradition, but no English source mentions such a status symbol in Powhatan's possession.

25. Ibid., 50 (1571), 46 (1572), 52ff. (hostages).

26. "The Spaniards, whose name is odious among them": Hamor 1957 [1615]: 13; Haile 1998: 811.

27. Lewis and Loomie 1953: 56.

28. Quinn 1955: 244–46.

29. Hulton 1984: 86.

30. The Carolina Sounds Algonquian speakers initially took the foreigners' technology, their relative immunity to (European) diseases, and their lack of women as evidence that they were "not born of women" (Hariot 1955 [1588]: 379–80). Martin Quitt has hinted (1995: 234) that the Powhatans may have considered that possibility as well. However, the presence of women and children in the "Lost Colony" and the aftermath of their abandonment would soon have dispelled any such notion in any native people who heard about them.

31. For a detailed discussion of these two different scenarios, see Rountree 1990: 21–23.

32. Strachey 1953 [1612]: 91; Haile 1998: 648.

33. Bows: Smith 1986b [1612]: 164; Strachey 1953 [1612]: 109; Haile 1998: 667. 100 yards: Greg Schneck, armorer at Jamestown Settlement Museum, speaking from extensive hands-on experience: personal communication, 2003. 300 yards: Featherstone 1998: 46–47, 59.

34. Smith 1986a [1608]: 89; Haile 1998: 179.

35. Strachey 1953 [1612]: 74–76 (expanded from Smith 1986b [1612]: 160); Haile 1998: 633–34.

36. Strachey 1953 [1612]: 85–86; Haile 1998: 642–43.

5. Watching from a Distance

1. Strachey 1953 [1612]: 105, also pp. 58–59; Haile 1998: 663, also pp. 615–16.

2. Percy 1969 [1608?]: 133; Smith 1986a [1608]: 27; Haile 1998: 90, 145. Percy has the attackers driven off by the ship's large guns; Smith has them "little respect[ing]" the guns and leaving when they had run out of arrows.

3. Percy 1969 [1608?]: 133–36; Haile 1998: 90–92.

4. Percy 1969 [1608?]: 136–37; Haile 1998: 92–93.

5. Smith 1986a [1608]: 51; Haile 1998: 160.

6. They left the impression that the district was called "Rappahannock"; that this was a mistake was found out later, but the name persisted in English usage (Strachey 1953 [1612]: 64; Haile 1998: 622).

7. Percy 1969 [1608?]: 137–38; Haile 1998: 93–94.

8. Compare the postholes from Jamestown Fort (Rountree and Turner 2002: 141) with those of a native one (ibid., 46, or see John White's illustration of Pomeioc, published in many places).

9. Percy 1969 [1608?]: 139; Haile 1998: 94–95.

10. Archaeologists have found a large amount of native-made pottery inside the bounds of Jamestown's fort; see Rountree and Turner 2002: chap. 4.

11. Probably the small unnamed village just upriver from Jamestown, i.e., not the district capital where Wowinchopunck lived.

12. Percy 1969 [1608?]: 139–40; Haile 1998: 95–96.

13 Archer 1969a [1607]: 81–95; Percy 1969 [1608?]: 140–41; Haile 1998: 102–15, 96–97.

14. Smith 1986a [1608]: 91; Strachey 1953 [1612]: 56–57; Haile 1998: 180, 614—Weyanocks. See chap. 4 for Appamattucks serving as guides later in the century.

15. Percy 1969 [1608?]: 140; Haile 1998: 96. The English probably did ask about this boy, because they had been ordered to inquire for the Roanoke colonists. There is no other mention of this part-European in the surviving records.

16. Archer 1969 [1607]: 92; Haile 1998: 113.

17. Smith 1986a [1608]: 31, 51; Haile 1998: 147, 159.

18. Archer 1969a [1607]: 94–95; Smith 1986a [1608]: 31, 33; Haile 1998: 114–15, 147.

19. Archer 1969a [1607]: 97–98; Haile 1998: 117.

20. Strachey 1953 [1612]: 67; Haile 1998: 625.

21. Corn: Percy 1969 [1608?]: 142; Haile 1998: 98. Drought: Stahle et al. 1998. Taunting: Archer 1969a [1607]: 98; Haile 1998: 117–18. Overtures: Smith 1986a [1608]: 33; Wingfield 1969 [1608]: 214–15; Haile 1998: 148, 184–85. Peace: Wingfield 1969 [1608]: 215–16; Percy 1969 [1608?]: 143; Haile 1998: 185–86, 98.

22. Smith 1986a [1608]: 35; Haile 1998: 148.

23. Wingfield 1969 [1608]: 216; Haile 1998: 186.

24. Percy 1969 [1608?]: 144; Smith 1986a [1608]: 33; Wingfield 1969 [1608]: 215; Haile 1998: 98–99, 148, 185.

25. Percy 1969 [1608?]: 143; Smith 1986a [1608]: 35; Smith 1986b [1612]: 210; Smith 1986c [1624]: 143; Haile 1998: 98, 148–49, 231.

26. Earle 1979: 103.

27. Percy 1969 [1608?]: 143; Perkins 1969 [1608]: 159–60; Haile 1998: 98, 133.

28. Probably nowhere near the 80 percent estimated by Strachey (1953 [1612]: 87; Haile 1998: 644), since no contemporary source mentions enough storage buildings connected with Powhatan to hold that much corn.

29. Smith 1986a [1608]: 37; Smith 1986b [1612]: 211; Smith 1986c [1624]: 144–45; Haile 1998: 149–50, 231–32. The 1624 version has Smith's party being taunted, at which they charged ashore and scattered the townsmen. Shortly afterward, sixty or seventy men attacked, bearing the image from their temple. A round of gunfire dispersed them, and Smith ransomed the image for corn. Exciting, but probably imaginary. Especially because Kecoughtan had only twenty or thirty fighting men (Smith 1986a [1608]: 146; Strachey 1953 [1612]: 68; Haile 1998: 627).

30. Smith 1986a [1608]: 37, 39; Haile 1998: 150–51.

31. Smith 1986a [1608]: 39, 41, 43; Haile 1998: 151, 154–55.

32. Worked out on USGS topographic maps by E. R. Turner III and me in 2003.

33. Smith 1986b [1612]: 164; Strachey 1953 [1612]: 83; Haile 1998: 640.

34. Smith 1986a [1608]: 47; Smith 1986c [1624]: 146; Haile 1998: 156–57, 235.

35. Smith 1986a [1608]: 89, 91; Haile 1998: 179.

6. Meeting a Captive Englishman

1. Smith 1986a [1608]: 45; Smith 1986c [1624]: 146; Haile 1998: 156, 234. The 1608 version has Smith going off to explore; the 1624 one says he was hunting for food for the men.

2. Worked out on USGS topographic maps by E. Randolph Turner III and me in 2003.

3. Smith 1986a [1608]: 45, 47; Smith 1986b [1612]: 212–13; Smith 1986c [1624]:

146–47; Haile 1998: 156–57, 234–35. 1608: holding off a handful of men with his pistol, without injury, until surrounded by 200 men. 1612 version: holding off 200 men with his pistol, without injury, until he became immobilized in a bog. 1624 version: holding off 300 men, sustaining several injuries, and sinking into the mud, after which he still held off his tormentors until he became too numb with cold.

4. Smith 1986c [1624]: 100; Haile 1998: 238: "They imagined the world to be flat and round like a trencher, and they in the middest."

5. Smith's 1624 account identifies it as Orapax, but that town did not exist until 1609.

6. Smith 1986a [1608]: 47, 49; Smith 1986c [1624]: 147–48; Haile 1998: 157–58, 235–36.

7. Percy 1969 [1608]: 136; Haile 1998: 92.

8. Smith 1986a [1608]: 49; Haile 1998: 158.

9. Smith 1986c [1624]: 148; Haile 1998: 236.

10. Smith 1986a [1608]: 49; Smith 1986c [1624]: 148–49; Haile 1998: 158–59, 236–37.

11. Smith 1986b [1612]: 160, 165; Strachey 1953 [1612]: 76, 104; Haile 1998: 634, 662.

12. Smith 1986b [1612]: 163; Strachey 1953 [1612]: 113; Haile 1998: 670–72.

13. Smith would write later that he was conjured at Pamunkey, after his around-the-countryside tour, but his 1608 letter (Smith 1986a [1608]: 59; Haile 1998: 163) shows otherwise: "Three or four days after my taking, seven of them [came] to the house where I lay. . . . Each morning, in the coldest frost, the principal [men] . . . assembled themselves in a round circle a good distance from the town, where they told me they consulted where to hunt the next day."

14. Smith 1986a [1608]: 59; Smith 1986b [1612]: 170–71; Strachey 1953 [1612]: 96–97; Smith 1986c [1624]: 149–50; Haile 1998: 163, 653–54, 237–38.

15. Smith 1986a [1608]: 49; Smith 1986c [1624]: 148; Haile 1998: 159, 236–37. In the 1624 version Smith's assailant was father to another man, mortally wounded, which gave the captive to show some English superiority. He offered to send to Jamestown for "a water"—aqua vitae, or brandy—to cure the man. The offer was declined because of plans to assault Jamestown, even though Smith says immediately afterward that he was allowed to send a note to the fort about his welfare. Illogical.

16. Wingfield 1969 [1608]: 227; Smith 1986a [1608]: 51; Haile 1998: 195, 160.

17. Smith 1986a [1608]: 49, 51; Smith 1986c [1624]: 149; Haile 1998: 159–60, 237.

18. It is tempting to call that settlement Opechancanough's capital. However, Strachey (1953 [1612]: 69; Haile 1998: 628) got his information from Machumps, and he listed Pomiscutuck as the chief of that town.

19. Smith was definite about a high-ranking chief living there, although Strachey (ibid.) listed a nonentity, Ottondeacommoc, as chief of the town. The Youghtanund River is now called the Pamunkey.

20. Barbour 1986: 1:9.

21. Much of this part of the trek probably followed the route of a modern road, U.S. Highway 17, allowing for the straightening needed for a high-speed motorway. Old land patents speak of a trail along several parts of its route, and until one nears Tappahannock, the road shows its antiquity in staying far enough inland to avoid nearly all swampy creek headwaters. Before the advent of the automobile, no one (Indian or non-Indian) wanted to maintain bridges of any size, so the really old trails and roads run high and dry. Date: ibid.

22. Conversation with the site's owners, 2002.

23. Smith 1986a [1608]: 67; Haile 1998: 168; Rountree 1989: 79.

24. Smith 1986a [1608]: 63, 73; Haile 1998: 166, 170–71.

25. "The waterside, which was some thirty score from" Powhatan's house" (Smith 1986a [1608]: 69; Haile 1998: 169). Barbour 1986: 1:69 n. 175: "Probably referring to paces: 3,000 ft., or more than half a mile." I doubt that one pace equaled five feet back then, any more than it does now, so for 600 paces I prefer a distance of 1,800 feet instead.

26. "Some 100. some 200 foot square" (Strachey 1953 [1612]: 79; Haile 1998: 636).

27. Hamor 1957 [1615]: 44, 43; Haile 1998: 835.

28. Spelman 1910 [1613?]: cvi; Haile 1998: 487.

29. Smith 1986a [1608]: 53; Haile 1998: 160–61. Smith was less complimentary in 1624 (1986c: 150–51; Haile 1998: 239); and there was a delay while Powhatan got dressed (unlikely!), during which "more than two hundred of those grim courtiers" (that is too many) stared him down.

30. Hamor 1957 [1615]: 39–40; Haile 1998: 832.

31. Smith 1986a [1608]: 53, 55, 57; Haile 1998: 160–62.

32. Smith 1986c [1624]: 150–51; Haile 1998: 239–40.

33. Smith 1986c [1624]: 151; Haile 1998: 239; brackets Haile's.

34. Rasmussen and Tilton 1994: 18.

35. Barbour 1970: 24–25.

36. Rountree 1989: 80–81.

37. Smith 1986c [1624]: 41; Smith 1986d [1630]: 186–88, 200, 201.

38. Barbour 1986: xxix–liv.

39. Barbour 1971: 12–13.

40. Beverley 1947 [1705]: 29–30.

41. For a detailed discussion of how much distant geography Powhatan and his people knew, and how it fits with archaeologists' knowledge, see Rountree 1993b, Turner 1993, Hantman 1993, and Clark and Rountree 1993.

42. Smith 1986a [1608]: 53, 55, 57; Haile 1998: 161–62.

43. My father spent time in rural Haiti in the late 1930s, and I remember his stories of people there asking him that question.

44. Smith 1986b [1612]: 139; Haile 1998: 209.

45. Smith 1986b [1612]: 274; Haile 1998: 336.

46. Smith 1986c [1624]: 151; Haile 1998: 240.

47. One proceeded by canoe down and across the York River and up Queens Creek, then cut overland for four miles—through the site of modern Williamsburg—and then, if a canoe was waiting, down College Creek and up the James River to Jamestown Island. If there was no canoe available, the overland walk to Neck of Land would be another four miles or so.

48. Barbour 1986: 1:61n.

7. The Alliance's Creaky Beginning

1. Smith 1986c [1624]: 260; Haile 1998: 864.

2. Smith 1986b [1612]: 213 (not in Haile); Smith 1986c [1624]: 152; Haile 1998: 240.

3. Perkins, letter, p. 133; Smith 1986a [1608]: 61; Wingfield 1969 [1608]: 228; Haile 1998: 133, 134, 165, 196.

4. The Powhatan language, like Southern American English, had separate forms for second person singular and second person plural (Siebert 1975: 326).

5. Words from Strachey 1953 [1612]: 85–86; Haile 1998: 642–43.

6. Smith 1986a [1608]: 61; Perkins 1969 [1608]: 160; Smith 1986b [1612]: 215; Smith 1986c [1624]: 152; Haile 1998: 134, 165, 243, 241.

7. Smith 1986a [1608]: 61; Smith 1986b [1612]: 215; Smith 1986c [1624]: 154; Haile 1998: 165, 243. The 1612 and 1624 versions have Newport sending lavish presents to Powhatan, so that the invitation sprang mainly from greed. Newport, as captain of the shipping that brought the personnel over, was the leader of the Jamestown colonization effort only when he was on the spot.

8. Smith 1986a [1608]: 63; Smith 1986b [1612]: 215–16; Smith 1986c [1624]: 155; Haile 1998: 166, 243–44. The identity of the guides comes from Smith's letter.

9. Smith 1986a [1608]: 63; Smith 1986b [1612]: 215–16; Smith 1986c [1624]: 155; Haile 1998: 166, 243–44.

10. Smith 1986a [1608]: 65, 67; Haile 1998: 167. The conversation does not appear in Smith's later accounts.

11. Smith 1986a [1608]: 69; Smith 1986b [1612]: 216; Smith 1986c [1624]: 156; Haile 1998: 168, 245.

12. Smith 1986a [1608]: 69, 71, 73, 75; Smith 1986b [1612]: 216–17; Smith 1986c [1624]: 156; Haile 1998: 169–71, 245–46.

13. Some have been found by the APVA Jamestown Rediscovery archaeologists. Those that are unfaded, after four centuries in the ground, really are a gorgeous sky blue.

14. Rountree 1989: 71–75.

15. Smith 1986a [1608]: 75; Haile 1998: 171.

16. Smith 1986a [1608]: 75, 77; Haile 1998: 171.

17. Smith 1986a [1608]: 75, 77; Smith 1986b [1612]: 217; Smith 1986c [1624]: 156–57; Haile 1998: 171, 246.

18. Smith 1986b [1612]: 166–67; Strachey 1953 [1612]: 109–10; Haile 1998: 667–68.

19. Smith 1986a [1608]: 77; Haile 1998: 171–72.

20. Smith 1986a [1608]: 77, 79; Haile 1998: 172.

21. Smith 1986a [1608]: 79; Haile 1998: 172–73.

22. Status: Brown 1964 [1890]: 172, 246–47. Jamestown: Hamor 1957 [1615]: 38; Haile 1998: 831.

23. Smith 1986b [1612]: 235 and Smith 1986c [1624]: 283 (return), 350 (death); Hamor 1957 [1615]: 38 (Powhatan asking about him in 1614); Haile 1998: 281, 831. Account of death is in part of *Generall Historie* not included in Haile.

24. Smith 1986c [1624]: 290; Nugent 1934: 1:30.

25. Purchas 1617: 954; Haile 1998: 880; brackets mine.

8. Allies Who Did Not Behave like Allies

1. Smith 1986a [1608]: 79; Smith 1986b [1612]: 220; Smith 1986c [1624]: 259; Haile 1998: 173, 249–50.

2. Smith 1986a [1608]: 79, 81; Smith 1986c [1624]: 191; Haile 1998: 173–74, 275–77. I follow the 1608 account, written closer to the time. The 1624 version has apparently friendly guides leading them upriver into an ambush. The hostilities halted only when the newcomers seized the people's canoes (equivalent in use and value to our cars) and threatened to chop them up. A promise of part of the fall's harvest got the invaders to go away. The level of hostility and the promise extracted both seem exaggerated for that early in the alliance with Powhatan.

3. Smith 1986a [1608]: 63; Haile 1998: 165. The intended route was probably by canoe as far as possible: down the James, up the Nansemond, overland some distance heading south-southwest, down the Blackwater and then the Chowan, and then across the head of Albemarle Sound to the mouth of the Roanoke.

4. Teaching: Perkins 1969 [1608]: 160; Haile 1998: 134; brackets mine. Spanish: Brown 1964 [1890]: 572, 632–33. Liaisons: Strachey 1953 [1612]: 113; Haile 1998: 670. Any resulting children seem to have remained among their mothers' people, as far as the surviving records show. If the Powhatans had been matrilineal, as many other Woodland Indian people were, remaining in the mother's family would have been the rule.

5. Archer 1969b [167]: 103; Haile 1998: 123.

6. Smith 1986a [1608]: 81, 83; Smith 1986b [1612]: 220; Smith 1986c [1624]: 259; Haile 1998: 174–75, 250.

7. Smith 1986a [1608]: 81, 83; Haile 1998: 174–75.

8. Smith 1986a [1608]: 87, 89, 91; Haile 1998: 178–79.

9. Strachey 1953 [1612]: 64 (name of weroance), 62 (Amocis's death); Smith 1986a [1608]: 91, 93 (departure), 87 and 93 (spying); Haile 1998: 622, 619–20,

178–80. Smith's later writings differ in tone: Smith terrorized would-be thieves until the local people captured two "foraging, disorderly soldiers." When the captors came to the fort, demanding an exchange, Smith attacked them then and there, not in a Paspahegh village, forcing them to give up their English prisoners (Smith 1986b [1612]: 220–21; Smith 1986c [1624]: 159–60; Haile 1998: 250).

10. Smith 1986b [1612]: 220–21; Smith 1986c [1624]: 159–60; Haile 1998: 250.

11. Smith 1986a [1608]: 93, 95; Haile 1998: 181.

12. Rountree 1998.

13. Smith 1986b [1612]: 274; Strachey 1953 [1612]: 62; Haile 1998: 336, 620.

14. Strachey 1953 [1612]: 72; Haile 1998: 630.

15. Smith 1986c [1624]: 257; Haile 1998: 862.

16. Smith 1986b [1612]: 225; Smith 1986c [1624]: 164; Haile 1998: 255.

17. Smith 1986b [1612]: 228; Smith 1986c [1624]: 168; Haile 1998: 262; brackets mine.

18. Smith 1986b [1612]: 225; Smith 1986c [1624]: 164; Haile 1998: 255.

19. Smith 1986b [1612]: 224–33; Smith 1986c [1624]: 162–80; Haile 1998: 254–78.

20. Smith 1986c [1624]: 167; Haile 1998: 261.

21. Smith 1986b [1612]: 229; Smith 1986c [1624]: 169; Haile 1998: 263.

22. Smith 1986b [1612]: 230–31; Smith 1986c [1624]: 170–71; Haile 1998: 265–66.

23. Smith 1986c [1624]: 175; Haile 1998: 272.

24. Strachey 1953 [1612]: 44; Haile 1998: 604.

25. Stahle et al. 1998: fig. 3-B.

26. Smith 1986b [1612]: 233–35, 238; Smith 1986c [1624]: 180–82, 184; Haile 1998: 278–80, 283.

27. Smith 1986b [1612]: 235; Smith 1986c [1624]: 182–83; Haile 1998: 280–81.

28. Smith 1986b [1612]: 236; Smith 1986c [1624]: 183; Haile 1998: 281–82.

29. Gifts: Smith 1986b [1612]: 234; Smith 1986c [1624]: 181. Orapax: Spelman 1910 [1613?]: cv; Haile 1998: 279, 486.

30. Smith 1986b [1612]: 237; Smith 1986c [1624]: 184; Haile 1998: 282.

31. Records: Feest 1983. Maryland: Jesuit Letters 1910 [1638]: 125.

32. Upstreaming from the 1620s, when Fleet (1876 [1631–32]: 25) learned about them all.

33. Smith 1986b [1612]: 238; Smith 1986c [1624]: 184; Haile 1998: 283–84.

9. The Breakdown of the Alliance

1. My 1995–96 experiments with tuckahoe digging, assisted by muscular males from Jamestown Settlement and Old Dominion University, showed that the most efficient way to excavate the tubers is to sit next to the plant and guddle up the deep roots with both hands and both feet, plus a digging stick for leverage. Whether the tide is high or low, it is an incredibly wet, muddy job. No one in her right mind would want to do it in the cold months of the year.

2. Smith 1986b [1612]: 239–40; Smith 1986c [1624]: 186–86; Haile 1998: 286; brackets mine.

3. Smith 1986b [1612]: 239–40, 242; Smith 1986c [1624]: 186–87, 191–92; Haile 1998: 285, 287, 293–94.

4. The 1624 version has the Strangers shooting and setting a house on fire, which made the Nansemonds beg for peace and promise "to plant purposely for us." That is unlikely, because the native side in Virginia still had the upper hand.

5. Smith 1986b [1612]: 246–47; Smith 1986c [1624]: 195; Haile 1998: 298–99.

6. Smith 1986b [1612]: 244–45; Smith 1986c [1624]: 193; Haile 1998: 296.

7. Smith 1986b [1612]: 265–66; Smith 1986c [1624]: 215; Haile 1998: 323.

8. Smith 1986b [1612]: 245; Smith 1986c [1624]: 194; Haile 1998: 297.

9. Smith 1986b [1612]: 245; Smith 1986c [1624]: 194; Haile 1998: 297.

10. Valuable: for childbearing and for farming and the other necessary work that was their province. Hence the region's wars being not "for lands or goods, but for women and children, and principally for revenge" (Smith 1986b [1612]: 165; Strachey 1953 [1612]: 104; Haile 1998: 662).

11. Strachey 1953 [1612]: 44; Haile 1998: 604.

12. Smith 1986b [1612]: 245–46; Smith 1986c [1624]: 194–95; Haile 1998: 297–98.

13. Smith 1986b [1612]: 246–50; Smith 1986c [1624]: 195–99; Haile 1998: 298–303; all brackets mine.

14. Smith 1986b [1612]: 274; Smith 1986c [1624]: 199–200; Haile 1998: 303, 336.

15. Smith 1986b [1612]: 250–51; Smith 1986c [1624]: 199–200; Haile 1998: 304–6.

16. Smith 1986b [1612]: 251–52; Smith 1986c [1624]: 200–201; Haile 1998: 304–6.

17. Spelman 1910 [1613?]: cvi; Haile 1998: 487.

18. Smith 1986b [1612]: 252–53; Smith 1986c [1624]: 201–2; Haile 1998: 306–7.

19. Smith 1986b [1612]: 253–54; Smith 1986c [1624]: 202–3; Haile 1998: 307–8.

20. Smith 1986b [1612]: 254; Smith 1986c [1624]: 203–4; Haile 1998: 308–9.

21. Smith 1986b [1612]: 254–56; Smith 1986c [1624]: 204–5; Haile 1998: 309–10.

22. The marlstone relic called "Powhatan's Chimney" in modern Gloucester County is the remnant of a later house that was located several miles from where Powhatan actually lived. There is no evidence of any English quarrying of such stone as early as 1609, much less for that barely begun, early abandoned structure at Werowocomoco.

23. Smith 1986b [1612]: 147; Strachey 1953 [1612]: 57; Haile 1998: 615; brackets mine.

24. Strachey 1953 [1612]: 69; Haile 1998: 628.

25. From the probable site of Orapax, it is eleven miles due north, as the crow flies, to the Pamunkey River at its nearest approach, and fourteen miles to the probable site of Youghtanund, upriver, with hilly country and swampy streams all along the way. Using Black Creek, a Pamunkey tributary, cut the overland trek down to about five miles. The town of Powhatan is thirteen miles due west of Orapax's site, with no convenient creeks to ascend and several streams' swampy heads to cross perpendicularly.

26. Strachey 1953 [1612]: 106; Haile 1998: 664.
27. E. R. Turner III, personal communication 2003; Turner and Opperman n.d.
28. Spelman 1910 [1613?]: cv; Haile 1998: 486.
29. Hamor 1957 [1615]: 38; Haile 1998: 831; brackets mine.
30. Worked out by archaeologist E. Randolph Turner III and me in 2003.
31. Haile 1996.

10. Contain Them, Then Let Them Starve

1. Strachey 1979 [1610]: 4ff.; Haile 1998: 384ff.; Stahle et al. 1998: fig. 3-B.
2. Strachey 1979 [1610]: 62; Haile 1998: 418.
3. Smith 1986b [1612]: 266; Smith 1986c [1624]: 215; Haile 1998: 323.
4. Smith 1986b [1612]: 259; Smith 1986c [1624]: 211, 208; Haile 1998: 317, 314–15.
5. Smith 1986b [1612]: 259–60; Smith 1986c [1624]: 209–10; Haile 1998: 315–16. The 1624 version omits the Poles and has Smith overcoming Wowinchopunck single-handed.
6. Probably the Paspahegh satellite town at Barrett's Point, excavated in the early 1990s as the Governor's Land site (Luccketti et al. n.d.).
7. Smith 1986b [1612]: 260–62; Smith 1986c [1624]: 210–11; Haile 1998: 316–18.
8. Hunger: Smith 1986b [1612]: 263–64; Smith 1986c [1624]: 212–13. Strachey 1953 [1612]: 83; Haile 1998: 319–21, 640.
9. Smith 1986b [1612]: 265; Smith 1986c [1624]: 214–15; McIlwaine 1915: 1:28; Haile 1998: 322–23, 894.
10. Smith 1986b [1612]: 266–67; Smith 1986c [1624]: 215–16; Haile 1998: 323–24.
11. Smith 1986b [1612]: 265; Smith 1986c [1624]: 216–17; Archer 1969c [1609]: 281–82; Haile 1998: 324–25, 352.
12. Smith 1986b [1612]: 269; Smith 1986c [1624]: 219–20 (reason was getting colonists away from quarrels in the fort); Strachey 1979 [1610]: 82, 83 (for health reasons; seconded by Earle 1979: 108); McIlwaine 1915: 1:29 (reason was hunger); Haile 1998: 327–29, 430–31, 895.
13. Siebert 1975: 354–55. Many Algonquian languages have variants of the same word, indicating that Algonquian speakers had been fighting head lice for a very long time before Europeans arrived.
14. Percy 1921–22 [1625?]: 262–65 (quotes from 263, 265); Smith 1986b [1612]: 269–70; Smith 1986c [1624]: 221; Haile 1998: 501–3, 329–30.
15. Smith 1986b [1612]: 270; Smith 1986c [1624]: 221; Haile 1998: 330; brackets mine.
16. Strachey 1953 [1612]: 56; Haile 1998: 614.
17. Percy 1921–22 [1625?]: 263–64; Smith 1986b [1612]: 270–71; Smith 1986c [1624]: 221–23; Haile 1998: 502, 330–32.
18. Smith 1986b [1612]: 271–72, 275; Smith 1986c [1624]: 223, 231–32; Haile 1998: 332, 339.

19. Percy 1921–22 [1625?]: 264; Haile 1998: 503.

20. Strachey 1953 [1612]: 61; Haile 1998: 619.

21. Spelman 1910 [1613?]: cii–ciii; Haile 1998: 482–83.

22. Dated by juxtaposition of Ratliffe 1969 [1609]: 283 and Percy 1921–22 [1625?]: 264 (Haile 1998: 354, 503).

23. Smith 1986b [1612]: 272; Smith 1986c [1624]: 223; Percy 1921–22 [1625?]: 264; Haile 1998: 332, 502.

24. Smith 1986b [1612]: 274; Haile 1998: 336.

25. Smith 1986c [1624]: 243; not in Haile.

26. Smith 1986c [1624]: 261; Haile 1998: 864.

27. Smith 1986b [1612]: 274; Haile 1998: 336; brackets mine.

28. Strachey 1953 [1612]: 62; Haile 1998: 620; brackets mine.

29. Implied in records about Pocahontas's capture in 1613. Ralph Hamor also found that after her English marriage, which removed her from her father's domain, another daughter had become Powhatan's favorite (see chap. 13).

30. Smith 1986b [1612]: 273, 275; Smith 1986c [1624]: 225, 232; Haile 1998: 335, 339.

31. Spelman 1910 [1613?]: ciii–cv; Haile 1998: 483–85. Briefer, secondhand accounts: White 1969 [1608?]: 150; Smith 1986b [1612]: 275; Smith 1986c [1624]: 232; Strachey 1979 [1610]: 99; Percy 1921–22 [1625?]: 265–66; Haile 1998: 141, 339, 441, 504.

32. Estimated from Ralph Hamor's saying that Savage had lived with the chief for "three years" (from February 1608) and Powhatan's saying in May 1614 that he had not seen Savage for "three or four years" (Hamor 1957 [1615]: 37, 38; Haile 1998: 830, 831).

33. Spelman 1910 [1613?]: ciii; Haile 1998: 485.

34. Percy 1921–22 [1625?]: 266; Haile 1998: 504–5.

35. Governor and Council, letter of July 7, 1610, in Brown 1964 [1890]: 405; Strachey 1979 [1610]: 64; Smith 1986b [1612]: 275–76; Smith 1986c [1624]: 232; Haile 1998: 457, 419, 339–40.

36. Strachey 1979 [1610]: 99; Haile 1998: 441.

37. Percy 1921–22 [1625?]: 269; Haile 1998: 507. Other accounts: George Somers, letter of June 15, 1610, in Brown 1964 [1890]: 401; McIlwaine 1915: 1:29; Smith 1986b [1612]: 275–76; Smith 1986c [1624]: 232; Haile 1998: 446, 339–40, 896.

38. Strachey 1979 [1610]: 99–100; Percy 1921–22 [1625?]: 267; Haile 1998: 446, 441, 506.

39. Strachey 1953 [1612]: 90 (hostility), 85–86 (prayers and song); Haile 1998: 647, 642–43.

40. Strachey 1979 [1610]: 64, 71; Smith 1986b [1612]: 276; Smith 1986c [1624]: 233–34; Haile 1998: 419, 424, 340–41.

11. Return with a Vengeance

1. Governor and Council, letter of July 7, 1610, in Brown 1964 [1890]: 403; Haile 1998: 455.

2. Kingsbury 1906–35: 3:17; Strachey 1953 [1612]: 58; Haile 1998: 616.

3. Strachey 1953 [1612]: 58–59; Haile 1998: 616.

4. Stahle et al. 1998: fig. 3-B.

5. Strachey 1979 [1610]: 86–87; Haile 1998: 433.

6. Extrapolated from other accounts given by his people, showing that they felt themselves innocent victims of the enemies who raided them, even though (of course) they kept the feuds alive by making return raids.

7. Percy 1921–22 [1625?]: 270–71; McIlwaine 1915: 1:30; Haile 1998: 508–9, 897–98.

8. Strachey 1979 [1610]: 88–89; Haile 1998: 434–35.

9. The records of the time do not specify what was being avenged, either.

10. The likely reason is that he wanted to avoid being grilled about the whereabouts of Namontack, whom he had killed on the way home (Smith 1986c [1624]: 350).

11. Strachey 1979 [1610]: 90–92 (quotes are on 92); Percy 1921–22 [1625?]: 271; Haile 1998: 436–37, 509. The plural in "Indians" indicates that he had heard from Machumps (returned with 3d Supply) as well as Namontack (returned with 2d Supply).

12. Strachey 1979 [1610]: 93 (quote is from this source); Percy 1921–22 [1625?]: 273; Haile 1998: 437–38, 511.

13. Smith 1986c [1624]: 236; Percy 1921–22 [1625?]: 272; Haile 1998: 509.

14. Hostages: Strachey 1979 [1610]: 94; Strachey 1953 [1612]: 65–66. Destruction: Percy 1921–22 [1625?]: 273. Haile 1998: 437–38, 624–25, 511.

15. Attack: Percy 1921–22 [1625?]: 273–75. Revenge: Smith 1986c [1624]: 242; Strachey 1953 [1612]: 64. Haile 1998: 511–13, 622.

16. Smith 1986c [1624]: 237; Percy 1921–22 [1625?]: 273–75; McIlwaine 1915: 1:30; Haile 1998: 511–13, 898.

17. Spelman 1910 [1613?]: cviii–cix; Haile 1998: 489–90.

18. Spelman 1910 [1613?]: civ; Smith 1986b [1612]: 277, 236; Dale, letter of May 25, 1611, to Council, in Brown 1964 [1890]: 493; De La Warre, ibid., 481–82; Strachey 1953 [1612]: 46–47, 101–2; Haile 1998: 486, 342, 524, 530, 606, 658–59.

19. Percy 1921–22 [1625?]: 274–75; Strachey 1953 [1612]: 66–67; Haile 1998: 512, 513, 625–26.

20. Dale visited the Paspahegh town nearest to Jamestown in that month and found it becoming overgrown with shrubs (letter, in Brown 1964 [1890]: 493; Haile 1998: 524); the visitors would have been repulsed if the people had still been inhabiting other parts of their territory.

21. Encounter: Percy 1921–22 [1625?]: 277–78; Whitaker, letter, in Brown 1964 [1890]: 498–99; Hamor 1957 [1610]: 26–27; Haile 1998: 514–15, 550, 822. Embittered: Ferrar Papers, 1992 ed., reel 1, item 40; published in Haile 1998: 778.

22. Strachey 1953 [1612]: 104–5; Haile 1998: 662–63.

23. Cleared: Kingsbury 1906–35: 3:708; Strachey 1953 [1612]: 39; Haile 1998: 601. Best: Kingsbury 1906–35: 3:557; in 1724 Hugh Jones would write (1956 [1724]: 55), "Wherever we meet with an old Indian field, or place where they have lived, we are sure of the best ground."

24. Strachey 1979 [1610]: 87–88; Haile 1998: 430. A piece of such matting has been found inside the original Jamestown fort by the APVA Jamestown Rediscovery archaeologists.

25. Argall and Dale, letters, in Brown 1964 [1890]: 641, 504; Whitaker 1936 [1613]: 40; Haile 1998: 753, 554, 742. Dale's letter includes a plan for settling the town of Chiskiack, the first of several such unfulfilled plans for that town in the next decade or so.

26. Percy 1921–22 [1625?]: 277–78, 280–81; Hamor 1957 [1615]: 27; Haile 1998: 514–15, 517–18, 822. Later accounts by Smith 1986c [1624]: 241; McIlwaine 1915: 1:31; Haile 1998: 900. The settlement was named Henricus; a historical park marks its site today.

27. Hex: Whitaker, letter, in Brown 1964 [1890]: 497–98. Hardening: Dale, Letter of June 15, 1613, Ferrar Papers, 1992 ed., reel 1, item 40; Percy 1921–22 [1625?]: 280–81. Haile 1998: 549–50, 777–79, 517–18.

28. Strachey 1953 [1612]: 105–7; Haile 1998: 663–65.

29. Sniping was still going on near the falls of the James in June (Dale, letter of June 15, 1613, Ferrar Papers, 1992 ed., reel 1, item 40; Haile 1998: 777).

30. Argall (eyewitness), Letter, in Brown 1964 [1890]: 641–43; Hamor 1957 [1615]: 4–6; Ancient Planters, in McIlwaine 1915: 1:33; Haile 1998: 753–55, 802–4, 903. Haile does not include Smith's version (1986c [1624]: 243–44), which is based upon Hamor's.

31. John Smith's version (1986c [1624]: 244; not in Haile 1998) has her "howling and crying."

12. Hostage Situation, with an Unusual Denouement

1. Hamor 1957 [1615]: 6; Haile 1998: 804.

2. Argall, letter, in Brown 1964 [1890]: 643; Haile 1998: 755; brackets mine.

3. Argall, letter, in Brown 1964 [1890]: 643; Hamor 1957 [1615]: 6–7; Haile 1998: 755, 804, 806; McClure 1939: 1:470–71.

4. Hamor 1957 [1615]: 7; Haile 1998: 806.

5. Haile 1998: 793n; Molina's letters are printed in Brown 1964 [1890].

6. Hamor 1957 [1615]: 56 (quoting Dale's letter of June 18, 1614), 59–60 (quoting Whitaker's letter of June 14, 1614); Haile 1998: 845, 848; brackets mine.

7. Strachey 1953 [1612]: 61; Haile 1998: 619.

8. Strachey 1953 [1612]: 98; Haile 1998: 655.

9. For a detailed comparison between Powhatan and English religion, see Rountree 1992.

10. Strachey 1953 [1612]: 95; Purchas 1617: 954–55; Haile 1998: 652, 881.

11. Smith 1986c [1624]: 258; Haile 1998: 861.

12. The best known is in Smith 1986c [1624]: 245, which is copied from Hamor 1957 [1615]: 10 (Haile 1998: 809).

13. See his agonized letter to Sir Thomas Dale, in Hamor 1957 [1615]: 61–68; Haile 1998: 850–56.

14. Strachey 1953 [1612]: 112–13; Haile 1998: 670.

15. Smith 1986c [1624]: 251.

16. Dale letter of June 18, 1614, in Hamor 1957 [1615]: 52–54; ibid., 7–10; Haile 1998: 843–45, 806–9. The Hamor version is paraphrased in Smith 1986c [1624]: 244–45. I have drawn more upon Dale's account, which was written closest to the events (three months later). All brackets are mine.

17. Hamor remembered a much more acrimonious encounter. Word of the boats' arrival would have been taken to both Powhatan and Opechancanough in any case.

18. Hamor remembered a fight, which the locals lost, after which they claimed that it had been started by "stragglers." He also remembered the promise of delivering weapons as being reneged upon, so that the ships took another day to push on to Matchut, where the defensive but nonviolent scene described by Dale was played by the residents there.

19. Stahle et al. 1998: fig. 3-B.

20. Hamor 1957 [1615]: 11; Haile 1998: 809; brackets mine. Paraphrased in Smith 1986c [1624]: 245–46.

21. Dale letter of June 18, 1614, in Hamor 1957 [1615]: 55–56; Whitaker letter of June 18, 1614, ibid.: 59–60; Haile 1998: 845, 848; brackets Haile's.

22. Purchas 1617: 943, marginal note (which reads: "Her true name was *Matokes*, which they concealed from the English, in a superstitious feare of hurt by the English if her name were knowne: she is now Christened *Rebecca*").

23. Smith 1986c [1624]: 258; Haile 1998: 861.

13. Interview with a Wily Old Man

1. Hamor 1957 [1615]: 37–46; Haile 1998: 830–37. Parallel version based on Hamor's in Smith 1986c [1624]: 248–50. All brackets mine.

2. Neither Haile nor I know the meaning of this word.

3. Native guests, because no English source mentions being so honored.

4. Machumps may still have been living at Jamestown; Namontack was dead, and there is no record of any other native person being fluent in English.

5. Purchas 1617: 956.

14. Pocahontas in England

1. Smith 1986c [1624]: 258; Haile 1998: 861; McClure 1939: 2:56–57.

2. Smith 1986c [1624]: 261; Haile 1998: 885.

3. Purchas 1617: 954, 955; Haile 1998: 880, 882. Purchas's subsequent editions follow Smith in saying he was Powhatan's councillor.

4. Dale, letter of June 3, 1616, from Plymouth, in Brown 1964 [1890]: 783; Haile 1998: 878–79.

5. McClure 1939: 2:12; Brown 1964 [1890]: 789.

6. Smith 1986c [1624]: 258; Haile 1998: 861.

7. Purchas 1904–6 [1625]: 19:118; Haile 1998: 883–84.

8. McClure 1939: 2:50; Sainsbury et al. 1860–1926: 1:18; brackets mine.

9. Smith 1986c [1624]: 261–62; Haile 1998: 864.

10. Beverley 1947 [1705]: 43–44.

11. Interpreter: Purchas 1617: 954; Haile 1998: 881. Interviews: Purchas 1904–6 [1625]: 19:117–19; Haile 1998: 884. Evangelize: Purchas 1617: 955; Haile 1998: 882.

12. Dog: a reference either to the greyhound Christopher Newport gave Powhatan in February 1608 or to the dog Powhatan asked Sir Thomas Dale for in May 1614. Smith 1986c [1624]: 261; Haile 1998: 885. Earlier account of the attempted tally (of both people and trees): Purchas 1617: 954; Haile 1998: 881–82.

13. McClure 1939: 2:50; Sainsbury et al. 1860–1926: 1:18.

14. The only source for this move is Smith 1986c [1624]: 261; Haile 1998: 863.

15. Barbour 1986: 1:xlv.

16. McClure 1939: 2:56–57.

17. Smith 1986c [1624]: 261; Haile 1998: 863–64.

18. Robert Beverley proposed tardiness as the only reason for her anger, adding that the pair were reconciled although she twitted him about his ingratitude to her father (Beverley 1947 [1705]: 43).

19. Ferrar Papers, 1992 ed., reel 1, item 72; published in Haile 1998: xviii.

20. Rolfe 1848 [1616]: 112–13; Haile 1998: 877.

21. Kingsbury 1906–35: 3:70; Haile 1998: 887.

22. Purchas 1904–6 [1625]: 19:118; Haile 1998: 884; Mossiker 1976: 279–80—in which she has Pocahontas dying as Matachanna wailed nearby.

23. Kingsbury 1906–35: 3:71; Haile 1998: 889.

24. John Rolfe, letter of June 8, 1617, in Kingsbury 1906–35: 3:71.

25. Ships: ibid., 70. Flux: McIlwaine 1915: 1:28; Haile 1998: 905. Well: Smith 1986c [1624]: 262. No records of 1617 mention the well at all. 1623: Kingsbury 1906–35: 4:25.

26. Earle 1979: 101–2, writing of the Jamestown colonists of 1607.

27. Mossiker 1976: 283–86. All but the final report is detailed in copies of correspondence, that report being briefly mentioned in a *Daily Mail* clipping of June 2, 1923, that Mr. Daniel McGuire recently acquired from the Home Office in Lon-

don and kindly reproduced for me. In spite of Sir Arthur's findings, rumors of the exhumation of Pocahontas's bones and hiding of them in various places persist.

28. Kingsbury 1906–35: 1:338–39 (medicines), 485, 496 (marriage).

29. Ibid., 3:71–72; Haile 1998: 888–90; Carson 1950.

30. Passage: Nugent 1934: 29. Visit: Robinson 1905–6: 394, 395. Fort: Nugent 1934: 234, 328, 384. Sales: ibid., 169, 353, 375. Death: Nugent 1977: 222.

31. For a succinct explanation of why, see Rountree and Turner 2002: 177–78.

32. Moore and Slatten 1985.

15. Unofficially in Control

1. Kingsbury 1906–35: 3:92.

2. Original is lost; mentioned in Smith 1986c [1624]: 265.

3. Smith 1986b [1612]: 169; Strachey 1953 [1612]: 94; Spelman 1910 [1613?]: cx; Haile 1998: 651, 491. 1621 ceremony: Kingsbury 1906–35: 4:10.

4. Kingsbury 1906–35: 3:438.

5. Purchas 1617: 956.

6. Ibid., 956–57.

7. Arrohatecks: Henrico, Coxendale, Rochedale, Curle's Neck. Appamattucks: Bermuda Hundred, Charles City Plantation. Weyanocks: Shirley Hundred. Based upon Nugent 1934: map facing 96 (note: 1963 reprint omits original edition's illustrations).

8. Rolfe 1848 [1616]: 106; Haile 1998: 870.

9. Hamor 1957 [1615]: 10 (Hamor's text), 53 (quoting Dale's letter); Haile 1998: 808, 843.

10. Nugent 1934: map facing 224 (note: 1963 reprint omits original edition's illustrations); Rolfe 1848 [1616]: 107; Haile 1998: 870.

11. Treaty: Hamor 1957 [1615]: 11–15; Dale letter, ibid., 56–57; Haile 1998: 809–13, 845–46. Fear: Smith 1986c [1624]: 247; Hamor 1957 [1615]: 14–15; Haile 1998: 812–13.

12. Kingsbury 1906–35: 4:5 (subjects), 93 (tribute); brackets mine.

13. Rainfall from dendrochronology: Stahle et al. 1998: fig. 3-B; poverty: Kingsbury 1906–35: 3:92. Dendrochronology was done on cypress trees, which catch water from a stream's whole drainage basin and average it to make an annual ring, while corn depends upon rain falling on the field in which it is planted and needs water at regular intervals during its 120-day growing cycle (Samuel Kisseadoo and Steve Wall, personal communications, 2003). Thus a "wet" year can still produce a poor crop or none at all, if all the rain falls at the wrong time.

14. Kingsbury 1906–35: 3:74.

15. Smith 1986c [1624]: 256 (poor hunters), 257 (teaching); McIlwaine 1979 [1924]: 28 (teaching); Haile 1998: 859, 860–61, 917.

16. Smith 1986c [1624]: 262, 285; brackets mine.

17. Ferrar Papers, 1992 ed., reel 1, item 113; brackets mine. The English source for this quote was Robert Poole, a qualified interpreter, who had heard Opechancanough make the statement.

18. Smith 1986c [1624]: 256–57; Haile 1998: 859–60; Kingsbury 1906–35: 4:117–18. Smith's is the longer account, followed here in detail because although it benefited from hindsight, its details ring true to me.

19. Purchas 1617: 956. Purchas added (1904–6 [1625]: 19:119; Haile 1998: 884) that Powhatan feared his brother would join the English against him, a very unlikely idea.

20. Flux: McIlwaine 1915: 1:28; Haile 1998: 905.

21. Kingsbury 1906–35: 1:220, 310.

22. Ibid.: 3:73–74; brackets mine.

23. That intention had been official policy since at least 1609 (ibid., 27) and had been attempted sporadically since at least 1613 (Ferrar Papers, 1992 ed., reel 1, item 40; published in Haile 1998: 777). Now there was a new, stronger policy (Kingsbury 1906–35: 1:310–11, 3:115, 117, 164–66). Rolfe letter, 1617: ibid., 71; Haile 1998: 888.

24. "Fostering out": Stone 1977: 106–7; emotionally cold: ibid., 99–102; obedience, ibid., 112; since 1500, Sneyd 1847: 24–26.

25. Kingsbury 1906–35: 3:128–29.

26. Ibid., 164–66.

27. McIlwaine 1915: 1:36; Haile 1998: 909; Smith 1986c [1624]: 268, 287.

28. The most specific statement on early mortality and poor premortem health for an early seventeenth-century English settlement (Jordan's Journey) is Owsley and Compton n.d.: 35, 36. Of the people there, 40 percent died in their teens, another one-third in their twenties, and 80 percent of the ones with permanent teeth had a dental anomaly indicating "prolonged periods of malnutrition or disease stress" during early childhood (i.e., back in England). Trying to escape poverty at home, they migrated and died.

29. Ibid., 266–67.

30. Old Paspahegh territory: Smith's/Southampton Hundred, Argall's Gift, Maycock's Plantation, Martin's Hundred, Archer's Hope. Weyanocks south of the James: Brandon, Jordan's Journey, Woodlief's Plantation, Chaplin's Choice, Merchant's Hope, Flowerdew Plantation, Ward's Plantation; Weyanocks north of the James: Berkeley Plantation, Westover, Smith's Plantation, Weyanoke (the capital's site). Appamattucks: Piercey's Manor. Powhatan townsfolk: Sheffield's Plantation, Proctor's Plantation, Falling Creek.

31. Quiyoughcohannocks: Pace's Pains. Warraskoyacks: Lawne's Plantation, which shortly failed (Kingsbury 1906–35: 3:246), Pace's Choice, Warraskoyack (capital site). Chiskiacks/Kecoughtans: Pierce's or Rolfe's Plantation, Water's Plantation, Buck Roe, Newport News. Nansemonds: Basse's Choice. Accomacs: Yeardley's Plantation, Willcock's Plantation. Based upon Nugent 1934: maps facing pp. 96, 224 (note: 1963 reprint omits original edition's illustrations).

32. Kingsbury 1906–35: 2:94.

33. A possibly inaccurate account of 1623 lists only ten actual settlements, "poorly housed," in 1619: McIlwaine 1915: 1:35; Haile 1998: 907.

34. Clay 1976; Hodges et al. 1985; Jones et al. 1985; Kitschel et al. 1986. The soil surveys for Surry and Charles City Counties were in galley proof at the time of this writing; I am grateful to the county agricultural agents' staffs who allowed me to photocopy parts of them.

35. Robinson 1905–6: 395; Kingsbury 1906–35: 3:79, 93.

36. See, for instance, Fausz 1987.

37. Ferrar Papers, 1992 ed., reel 1, item 113.

38. There was, in fact, no new governor coming. Yeardley was not replaced until the fall of 1621, when Sir Francis Wyatt took over. There may have been a plan that early to push out the Chiskiacks; Yeardley heard something to that effect, planned by the Virginia Company, in early 1621 (Kingsbury 1906–35: 3:451).

39. Haile 1998: 67.

40. Kingsbury 1906–35: 1:310, 3:174–75 (alienation), 242 (sentence), 251 and 253 (Poole).

41. Ibid., 244, 247; Smith 1986c [1624]: 267–68.

42. Isolation: Rountree and Davidson 1997: 41, 46, chap. 2. Gift: Nugent 1934: map facing 96 and patent on 30.

43. Smith 1986c [1624]: 289–91. The governor was Samuel Argall, for the incidents occurred before April 1619.

44. Ibid., 264–65 (promises), 291 (events at Accomac).

45. Kingsbury 1906–35: 3:147–48, 372.

46. Ibid., 244–45.

47. Ibid., 228.

48. Harvest: ibid., 220. Proclamation: Ferrar Papers, 1992 ed., reel 1, item 164.

16. The Great Assault of 1622

1. Kingsbury 1906–35: 4:10. Archaeological evidence of trophy taking: Noël Hume 1982: 243–44, 287ff.

2. Esmy Shichans was a weroance under Opechancanough, although he was the paramount chief in his own right of both the Accomacs and the Occohannocks.

3. Kingsbury 1906–35: 3:556, 4:10; Smith 1986c [1624]: 298. The governor was Yeardley, according to the records, which places the events before November 1621, when Sir Francis Wyatt took over the governorship. Land: ibid., 288.

4. Kingsbury 1906–35: 4:10.

5. Ibid., 3:446 (fashions), 462 (visits).

6. Ibid., 552–53; Anonymous 1900–1901: 210–12.

7. Percy 1921–22 [1625?]: 280; Haile 1998: 517–18.

8. Smith 1986c [1624]: 293; Anonymous 1900–1901: 213. Smith has Opechan-

canough pulling off the Great Assault only two weeks later (he is the only contemporary writer to do so), which has led some later historians to place Nemattanow's death in the late winter of 1622. However, the governor who dealt with the matter was George Yeardley (Kingsbury 1906–35: 4:11), who remained in office until October 1621 (Barbour 1986: 2:283n).

9. Kingsbury 1906–35: 4:11.

10. Ibid., 3:549–50; Anonymous 1900–1901: 208.

11. It's not that hard, when living in a place without light pollution, to notice that stars form patterns and that those patterns rotate around the heavens in the course of a year.

12. Stahle et al. 1998: fig. 3-B.

13. Kingsbury 1906–35: 3:583–84.

14. Strachey 1953 [1612]: 113–14; Haile 1998: 671.

15. Scattering: Kingsbury 1906–35: 4:178; Smith 1986c [1624]: 293. Confidence that Indians were harmless: ibid.; Kingsbury 1906–35: 3:550; Anonymous 1900–1901: 208–10.

16. Calculated on the websites www.SUNearth.gsfc.nasa.gov/eclipse/phase/phasecat.html and adjusted for England's then being on the Julian calendar (ten days behind the Gregorian one we now use). I am indebted to Morris Bander and Thomas Finderson for finding this site for me.

17. Strachey 1953 [1612]: 104; Haile 1998: 662; brackets mine.

18. Kingsbury 1906–35: 3:550, 554.

19. Ibid., 555–56; Smith 1986c [1624]: 297–98; Anonymous 1900–1901: 212–13.

20. Kingsbury 1906–35: 3:554 (warnings), 4:98 (Chauco).

21. One hour: Anonymous 1900–1901: 212. Warning and mutilation: Kingsbury 1906–35: 3:551–53; Smith 1986c [1624]: 295.

22. Kingsbury 1906–35: 3:550–51, 4:516; Smith 1986c [1624]: 294–96; Anonymous 1900–1901: 211, 213.

23. Smith 1986c [1624]: 308–9.

24. Kingsbury 1906–35: 4:9, 250.

25. Smith 1986c [1624]: 304–5.

26. Ibid., 309.

27. Ferrar Papers, 1992 ed., reel 2, item 364. The text of this previously unpublished document shows clearly that the Jamestown leadership was still more afraid of the Spanish than of the Powhatans.

28. Smith 1986c [1624]: 303.

29. Kingsbury 1906–35: 3:557–58, 704–10.

17. A War of Attrition, Including an English Massacre

1. Stahle et al., "Jamestown Droughts," fig. 3-B.

2. Kingsbury 1906–35: vols. 3 and 4. We know the hunger was mutual because

of the account of one prisoner that Opechancanough released early (ibid., 4:98–99, 239).

3. Smith 1986c [1624]: 312; Kingsbury 1906–35: 3:652–53.

4. Commissions to trade: Kingsbury 1906–35: 3:622, 654–57, 697–98, 700, 4:7. Trouble: Smith 1986c [1624]: 304–5, 308–10, 312–14. Accomacs: McIlwaine 1979 [1924]: 11.

5. Kingsbury 1906–35: 3:556.

6. Men: ibid., 4:238. Twenty left: Smith 1986c [1624]: 309–10; nineteen or fifteen left: Kingsbury 1906–35: 4:232, 41. Slavery: ibid., 232, 473.

7. Kingsbury 1906–35: 4:41, 25.

8. Ibid., 41 and 25 (disease), 22 (raids); Smith 1986c [1624]: 310 (raids).

9. Smith 1986c [1624]: 314–15.

10. On Aug. 1, 1622: Kingsbury 1906–35: 3:671–73.

11. Chickahominy: Smith 1986c [1624]: 318; James River: Kingsbury 1906–35: 4:10.

12. Kingsbury 1906–35: 4:37, 75.

13. Ibid., 58, 61–62, 83, 108–9, 228–29, 234, 238, 450 (revenge taken on Piscataways); Smith 1986c [1624]: 320–21.

14. Kingsbury 1906–35: 4:98–99.

15. Ibid.

16. Jane Dickenson: ibid., 473. The "creditor" was Dr. John Pott, who was later labeled "the poisoner of the savages" (see below). There is no record of the outcome of her suit against him.

17. Ibid., 102 (general letter from council), 221–22 (detailed letter from participant); brackets mine.

18. Poison used: ibid., 221; colony's doctor, John Pott, censured for it: Sainsbury et al. 1860–1926: 3:69; governor's feeble denial of using poison: Ferrar Papers, 1992 ed., reel 3, item 556. The type of poison is never specified.

19. Toast and shooting: Kingsbury 1906–35: 4:222; shooting: Sainsbury et al. 1860–1926: 2:48.

20. Sainsbury et al. 1860–1926: 2:48, 4:102; Kingsbury 1906–35: 2:482–83; Purchas 1904–6 [1625]: 19:170.

21. Kingsbury 1904–6: 4:186, 216, 228–29.

22. Ibid., 189, 190, 235, 250 (tribes listed); Purchas 1904–6 [1625]: 19:170.

23. Kingsbury 1906–35: 4:277, 446, 447–48, 450–51 (specific mention of being allies).

24. Ibid., 583–84; Hening 1809–23: 1:126.

25. Kingsbury 1906–35: 4:476.

26. Stahle et al. 1998: fig. 3-B.

27. Kingsbury 1906–35: 4:507–8. Most of the colony's ammunition was used in that Pamunkey raid. Given their small number, the English must have worn armor.

28. Ibid., 566 and 568–69 (late arrival), 569 (truce); McIlwaine 1979 [1924]: 57, 48 (interpreters).

29. McIlwaine 1979 [1924]: 128 (Pamunkey); Sainsbury 1860–1926: 4:80 et passim (other trade).

30. McIlwaine 1979 [1924]: 111, 116.

31. Ibid., 483, 129, 147. The enemy, for their part, were planning to seat the town of Chiskiack (ibid., 136).

32. Ibid., 151, 155; the plans in these records were made in early July and mid-October, respectively, indicating that there was enough ammunition to mount the raids.

33. Ibid., 155.

34. Ibid., 172, 484.

35. Date: ibid., 184; clauses: ibid., 190, 198.

36. Ibid., 189.

37. Report of William Pierce, quoted in Neill 1866: 60; the abstract in Sainsbury 1860–1926: 1:100 mentions no one by name. Poole: McIlwaine 1979 [1924]: 198.

38. Robinson 1905–6: 400; McIlwaine 1915: 1:52; Hening 1809–23: 1:140, 141, 153.

39. McIlwaine 1979 [1924]: 482 (Cantaunkack). Sainsbury 1860–1926: 5:116 (Chiskiack). Meanwhile, Dr. Pott, the "poisoner of the savages" in 1623, was prosecuted for various crimes and found guilty of cattle stealing (ibid.).

40. Hostilities: McIlwaine 1979 [1924]: 484; Hening 1809–23: 1:167, 173, 176. Chiskiack: McIlwaine 1979 [1924]: 479; Nugent 1934: 44.

41. McIlwaine 1979 [1924]: 484; corroborated by dendrochronology: Stahle et al. 1998: fig. 3-B.

42. McIlwaine 1979 [1924]: 480. Law: Hening 1806–23: 1:193. Peace: McIlwaine 1979 [1924]: 480; brackets mine.

43. Robinson 1905–6: 390.

18. Running Out of Time

1. Robinson 1905–6: 394, 395; brackets mine.

2. Brit. Col. Papers, vol. 8, 1634–35, no. 3, cited in Bruce 1910: 2:72.

3. Forbidding: Hening 1809–23: 1:219 (selling of arms and ammunition, cloth). "Illegal" trading: Robinson 1905–6: 390 [1633]; Sainsbury et al. 1860–1926: 9:268, 269 (ca. 1638). Buying food: ibid., 250 (1637), Hening 1809–23: 1:227 (1639); McIlwaine 1979 [1924]: 492.

4. Tuckahoe, or *Peltandra virginica,* a freshwater emergent plant, does not grow in the salty estuary waters surrounding the Virginia Eastern Shore.

5. True on the mainland at this period; some Eastern Shore land was given away by the Accomac chief in the 1630s. The major period when native people sold land to settlers in Virginia was the 1650s–60s, and most of that occurred on the Eastern Shore. See Rountree 1990: chaps. 4 and 5.

6. Nugent 1934: 10, 31, et passim (Warraskoyacks); 3, 8 (Quiyoughcohannocks); 21, 34 (Nansemonds); 18, 98 (Chickahominies); 31, 49 (Appamattucks); 126,

131 (north bank of York River); 172, 188 (Pamunkey and Mattaponi Rivers); 131 (Chiskiacks); 132, 137 (Rappahannock River); 144 (Wiccocomicos); 149 (Sekakawon/Yoacomocos). Chiskiack "trouble": McIlwaine 1979 [1924]: 499.

7. Genealogy page in 1675 Sermon Book, in descendants' possession; photo published in Rountree 1990: 85. Most of the people in the modern Nansemond tribe descend from that marriage.

8. Funding: Robinson 1905–6: 391 (1640), 500 (1642). Child: McIlwaine 1979 [1924]: 477–78.

9. McIlwaine 1979 [1924]: 478 (prosecution), 476 and 482 (interceding). Law: Anonymous 1901: 53–54.

10. Hening 1809–23: 1:255–56; McIlwaine 1979 [1924]: 500.

11. The York County Order Books survive, though for reasons unknown, most of the pages for sessions in the 1630s–40s are blank, as though someone didn't get around to transcribing notes from the court sessions.

12. Deduced from three sources: Robert Beverley (1947 [1705]: 60) saying that the greatest blows fell on Southside Virginia, the York River, and the "heads" (near the fall line) of the other rivers (meaning the James and Rappahannock); lawyer Conway Robinson's terse notes about the Rappahannock River area (McIlwaine 1979 [1924]: 501, 502); and Mr. Streeter's extracts (ibid., 563).

13. Anonymous 1947 [1649]: 11.

14. Beverley 1947 [1705]: 50.

15. Hening 1809–23: 1:289. Among the Strangers, April 18 was Maundy Thursday, the Thursday before Easter when the original Last Supper is celebrated (see Ely Cathedral's website: www.ely.anglican.org/cgi-bin/easter), but that would have been irrelevant to the Powhatans. I am indebted to Mary Theobald for pointing out the reference.

16. I.e., the night before was five nights past full moon (see chap. 16, n. 16), probably not useful for setting a date.

17. McIlwaine 1979 [1924]: 501.

18. Withdrawing: Anonymous 1947 [1649]: 11. Fleeing: Anonymous 1900: 349–50. Subsequent history: Rountree 1990: 108–9.

19. McIlwaine 1979 [1924]: 564 (Pamunkey campaign); ibid., 501, 502, 563, and Hening 1809–23: 1:287–88 (raid, Rappahannocks).

20. Fort established: Hening 1809–23: 1:298–93. Location: E. Randolph Turner III, personal communication, 2003.

21. McIlwaine 1979 [1924]: 564, 565.

22. They may not have known that some of the personnel the foreigners used were indentured servants, impressed unwillingly into service (York Co., Records 2:361 [claim made based on 1645 council order to that effect]).

23. Hening 1809–23: 1:315 (Nansemonds), 318–19 (peace).

24. Age: Anonymous 1947 [1649]: 7. Beverley 1947 [1705]: 62.

25. It is fairly common in the United States today, with its medical technology

and its aging population, to have surgery if those folds droop enough to interfere with seeing.

Epilogue

1. Rountree 1990: chaps. 5–10; Rountree and Turner 2002: chaps. 5–7. I still do active fieldwork among the seven major organized tribes, and I have testified for them in state and federal recognition cases.

2. Fausz, 1981.

3. Beverley 1947 [1705]: 61.

4. Hamor 1957 [1615]: 13; Haile 1998: 811.

5. I was invited to be a consultant on that film, an offer I flatly refused.

6. Fausz 1981 and mentions of the three people in Rountree 1989 were the early attempts.

BIBLIOGRAPHY

Anonymous. 1900. Indians of Southern Virginia, 1650–1711: Depositions in the Virginia and North Carolina Boundary Case. *Virginia Magazine of History and Biography* 7:337–52, 8:1–11.

Anonymous. 1900–1901. Two Tragicall Events: The Voyage of Anthony Chester, Made in the Year 1620 . . . . *William and Mary Quarterly,* 1st ser., 9:203–14.

Anonymous. 1901. The Virginia Assembly of 1641: A List of Members and Some of the Acts. *Virginia Magazine of History and Biography* 9:50–59.

Anonymous. 1947 [1649]. *A Perfect Description of Virginia* . . . . In *Tracts and Other Papers.* Ed. Peter Force. Rept. New York: Peter Smith. Vol. 2, no. 8.

Anonymous. 1947 [1612]. *For the Colony in Virginea Britannia. Lavves Diuine, Morall and Martiall, etc.* In *Tracts and Other Papers.* Ed. Peter Force. Rept. New York: Peter Smith. Vol. 3, no. 2. [Attributed now to William Strachey as compiler.]

Archer, Gabriel. 1969a [1607]. Relatyon of the Discovery of Our River. In *The Jamestown Voyages under the First Charter.* Ed. Philip L. Barbour. Cambridge: Hakluyt Society. Ser. 2, vol. 136, pp. 80–98. Also printed, verbatim but with modernized spelling, in *Jamestown Narratives: Eyewitness Accounts of the Virginia Colony: The First Decade, 1607–1617.* Ed. Edward W. Haile. Champlain, Va.: RoundHouse, 1998. Pp. 101–18.

———. 1969b [1607]. Description of the People [authorship uncertain]. In *The Jamestown Voyages under the First Charter.* Ed. Philip L. Barbour. Cambridge: Hakluyt Society. Ser. 2, vol. 136, pp. 102–4. Also printed, verbatim but with modernized spelling, in *Jamestown Narratives: Eyewitness Accounts of the Virginia Colony: The First Decade, 1607–1617.* Ed. Edward W. Haile. Champlain, Va.: RoundHouse, 1998. Pp. 122–24.

———. 1969c [1609]. Letter from Jamestown. In *The Jamestown Voyages under the First Charter.* Ed. Philip L. Barbour. Cambridge: Hakluyt Society. Ser. 2, vol. 136, pp. 279–82. Also printed, verbatim but with modernized spelling, in *Jamestown Narratives: Eyewitness Accounts of the Virginia Colony: The First*

Decade, 1607–1617. Ed. Edward W. Haile. Champlain, Va.: RoundHouse, 1998. Pp. 350–53.

Argall, Samuel. 1904–6 [1613]. A Letter of Sir Samuel Argall Touching His Voyage to Virginia, and Actions There: Written to Master Nicholas Hawes. In *Hakluytus Posthumus or Purchas His Pilgrimes.* Ed. Samuel Purchas. Rept. Glasgow: James MacLehose and Sons. 19:90–95. Also printed, verbatim but with modernized spelling, in *Jamestown Narratives: Eyewitness Accounts of the Virginia Colony: The First Decade: 1607–1617.* Ed. Edward W. Haile. Champlain, Va.: RoundHouse, 1998. Pp. 752–56.

Bailey, Kent P., and Ransom B. True. 1980. *A Guide to Seventeenth-Century Virginia Court Writing.* Richmond: Association for the Preservation of Virginia Antiquities.

Barbour, Philip L. 1964. *The Three Worlds of Captain John Smith.* Boston: Houghton Mifflin.

———. 1970. *Pocahontas and Her World.* Boston: Houghton Mifflin.

———. 1971. The Honorable George Percy, Premier Chronicler of the First Virginia Voyage. *Early American Literature* 6:7–17.

———. 1986. Notes to texts, redaction of dates, etc. In *The Complete Works of Captain John Smith (1580–1631).* Ed. Philip L. Barbour. 3 vols. Chapel Hill: Univ. of North Carolina Press.

Beverley, Robert. 1947 [1705]. *History and Present State of Virginia.* Ed. Louis B. Wright. Chapel Hill: Univ. of North Carolina Press.

Bland, Edward, Abraham Wood, Sackford Brewster, and Elias Pennant. 1911 [1651]. *The Discovery of New Brittaine, Began August 27, Anno Dom. 1650 . . . .* In *Narratives of Early Carolina, 1650–1708.* Ed. Alexander S. Salley. New York: Charles Scribner's Sons. Pp. 5–19.

Bridenbaugh, Carl. 1967. *Vexed and Troubled Englishmen, 1590–1642.* New York: Oxford Univ. Press.

———. 1981. *Jamestown, 1544–1699.* New York: Oxford Univ. Press.

Brown, Alexander, ed. 1964 [1890]. *The Genesis of the United States.* 2 vols. Rept. New York: Russell and Russell.

Browne, William Hand, et al., eds. 1883–1972. *The Archives of Maryland.* 72 vols. Baltimore: Maryland Historical Society.

Bruce, Philip Alexander. 1910. *Institutional History of Virginia in the Seventeenth Century.* 2 vols. New York: G. P. Putnam's Sons.

Brush, Grace S. 2001. Forests before and after the Colonial Encounter. In *Discovering the Chesapeake: The History of an Ecosystem.* Ed. Philip D. Curtin, Grace S. Brush, and George W. Fisher. Baltimore: Johns Hopkins Univ. Press. Pp. 40–59.

Byrd, William. 1966. *The Prose Works of William Byrd of Westover.* Ed. Louis B. Wright. Cambridge, Mass.: Harvard Univ. Press.

Carson, Jane. 1950. The Will of John Rolfe. *Virginia Magazine of History and Biography* 58:58–65.

Clark, Wayne E., and Helen C. Rountree. 1993. The Powhatans and the Maryland

Mainland. In *Powhatan Foreign Relations, 1500–1722.* Ed. Helen C. Rountree. Charlottesville: Univ. Press of Virginia. Pp. 112–35.

Clay, John W. 1976. *Soil Survey of Henrico County, Virginia.* Washington, D.C.: U.S. Department of Agriculture.

Clayton, John. 1965 [1687]. "The Aborigines of the Country": Letter to Dr. Nehemiah Grew. In *The Reverend John Clayton.* Ed. Edmund Berkeley and Dorothy S. Berkeley. Charlottesville: Univ. Press of Virginia. Pp. 21–39. Also published in 1964 as "John Clayton's 1687 Account of the Medicinal Practices of the Virginia Indians." Ed. Bernard G. Hoffman. *Ethnohistory* 11:1–40.

Culliford, S. G. 1965. *William Strachey, 1572–1621.* Charlottesville: Univ. Press of Virginia.

Dale, Thomas. 1998 [1613]. Letter [of June 10] to Sir Thomas Smythe. In Ferrar Papers, 1992 ed. Reel 1, item 40. Printed, verbatim but with modernized spelling, in *Jamestown Narratives: Eyewitness Accounts of the Virginia Colony: The First Decade, 1607–1617.* Ed. Edward W. Haile. Champlain, Va.: RoundHouse, 1998. Pp. 760–83.

Denton, Daniel. 1937 [1670]. *A Brief Description of New-York, with the Places Thereunto Adjoining, Formerly Called the New Netherlands, etc.* New York: Columbia Univ. Press.

Earle, Carville V. 1979. Environment, Disease, and Mortality in Early Virginia. In *The Chesapeake in the Seventeenth Century: Essays on Anglo-American Society.* Ed. Thad W. Tate and David L. Ammerman. Chapel Hill: Univ. of North Carolina Press. Pp. 96–125.

Fausz, J. Frederick. 1981. Opechancanough, Indian Resistance Leader. In *Struggle and Survival in Colonial America.* Ed. David G. Sweet and Gary B. Nash. Berkeley: Univ. of California Press. Pp. 21–37.

———. 1987. Middlemen in Peace and War: Virginia's Earliest Indian Interpreters, 1608–1632. *Virginia Magazine of History and Biography* 95:41–64.

Featherstone, Donald. 1998. *Armies and Warfare in the Pike and Shot Era, 1422–1700.* London: Constable & Co.

Feest, Christian F. 1983. Powhatan's Mantle. In *Tradescant's Rarities.* Ed. Arthur MacGregor. Oxford: Clarendon Press. Pp. 130–35.

The Ferrar Papers. 1992 [1590–1790]. Originals housed in Magdalene College, Cambridge Univ.. First published in 6 microfilm reels in 1960; more complete collection published in 14 microfilm reels in 1992.

Fleet, Henry. 1876 [1631–32]. A Brief Journal of a Voyage Made in the Bark *Virginia,* to Virginia and Other Parts of the Continent of America. In *Founders of Maryland.* Ed. Edward D. Neill. Albany: Joel Munsell. Pp. 19–37.

Gibbs, W. Wayt. 2002. Saving Dying Languages. *Scientific American* 287 (2): 79–85.

Gleach, Frederick W. 1997. *Powhatan's World and Colonial Virginia: A Conflict of Cultures.* Lincoln: Univ. of Nebraska Press.

Haile, Edward Wright, ed. 1995. *Virginia Discovered and Discribed by Captayn John Smith 1608.* Champlain, Va.: Globe Sales Publications. Map, based upon Smith and Zuniga maps; base map is Smith n.d.

————, comp. 1996. *England in America: The Chesapeake Bay from Jamestown to St. Mary's City, 1607–1634.* Richmond: Dietz Press. Modern base map with towns from Smith and Zuniga added.

————, ed. 1998. *Jamestown Narratives: Eyewitness Accounts of the Virginia Colony: The First Decade, 1607–1617.* Champlain, Va.: RoundHouse.

Hamor, Ralph. 1957 [1615]. *A True Discourse of the Present State of Virginia, and the Success of the Affairs There till the 18 of June, 1614.* Facsimile issue. Richmond: Virginia State Library. Also printed, verbatim but with modernized spelling, in *Jamestown Narratives: Eyewitness Accounts of the Virginia Colony: the First Decade: 1607–1617.* Ed. Edward W. Haile, ed. Champlain, Va.: RoundHouse, 1998. Pp. 795–856.

Hantman, Jeffrey L. 1990. Between Powhatan and Quirank: Reconstructing Monacan Culture and History in the Context of Jamestown. *American Anthropologist* 92:676–90.

————. 1993. Powhatan's Relations with the Piedmont Monacan. In *Powhatan Foreign Relations, 1500–1722.* Ed. Helen C. Rountree. Charlottesville: Univ. Press of Virginia. Pp. 94–111.

Hariot, Thomas. 1955 [1588]. *A Briefe and True Report of the New Found Land of Virginia.* In *The Roanoke Voyages, 1584–1590.* Ed. David B. Quinn. Cambridge: Hakluyt Society. Ser. 2, vol. 104, pp. 317–87. Facsimile reprint: New York: Dover, 1972.

Hening, William Waller, comp. 1809–23. *The Statutes at Large, Being a Collection of All the Laws of Virginia from the First Session of the Legislature.* 13 vols. Richmond, etc.: R. & W. & G. Bartow.

Hodges, Robert L., P. Ben Sabo, David McCloy, and C. Kent Staples. 1985. *Soil Survey of James City and York Counties and the City of Williamsburg, Virginia.* Washington, D.C.: U.S. Department of Agriculture.

Hoffman, Paul. 1990. *A New Andalucia and a Way to the Orient: The American Southeast during the Sixteenth Century.* Baton Rouge: Louisiana State Univ. Press.

Hulton, Paul. 1984. *America in 1585: The Complete Drawings of John White.* Chapel Hill: Univ. of North Carolina Press.

Jesuit Letters. 1910 [various years, 1634 onward]. Extracts from the Annual Letters of the English Province. In *Narratives of Early Maryland, 1633–1684.* Ed. Clayton Colman Hall. New York: Charles Scribner's Sons. Pp. 118–44.

Jones, David L., Ian A. Rodihan, Louis E. Cullipher, John W. Clay, and Michael J. Marks. 1985. *Soil Survey of Prince George County, Virginia.* Washington, D.C.: U.S. Department of Agriculture.

Jones, Hugh. 1956 [1724]. *The Present State of Virginia.* Ed. Richard L. Morton. Chapel Hill: Univ. of North Carolina Press.

Kingsbury, Susan Myra, comp. 1906–35. *Records of the Virginia Company of London.* 4 vols. Washington, D.C.: Library of Congress. Half-sized facsimile reprint: Heritage Books, Bowie, Md., 1995.

Kitchel, William F., H. Thomas Saxton III, Ruch A. Strauss, Steve K. Thomas, and Carl D. Peacock, Jr. 1986. *Soil Survey of Isle of Wight County, Virginia*. Washington, D.C.: U.S. Department of Agriculture.

Lederer, John. 1958 [1672]. *The Discoveries of John Lederer*. Ed. William P. Cumming. Charlottesville: Univ. of Virginia Press.

Lewis, Clifford M., and Albert J. Loomie. 1953. *The Spanish Jesuit Mission in Virginia, 1570–1572*. Chapel Hill: Univ. of North Carolina Press.

Luccketti, Nicholas M., Mary Ellen N. Hodges, and Charles T. Hodges, eds. N.d. Paspahegh Archaeology: Data Recovery Investigations of Site 44JC308 at the Governor's Land at Two Rivers, James City County, Virginia. Report (1994) on file, Virginia Department of Historic Resources, Richmond.

Mathew, Thomas. 1947 [1705]. *The Beginning, Progress and Conclusion of Bacon's Rebellion in Virginia in the Years 1675 & 1676*. In *Tracts and Other Papers*. Peter Force, ed. Rept. New York: Peter Smith. Vol. 1, no. 8.

McClure, Norman Egbert, ed. 1939. *Letters of John Chamberlain*. Philadelphia: American Philosophical Society. Memoir 12, pts. 1 and 2.

McIlwaine, H. R., comp. 1915. *Journal of the House of Burgesses*. 13 vols. Richmond: Virginia State Library.

———. 1979 [1924]. *Minutes of the Council and General Court of Virginia, 1622–1632, 1670–1676*. 2d ed. Richmond: Virginia State Library.

Mook, Maurice M. 1944. The Aboriginal Population of Tidewater Virginia. *American Anthropologist* 46:193–208.

Moore, Elizabeth Vann, and Richard Slatten. 1985. The Descendants of Pocahontas: An Unclosed Case. *Magazine of Virginia Genealogy* 23 (3): 3–16.

Mossiker, Frances. 1976. *Pocahontas: The Life and Legend*. New York: Knopf.

Neill, Edward E. 1866. *Virginia Carolorum*. Albany: John Munsell's Sons.

Noël Hume, Ivor. 1982. *Martin's Hundred*. New York: Knopf.

Norwood, Col. Henry. 1947 [1650; 1732]. A Voyage to Virginia by Col. Norwood. In *Tracts and Other Papers*. Ed. Peter Force. Rept. New York: Peter Smith. Vol. 3, no. 10.

Nugent, Nell Marion, comp. 1934. *Cavaliers and Pioneers: Abstracts of Virginia Land Patents and Grants, 1623–1800*. Vol. 1. Richmond: Dietz Press. The 1963 reprint of this volume omits the original edition's illustrations.

———. 1977. *Cavaliers and Pioneers: Abstracts of Virginia Land Patents and Grants, 1623–1800*. Vol. 2. Richmond: Virginia State Library.

Owsley, Douglas, and Bertita Compton. N.d. Osteological Investigation of Human Remains from Jordan's Journey (Site 44PG302), a 17th Century Fortified Settlement in Prince George County, Virginia. Appendix 2 of Douglas C. McLearen and L. Daniel Mouer. N.d. Jordan's Journey II: Preliminary Report on the 1992 Excavations at Archaeological Sites 44 PG302, 44PG303, and 44PG315. Report (1993) on file, Virginia Department of Historic Resources, Richmond.

Pendergast, James. 1991. The Massawomeck: Raiders and Traders into the Chesapeake Bay in the Seventeenth Century. *Transactions of the American Philosophical Society* 81 (2).

Percy, George. 1608. Letter of March 28, 1608. In *The Jamestown Voyages under the First Charter*. Ed. Philip L. Barbour. Cambridge: Hakluyt Society. Ser. 2, vol. 136, pp. 158–62. Also printed, verbatim but with modernized spelling and a different translator, in *Jamestown Narratives: Eyewitness Accounts of the Virginia Colony: The First Decade, 1607–1617*. Ed. Edward W. Haile. Champlain, Va.: RoundHouse, 1998. Pp. 131–36.

————. 1921–22 [1625?]. *A Trewe Relacyon*. In *Tyler's Quarterly* 3:259–82. Also printed, verbatim but with modernized spelling, in *Jamestown Narratives: Eyewitness Accounts of the Virginia Colony: The First Decade, 1607–1617*. Ed. Edward W. Haile. Champlain, Va.: RoundHouse, 1998. Pp. 499–519.

————. 1969 [1608?]. *Observations Gathered out of a Discourse of the Plantation of the Southern Colony in Virginia by the English, 1606*. In *The Jamestown Voyages under the First Charter*. Ed. Philip Barbour. Cambridge: Hakluyt Society. Ser. 2, vol. 136, pp. 129–46. Also printed, verbatim but with modernized spelling, in *Jamestown Narratives: Eyewitness Accounts of the Virginia Colony: The First Decade, 1607–1617*. Ed. Edward W. Haile. Champlain, Va.: RoundHouse, 1998. Pp. 85–100.

Perkins, Francis. 1969 [1608]. Letter of March 18, 1608. In *The Jamestown Voyages under the First Charter*. Ed. Philip L. Barbour. Cambridge: Hakluyt Society. Ser. 2, vol. 136, pp. 158–62. Also printed, verbatim but with modernized spelling, in *Jamestown Narratives: Eyewitness Accounts of the Virginia Colony: The First Decade, 1607–1617*. Ed. Edward W. Haile. Champlain, Va.: RoundHouse, 1998. Pp. 131–36.

Petersson, Harold L. 2000 [1956]. *Arms and Armor in Colonial America, 1526–1783*. Rept. New York: Dover.

Potter, Stephen R. 1993. *Commoners, Tribute, and Chiefs: The Development of Algonquian Culture in the Potomac Valley*. Charlottesville: Univ. Press of Virginia.

Purchas, Samuel, comp. and ed. 1614. *Purchas His Pilgrimes*. 2d ed. London.

————. 1617. *Purchas His Pilgrimes*. 3d ed. London. Account of Uttamatomakkin (pp. 954–55) printed, verbatim but with modernized spelling, in *Jamestown Narratives: Eyewitness Accounts of the Virginia Colony: The First Decade, 1607–1617*. Ed. Edward W. Haile. Champlain, Va.: RoundHouse, 1998. Pp. 880–83.

————. 1626. *Purchas His Pilgrimes*. 4th ed. London.

————. 1904–6 [1625]. *Hakluytus Posthumus or Purchas His Pilgrimes*. Rept. Glasgow: James MacLehose and Sons. 20 vols. Account of Uttamatomakkin (19:117–19) printed, verbatim but with modernized spelling, in *Jamestown Narratives: Eyewitness Accounts of the Virginia Colony: The First Decade, 1607–1617*. Ed. Edward W. Haile, ed. Champlain, Va.: RoundHouse, 1998. Pp. 883–84.

Quinn, David Beers, ed. 1955. *The Roanoke Voyages, 1584–1590*. Cambridge: Hakluyt Society. Ser. 2, vol. 104.

Quitt, Martin H. 1995. Trade and Acculturation at Jamestown, 1607–1609: The Limits of Understanding. *William and Mary Quarterly*, 3d ser., 52:227–58.

Rasmussen, William M. S., and Robert S. Tilton. 1994. *Pocahontas: Her Life and Legend*. Richmond: Virginia Historical Society.

Ratliffe, John. 1969 [1609]. Letter [of October 4] to Lord Salisbury. In *The Jamestown Voyages under the First Charter*. Ed. Philip Barbour. Cambridge: Hakluyt Society. Ser. 2, vol. 136, p. 283. Also printed, verbatim but with modernized spelling, in *Jamestown Narratives: Eyewitness Accounts of the Virginia Colony: The First Decade, 1607–1617*. Ed. Edward W. Haile. Champlain, Va.: RoundHouse, 1998. Pp. 354–55.

Robinson, Conway. 1905–6. Notes from the Council and General Court Records, 1641–1659. *Virginia Magazine of History and Biography* 13:389–401.

Rolfe, John. 1848 [1616]. A True Relation of the State of Virginia. *Virginia Historical Register* 1 (3). Also printed, verbatim but with modernized spelling, in *Jamestown Narratives: Eyewitness Accounts of the Virginia Colony: The First Decade, 1607–1617*. Ed. Edward W. Haile. Champlain, Va.: RoundHouse, 1998. Pp. 866–77.

Rountree, Helen C. 1989. *The Powhatan Indians of Virginia: Their Traditional Culture*. Norman: Univ. of Oklahoma Press.

———. 1990. *Pocahontas's People: The Powhatan Indians of Virginia through Four Centuries*. Norman: Univ. of Oklahoma Press.

———. 1992. Powhatan Priests and English Rectors: Worldviews and Congregations in Conflict. *American Indian Quarterly* 16:485–500.

———. 1993a. Who Were the Powhatans and Did They Have a Unified "Foreign Policy"? In *Powhatan Foreign Relations, 1500–1722*. Ed. Helen C. Rountree. Charlottesville: Univ. Press of Virginia. Pp. 1–19.

———. 1993b. The Powhatans and Other Woodland Indians as Travelers. In *Powhatan Foreign Relations, 1500–1722*. Ed. Helen C. Rountree. Charlottesville: Univ. Press of Virginia. Pp. 21–52.

———. 1996. A Guide to the Late Woodland Indians' Use of Ecological Zones in the Chesapeake Region. *The Chesopiean, a Journal of Archaeology* 34 (2–3).

———. 1998. Powhatan Indian Women: The People Captain John Smith Barely Saw. *Ethnohistory* 45:1–29.

Rountree, Helen C., and Thomas E. Davidson. 1997. *Eastern Shore Indians of Virginia and Maryland*. Charlottesville: Univ. Press of Virginia.

Rountree, Helen C., Martha W. McCartney, and Blair A. Rudes. N.d. Powhatan Words and Names (In progress).

Rountree, Helen C., and E. Randolph Turner III. 1994. On the Fringe of the Southeast: The Powhatan Paramount Chiefdom in Virginia. In *The Forgotten Centuries: Europeans and Indians in the American South, 1513–1704*. Ed. Charles Hudson and Carmen Chaves Tesser. Athens: Univ. of Georgia Press. Pp. 355–72.

———. 1999. The Evolution of the Powhatan Paramount Chiefdom. In *Chiefdoms and Chieftaincy: An Integration of Archaeological, Ethnohistorical, and Ethnographic*

Approaches. Ed. Elsa M. Redmond. Gainesville: Univ. Presses of Florida. Pp. 265–96.

———. 2002. *Before and after Jamestown: Virginia's Powhatans and Their Predecessors.* Gainesville: Univ. Press of Florida.

Rutman, Darrett B., and Anita H. Rutman. 1976. Of Agues and Fevers: Malaria in the Early Chesapeake. *William and Mary Quarterly,* 3d ser., 33:31–60.

———. 1979. "Now-Wives and Sons-in-Law": Parental Death in a Seventeenth Century Virginia County. In *The Chesapeake in the Seventeenth Century: Essays on Anglo-American Society.* Ed. Thad W. Tate and David L. Ammerman. Chapel Hill: Univ. of North Carolina Press. Pp. 153–82.

Sainsbury, W. Noel, J. W. Fortescue, and Cecil Headham, comps. 1860–1926. *Calendar of State Papers, Colonial Series.* 60 vols. London: Longman, Green and Roberts.

Siebert, Frank T., Jr. 1975. Resurrecting Virginia Algonquian from the Dead: The Reconstituted and Historical Phonology of Powhatan. In *Studies in Southeastern Indian Languages.* Ed. James M. Crawford. Athens: Univ. of Georgia Press. Pp. 285–453.

Smith, John. n.d. [1612]. *Virginia Discouered and Described by Captayn John Smith, 1606.* [Map, in various editions.] Richmond: Library of Virginia.

——— 1986a [1608]. *A True Relation.* In *The Complete Works of Captain John Smith (1580–1631).* Ed. Philip L. Barbour. 3 vols. Chapel Hill: Univ. of North Carolina Press. 1:3–118. Also printed, verbatim but with modernized spelling, in *Jamestown Narratives: Eyewitness Accounts of the Virginia Colony: The First Decade, 1607–1617.* Ed. Edward W. Haile. Champlain, Va.: RoundHouse, 1998. Pp. 143–82.

———. 1986b [1612]. *A Map of Virginia* [with historical section compiled from various texts by William Simmond]. In *The Complete Works of Captain John Smith (1580–1631).* Ed. Philip L. Barbour. 3 vols. Chapel Hill: Univ. of North Carolina Press. 1:119–90. Also printed in part, verbatim but with modernized spelling, in *Jamestown Narratives: Eyewitness Accounts of the Virginia Colony: The First Decade, 1607–1617.* Ed. Edward W. Haile. Champlain,. Va.: RoundHouse, 1998. Pp. 205ff., 569ff.

———. 1986c [1624]. *The Generall Historie of Virginia, New England, and the Summer Isles, 1624.* In *The Complete Works of Captain John Smith (1580–1631).* Ed. Philip Barbour. 3 vols. Chapel Hill: Univ. of North Carolina Press. 2: 25–488. Also printed in part, verbatim but with modernized spelling, in *Jamestown Narratives: Eyewitness Accounts of the Virginia Colony: The First Decade, 1607–1617.* Ed. Edward W. Haile. Champlain, Va.: RoundHouse, 1998. Pp. 215–347, 857–64.

———. 1986d [1630]. *The True Travels, Adventures, and Observations of Captaine John Smith.* In *The Complete Works of Captain John Smith (1580–1631).* Ed. Philip Barbour. 3 vols. Chapel Hill: Univ. of North Carolina Press. 3:125–251.

Sneyd, Charlotte Augusta, trans. 1847. *A Relation, or rather A True Account, of the*

Island of England, with Sundry Particulars of the Customs of These People, and of the Royal Revenues under King Henry the Seventh, about the Year 1500. London: Printed for the Camden Society by John Bowyer Nichols & Son.

Speck, Frank G. 1927. *The Nanticoke and Conoy Indians with a Review of Linguistic Material from Manuscript and Living Sources: An Historical Study.* Papers of the Historical Society of Delaware, new ser., 1. Wilmington.

Spelman, Henry. 1910 [1613?]. Relation of Virginea. In *The Travels and Works of Captain John Smith.* Ed. Edward Arber and A. G. Bradley. New York: Burt Franklin. Pp. ci–cxiv. Also published, verbatim but with modernized spelling, in *Jamestown Narratives: Eyewitness Accounts of the Virginia Colony: The First Decade, 1607–1617.* Ed. Edward W. Haile. Champlain, Va. RoundHouse, 1998. Pp. 481–95.

Stahle, David W., Malcom K. Cleaveland, Dennis B. Blanton, Matthew D. Therrell, and David A. Gay. 1998. The Lost Colony and Jamestown Droughts. *Science* 280:564–67.

Stone, Lawrence. 1977. *The Family, Sex, and Marriage in England, 1500–1800.* New York: Harper and Row.

Strachey, William. 1953 [1612]. *Historie of Travel into Virginia Britania.* Ed. Louis B. Wright and Virginia Freund. Cambridge: Hakluyt Society. Ser. 2, vol. 103. Also printed (first book only), verbatim but with modernized spelling, in *Jamestown Narratives: Eyewitness Accounts of the Virginia Colony: The First Decade, 1607–1617.* Ed. Edward W. Haile. Champlain, Va.: RoundHouse, 1998. Pp. 569–689.

———. 1979 [1610]. *True Reportory.* In *New American World: A Documentary History of North America to 1612.* Ed. David B. Quinn. New York: Arno Press. Pp. 288–301. Also printed, verbatim but with modernized spelling, in *Jamestown Narratives: Eyewitness Accounts of the Virginia Colony: The First Decade, 1607–1617.* Ed. Edward W. Haile. Champlain, Va.: RoundHouse, 1998. Pp. 382–443.

Turner, E. Randolph, III. 1993. Native American Protohistoric Interactions in the Powhatan Core Area. In *Powhatan Foreign Relations, 1500–1722.* Ed. Helen C. Rountree. Charlottesville: Univ. Press of Virginia. Pp. 76–93.

Turner, E. Randolph, III, and Antony F. Opperman. N.d. Searching for Virginia Company Period Sites: An Assessment of Surviving Archaeological Manifestations of Powhatan-English Interactions, A.D. 1607–1624. MS-in-progress on file, Virginia Department of Historic Resources, Richmond.

Ubelaker, Douglas H. 1993. Human Biology of Virginia Indians. In *Powhatan Foreign Relations, 1500–1722.* Ed. Helen C. Rountree. Charlottesville: Univ. Press of Virginia. Pp. 53–75.

Ubelaker, Douglas H., and Philip D. Curtin. 2001. Human Biology of Populations in the Chesapeake Watershed. In *Discovering the Chesapeake: The History of an Ecosystem.* Ed. Philip D. Curtin, Grace S. Brush, and George W. Fisher. Baltimore: Johns Hopkins Univ. Press. Pp. 127–48.

Virginia Company of London. 1617. Warrant [of March 10]. In Ferrar Papers. 1992 ed. Reel 1, item 72.

Whitaker, Alexander. 1936 [1613]. *Good Newes from Virginia*. New York: Scholars' Facsimiles & Reprints. Also printed, verbatim but with modernized spelling, in *Jamestown Narratives: Eyewitness Accounts of the Virginia Colony: The First Decade, 1607–1617*. Ed. Edward W. Haile. Champlain, Va.: RoundHouse, 1998. Pp. 697–745.

White, Fr. Andrew. 1910 [1634]. A Briefe Relation of the Voyage unto Maryland. In *Narratives of Early Maryland, 1633–1684*. Ed. Clayton Colman Hall. New York: Charles Scribner's Sons. Pp. 25–45.

White, William. 1969 [1608?]. Fragments Published before 1614. In *The Jamestown Voyages under the First Charter*. Ed. Philip L. Barbour. Cambridge: Hakluyt Society. Ser. 2, vol. 136, pp. 147–50. Also printed, verbatim but with modernized spelling, in *Jamestown Narratives: Eyewitness Accounts of the Virginia Colony: The First Decade, 1607–1617*. Ed. Edward W. Haile. Champlain, Va.: RoundHouse, 1998. Pp. 138–41.

Williamson, Margaret Holmes. 2003. *Powhatan Lords of Life and Death: Command and Consent in Seventeenth-Century Virginia*. Lincoln: Univ. of Nebraska Press.

Wingfield, Edward Maria. 1969 [1608]. Discourse. In *The Jamestown Voyages under the First Charter*. Ed. Philip L. Barbour. Cambridge: Hakluyt Society. Ser. 2, vol. 136, pp. 213–34. Also printed, verbatim but with modernized spelling, in *Jamestown Narratives: Eyewitness Accounts of the Virginia Colony: The First Decade, 1607–1617*. Ed. Edward W. Haile. Champlain, Va.: RoundHouse, 1998. Pp. 184–201.

Winne, Peter. 1969 [1609]. Letter [of November 16, 1608] to Sir John Egerton. In *The Jamestown Voyages under the First Charter*. Ed. Philip L. Barbour, Cambridge: Hakluyt Society. Ser. 1, vol. 136, pp. 245–46. Also printed, verbatim but with modernized spelling, in *Jamestown Narratives: Eyewitness Accounts of the Virginia Colony: The First Decade, 1607–1617*. Ed. Edward W. Haile. Champlain, Va.: RoundHouse, 1998. Pp. 203–4.

York County, Virginia. 1633 to present. Records (incomplete). County records. Housed in the courthouse in Yorktown, Virginia; copies in the Library of Virginia, Richmond.

INDEX